U0069877

國中小實用 2000單字辭典

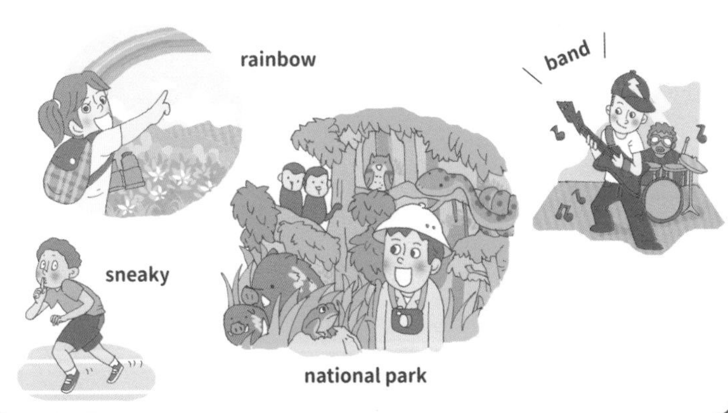

序

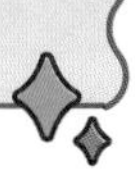

這是一本實用、好用的優質中小學生英文辭典。

實用的理由

❶ 完全按照教育部頒定 108 課綱之國中小基本 1,200 字與常用 800 字編寫。

❷ 所有單字均附美語人士實際發音的音標。

❸ 所有單字均附實用例句及淺顯易懂的文字，告訴中小學生如何將單字活用於日常會話中。

❹ 與單字相關的重要片語、用法詳細列舉，提升單字的實用性。

好用的理由

❶ 每則單字均配合例句內容手繪精緻插圖，強化視覺記憶效果。

❷ 單字例句簡短精確，極利背誦。

❸ 所有單字例句均由發音精確、口齒清晰的專業外籍老師朗讀，便於學生模仿，可大幅改善發音並有助於聽力的培養。

我們的建議

♡ 隨身攜帶，利用零星時間不時翻閱並掃描 QR Code 聆聽音檔內容。熟悉單字唸法，以朗讀例句取代死記單字。

♡ 每天重複閱讀 2 至 3 頁，不出一年，整本書所蒐集的單字就可牢記在心。

學英文貴在恆心，只要肯努力，每位讀者將來一定會成為英文高手！

使用說明

該單字詞性與中解。清晰又易懂。

每字母首頁均有 QR Code，只需使用手機輕輕一掃，即可聆聽該字母所有音檔。方便好學習。

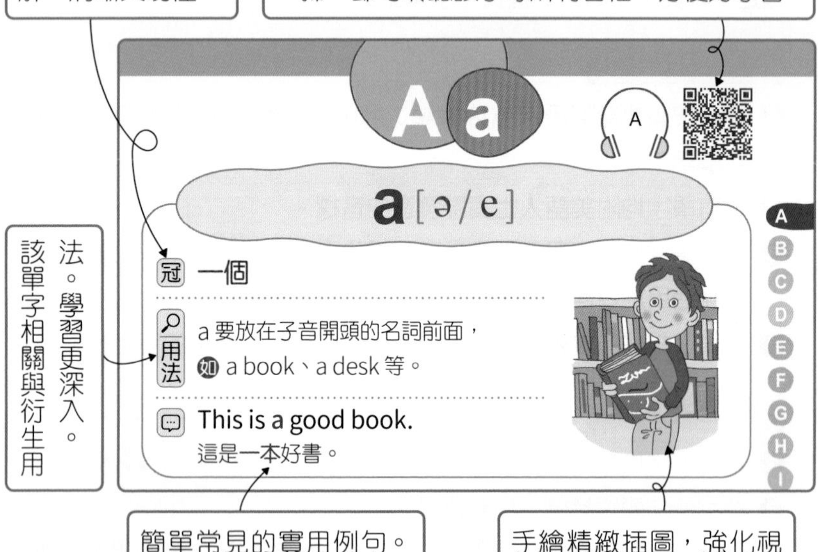

A a
A
a [ə / e]
冠 一個
用法 a 要放在子音開頭的名詞前面，
如 a book、a desk 等。
This is a good book.
這是一本好書。
A B C D E F G H I

該單字相關與衍生用法。學習更深入。

簡單常見的實用例句。好讀好吸收。

手繪精緻插圖，強化視覺記憶效果。

代號說明

動	動詞	冠	冠詞
名	名詞	助	助動詞
形	形容詞	限	限定詞
副	副詞	感歎	感歎詞
介	介詞	sb	人
連	連接詞	sth	事物
代	代名詞		

索引

A	
a	1
able	3
about	4
above	4
abroad	4
absent	5
accept	5

頁數

全書音檔

詞類用法說明

本書單字中文前均標有該單字的詞性，舉例來說：

名 老闆；上司
形 中心的，中央的

上列單字的 名 及 形 分別是 boss 及 central 的詞性。名 代表「名詞」，形 代表「形容詞」。換言之，我們若想正確使用英文單字就須先了解該字的詞性，否則徒然記了一大堆單字卻不會使用它們，任憑我們再怎麼努力學英文都是白費工夫的。

現在，我們就依本書所列的各種詞性及其用法，以淺顯的文字舉例如下，希望藉此增進大家用字的能力：

❶ 名 → 名詞

詞性 名詞就是指有名稱的人或物。

人：man（男人）、woman（女人）、boy（男孩）、girl（女孩）、son（兒子）、daughter（女兒）、John（約翰）、Mary（瑪麗）等。

物：desk（書桌）、house（房子）、dog（狗）、tree（樹）等。

一些看不見的意境或抽象概念也有名稱，因此也稱作名詞。如 beauty（美麗）、knowledge（知識）等。

用法 中文的名詞與英文的名詞在句中的用法完全相同。

中文：瑪麗喜歡狗。

英文：Mary likes dogs.
　　　名　　　名

中文：知識就是力量。

英文：Knowledge is power.
　　　名　　　名

❷ 代 → 代名詞

詞性 代名詞就是代替人或物的名詞。

代替人：

種類	放在句首	放在動詞 / 介詞之後（受格）	放在名詞前面（所有格）	之後無需名詞（所有格代名詞）	指自己的代名詞（反身代名詞）
我	I	me	my（我的）	mine（我的東西）	myself（我自己）
你 / 妳	you	you	your（你 / 妳的）	yours（你 / 妳的東西）	yourself（你 / 妳自己）
他	he	him	his（他的）	his（他的東西）	himself（他自己）
她	she	her	her（她的）	hers（她的東西）	herself（她自己）

我們	we	us	our（我們的）	ours（我們的東西）	ourselves（我們自己）
你們 / 妳們	you	you	your（你們 / 妳們的）	yours（你們 / 妳們的東西）	yourselves（你們 / 妳們自己）
他們 / 她們	they	them	their（他們 / 她們的）	theirs（他們 / 她們的東西）	themselves（他們 / 她們自己）

代替物：

種類	放在句首	放在動詞 / 介詞之後（受格）	放在名詞前面（所有格）	之後無需名詞（所有格代名詞）	指自己的代名詞（反身代名詞）
它 / 牠	it	it	its（它 / 牠的）	its（它 / 牠的東西）	itself（它 / 牠自己）
它們 / 牠們	they	them	their（它們 / 牠們的）	theirs（它們 / 牠們的東西）	themselves（它們 / 牠們自己）

用法 中文的代名詞與英文的代名詞在句中的用法完全相同。

ⓐ 放在句首

中文：我喜歡音樂。

英文：I love music.

ⓑ 放在動詞之後

中文：班喜歡 我。

英文：Ben likes me.

ⓒ 放在介詞之後

中文：我坐在她旁邊。

英文：I sit beside her.

ⓓ 放在名詞前面

中文：這是我的 書。

英文：This is my book.

ⓔ 之後無需名詞

中文：這隻筆是我的。

英文：This pen is mine.

ⓕ 指自己的代名詞

中文：你應愛你自己 / 你應自愛。

英文：You should love yourself.

❸ 形 → 形容詞

詞性 英文的形容詞相當於中文「……的」之意，用來形容名詞或代名詞。

用法 a 形容詞可置於名詞前。

中文：那個漂亮的 女孩是我妹妹。

英文：That beautiful girl is my sister.

形　名

b 形容詞可置於 is、am、are 等 be 動詞之後，形容名詞或代名詞。

中文：瑪麗很漂亮。

英文：Mary is beautiful.

名　形

中文：他們很忙。

英文：They are busy.

代　形

4 冠 → 冠詞

詞性 冠詞就像頭冠一樣，置於名詞前面。有 a / an / the 三種。用法請參考內文。

5 動 → 動詞

詞性 動詞就是有「動作功能」的詞類。它就像人體的心臟一樣，沒有它，句子就無法形成。動詞出現在名詞或代名詞之後。

用法 a 名詞之後

中文：約翰 住在臺北。

英文：John lives in Taipei.

b 代名詞之後

中文：他 是我朋友。

英文：He is my friend.

代 動

名詞或代名詞之後若有動詞，這個名詞或代名詞就稱作主詞。

6 助 → 助動詞

詞性 助動詞就是幫忙動詞的詞類。常用的助動詞有 will（將）、can（能夠）、may（也許）、should（應當）、must（必須）、have（已經）等。

用法 a 助動詞要放在動詞前

中文：艾德將要 來。

英文：Ed will come.

助 動

中文：約翰已經 走了。

英文：John has left.

助 動

b 助動詞也可用來形成問句，此時要將助動詞放在句首，如：

中文：艾德將要來嗎？

英文：Will Ed come?

助

中文：約翰已經走了嗎？

英文：Has John left?

助

❼ 副 → 副詞

詞性 副詞是用來修飾動詞、形容詞的詞類，副詞也可用來修飾副詞。

用法 ⓐ 修飾動詞

此時，副詞通常放在動詞之後。

中文：湯姆跑得很快。

英文：Tom runs fast.

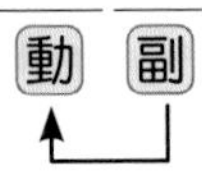

ⓑ 修飾形容詞

此時，副詞要放在形容詞之前。

中文：瑪麗很美。

英文：Mary is very beautiful.

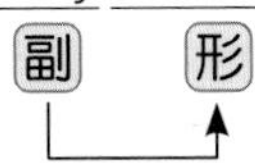

ⓒ 修飾副詞

此時，副詞要放在副詞之前。

中文：彼得很用功。

英文：Peter studies very hard.

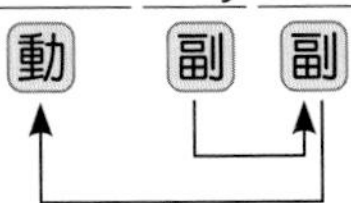

❽ 介 → 介詞

詞性 介詞就是介於名詞、代名詞之前的詞類，常用的有 in（在……之內）、on（在……之上）、under（在……之下）、before（在……之前）、after（在……之後）、beside（在……之旁）等。

用法 ⓐ 介於名詞之前

中文：我住在那棟房子裡。

英文：I live in that house.

in 介　house 名

ⓑ 介於代名詞之前

中文：我看到桌上有個盒子。裡面有什麼東西？

英文：I see a box on the table. What's in it?

on 介　table 名　in 介　it 代

ⓒ 動詞也可放在介詞之後，不過動詞一定要變成動名詞才行。動名詞就是動詞變成的名詞（動詞字尾加 -ing）。

中文：我對唱歌有興趣。

英文：I'm interested in sing.（×）

in 介　sing 動

→ I'm interested in singing.（○）

in 介　singing 動名詞

❾ 連 → 連接詞

詞性 連接詞就是用來連接句子或相等詞類的字。

用法 a 連接句子

此時，常用的連接詞有 and（同時）、but（但是）、or（否則）、because（因為）、so（所以）、although（雖然）等。

John is friendly, so we all like him.

（約翰很友善，所以我們都喜歡他。）

Mary sings well, and she can also dance.

（瑪麗很會唱歌，同時她也會跳舞。）

You should study hard, or you'll be sorry.

（你應用功，否則你會後悔。）

英文的兩句之間，只可使用一個連接詞。

中文：雖然班很好，但是我不喜歡他。（○）

英文：Although Ben is nice, but I don't like him.（×）

→ Although Ben is nice, I don't like him.（○）

或：Ben is nice, but I don't like him.（○）

中文：因為彼得很好，所以瑪麗很愛他。（○）

英文：Because Peter is nice, so Mary loves him.(×)

→ Because Peter is nice, Mary loves him.（○）

或：Peter is nice, so Mary loves him.（○）

b 連接對等的詞類

此時，常用的連接詞有 and（和）、but（而、卻）、or（或者）。

John is nice and handsome.

（約翰人好又英俊。）

Anna is not a student but a teacher.

（安娜不是學生，而是老師。）

Is Ted good or bad?

形 連 形

（泰德是好人還是壞人？）

以上是各詞類的基本介紹及用法。我們只要勤用本辭典，不斷複習所學的單字及例句，相信我們的英文程度會在短期之內大大提升，遠遠超越父母師長的期許。

目錄

Aa

A B C D E F G H I J K L M N O P Q R S T U V W X Y Z

a [ə/e]

冠 一個

用法 a 要放在子音開頭的名詞前面，
如 a book、a desk 等。

This is a good book.
這是一本好書。

an [æn]

冠 一個

用法 an 要放在母音開頭的名詞前面，
如 an orange（一粒柳橙）、
an apple（一顆蘋果）等。

Alan eats an orange every day.
艾倫每天都吃一顆柳橙。

a few [ə ˋfju]

形 一些，幾個

用法 a few 要放在複數可數名詞之前，
如 a few boys（一些男孩）、
a few books（幾本書）。

Sam will stay here for a few days.
山姆會在這裡待上幾天。

A a

few [fju]

形 **沒幾個，幾乎沒有**

用法 few 也放在複數名詞之前，但有否定的意味，表示「沒幾個」。

Ben has few friends.
班沒幾個朋友。

a little [ə ˋlɪtḷ]

形 **一些**

用法 a little 要放在不可數名詞之前，
如 a little water（一些水）、
a little sugar（一些糖）。

Terry needs a little money to buy a book.
泰瑞需要一些錢來買書。

little [ˋlɪtḷ]

形 **沒多少，幾乎沒有**

用法 little 也放在不可數名詞之前，但有否定的意味，表示「沒多少」。

Amy has little money to lend Ted.
艾咪沒什麼錢借給泰德。

a lot [ə ˋlɑt]

副 很，非常

用法 若要表達非常感謝，a lot 要放在 thanks 之後。Thanks a lot.
= Thank you very much.（很謝謝你。）

Thanks a lot for your help.
非常感謝您的幫忙。

a lot of [ə ˋlɑt ˏəv]

形 許多的

用法 a lot of 之後可接複數或不可數名詞，
如 a lot of friends（許多朋友）、
a lot of money（許多錢）。

Andy has a lot of work to do.
安迪有許多工作要做。

able [ˋebḷ]

形 有能力的

用法 本字一定用於下列結構中：
be able to + V　能夠……
= can + V

Don't worry. Barry is able to do the work.
別擔心。這工作貝瑞做得來。

Aa

about [əˋbaʊt]

介 有關，關於

用法 ⓐ about 也可表示「大約」，常與數字並用，
如 about 10 dollars（大約十元）。
ⓑ about 又可表示「即將」。

What are you talking about?
你們在談關於什麼？

above [əˋbʌv]

介 在……的上方

用法 above 與 on 均表「在……之上」，但 on 指兩物間有接觸，而 above 則指兩物間無接觸且懸空的狀況。

The mountain rises above the clouds.
這座山聳立於雲層上方。

abroad [əˋbrɔd]

副 在國外，到國外

用法 abroad 一定放在動詞之後，
如 study abroad（留學）、
go abroad（出國）。

Adam will study abroad next year.
亞當明年要出國念書。

Aa

absent [ˋæbsənt]

形 缺席的

用法 be absent from...
從……中缺席

John was **absent** from the meeting this morning.
今天早上的會議約翰缺席了。

accept [əkˋsɛpt]

動 接受

用法 accept + N/V-ing
接受……

I think I'll **accept** Amy's invitation.
我想我會接受艾咪的邀請。

accident [ˋæksədənt]

名 意外事故

用法 by accident　意外地
Nina found the secret by accident.
（妮娜意外地發現了這個祕密。）

Ted was badly hurt in a car **accident**.　泰德因車禍嚴重受傷。

A

across [əˋkrɔs]

介 越過

用法 across 一定放在動詞後面，
如 swim across the river（游過河）、
run across the street（跑步過街）。

Be careful when you walk across the street. 你步行過街時要小心。

act [ækt]

動 行動；表現

用法 act 也可作名詞，表示「行為」，
如 Cheating is a bad act.
（作弊是不好的行為。）

Little Peter acts badly at school.
小彼得在校行為不佳。

action [ˋækʃən]

名 行動

用法 action 指「行動」，非「行為」；
action 常與 take 並用。
take action　採取行動

We should take action to help the poor girl.
我們應該採取行動來幫助這個可憐的女孩。

active [ˋæktɪv]

形 活躍的；積極的

用法 an active volcano
活火山

My grandfather is old, but he is still very active. 我爺爺歲數大了，但仍舊很活躍。

activity [ækˋtɪvətɪ]

名 活動

用法 an outdoor activity
戶外活動

Anthony can take part in a lot of activities here.
安東尼可以參加這裡的很多活動。

actor [ˋæktɚ]

名（男）演員

用法 actor 指在話劇（plays）、電影（movies）或電視（television）演出的男演員。

My friend John is a famous actor.
我的朋友約翰是個知名演員。

actress [ˋæktrɪs]

名 （女）演員

用法 如同 actor，actress 也指在話劇、電影或電視演出的女演員。

My sister wants to be an actress.
我妹妹想要當女演員。

actually [ˋæktʃuəlɪ]

副 事實上

用法 actually 和 in fact 都表示「事實上」，不過 actually 通常用在不完全同意的話；in fact 則主要用在對之前的話做補充。

Actually, Arthur is very busy at this moment.
事實上，亞瑟此刻正在忙著。

add [æd]

動 加入

用法 add A to B
將 A 添加到 B

Add some milk to your coffee.
在你的咖啡裡加點牛奶吧。

address [ə`drɛs]

名 地址；演講（= speech）

用法 e-mail address 電子郵件
What's Angela's e-mail address?
（安琪拉的電子郵件地址是什麼？）

Steven made a wonderful address at the meeting.
會議上史蒂芬發表了一篇精彩的演講。

admire [əd`maɪr]

動 欽佩，讚賞

用法 admire sb for sth
讚賞某人某事

We all admire John for his courage.
我們都欽佩約翰的勇氣。

adult [ə`dʌlt]

名 成人

用法 adult 也可以做形容詞使用，
意思為「成年的」。
an adult male 成年男子

Tickets are NT$300 for adults.
成人票價為新臺幣三百元。

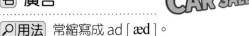

advertisement

[ˌædvɚˋtaɪzmənt]

名 廣告

CAR SALE

用法 常縮寫成 ad [æd]。

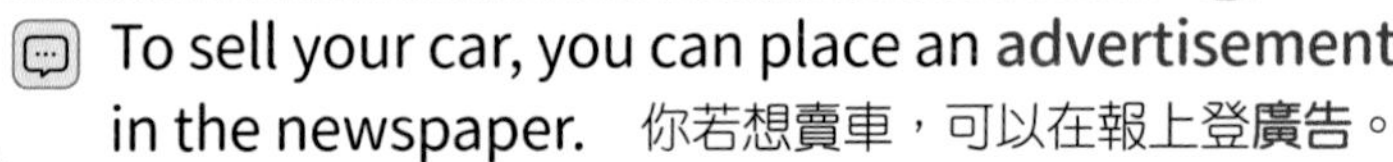

To sell your car, you can place an **advertisement** in the newspaper. 你若想賣車，可以在報上登廣告。

advice [ədˋvaɪs]

名 忠告，建議（不可數）

用法 an advice (×)
→ a piece of advice (○) 一則建議

Let me give you a piece of **advice**.
讓我給你一個忠告吧。

advise [ədˋvaɪz]

動 勸告；忠告

用法 advise sb to do sth
勸告某人某事

The doctor **advised** me to get more rest.
醫生勸我多休息。

affect [əˋfɛkt]

動 影響

用法 affect 指的是負面的影響。

Smoking too much may **affect** your health.
吸菸過量會影響你的健康。

afraid [əˋfred]

形 害怕的

用法 be afraid of + N　害怕……
be afraid to + V　害怕……

Eliot is **afraid** of the bad dog.
艾略特很怕這隻惡狗。

after [ˋæftɚ]

介 連 在……之後

用法 after school　放學後（after 為介詞）
= after school is over（after 為連接詞）

What are you going to do **after school**?
放學後你要做什麼？

afternoon [ˌæftɚˋnun]

名 下午

用法
this afternoon 今天下午
tomorrow afternoon 明天下午
yesterday afternoon 昨天下午

I will be very busy this afternoon.
我今天下午會很忙。

again [əˋgɛn]

副 再一次，又

用法
again and again 一再，屢次
Duncan made the same mistake again and again.（當肯一犯再犯同樣的錯誤。）

Come back to see us again.
要再回來見我們喲。

against [əˋgɛnst]

介 反對

用法
vote against / for...
投票反對 / 贊成……

Is your brother for or against it?
你弟弟對這件事是贊成還是反對？

A a

age [edʒ]

名 年齡；時代

用法 ⓐ the space age　太空時代
ⓑ Harry is five years of age.
= Harry is five years old.（哈利五歲了。）

Jane is five years of age now.
珍現在五歲了。

ago [əˋgo]

副 （某段時間）之前

用法 ago 之前要置一段時間，
如 two days ago（兩天前）、
five weeks ago（五個星期前）。

Peter was here two minutes ago.
兩分鐘前彼得還在這裡。

agree [əˋgri]

動 同意

用法 agree with + sb　同意某人的看法
agree to sth　同意……；答應……

When I said Mary was beautiful, nobody agreed with me.　我說瑪麗很漂亮時，沒人同意我的看法。

ahead [ə`hɛd]

副 在前方

用法 ahead of...
在……前方

Watch out! There is a car **ahead of** us.
小心！我們**前方**有一輛車子。

aim [em]

名 目標，目的　動 瞄準

用法 aim (sth) at...
（將某物）瞄準……

Edward **aimed** his gun at the snake but missed.
愛德華舉槍**瞄準**那條蛇但卻沒打著。

air [ɛr]

名 空氣

用法 air 也可以表示「空中」，
如 My sister sees a bird in the air.
（我妹妹看到天空有隻鳥。）

We can't live without **air**.
沒有**空氣**我們就無法生存。

air conditioner

[ˋɛr kən͵dɪʃənɚ]

名 冷氣機

用法 air conditioner 簡稱 AC。

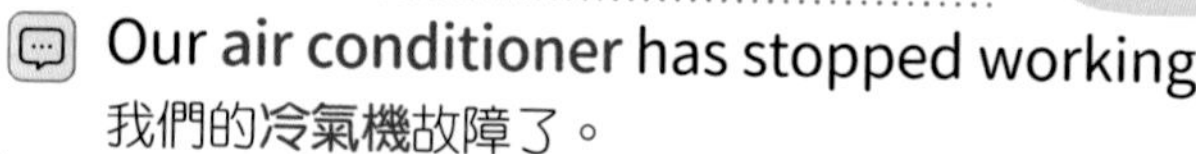

Our **air conditioner** has stopped working.
我們的**冷氣機**故障了。

airline [ˋɛrlaɪn]

名 航空公司

用法 airline 指「航空公司」；airplane 指「飛機」；flight 則是指「班次」。

Linda's father is an **airline** pilot.
琳達的爸爸是某**航空公司**的飛行員。

airplane [ˋɛr͵plen]

名 飛機

用法 airplane 常簡稱為 plane [plen]。
fly an airplane　開飛機

Can you **fly an airplane**?
你會**開飛機**嗎？

airport [ˋɛrˏpɔrt]

名 機場

用法 at the airport
在機場

Greg will see his friend off at the airport today. 葛瑞格今天會到機場為他朋友送行。

alarm [əˋlɑrm]

名 鬧鐘

用法 講「設（幾點）的鬧鐘」搭配詞用 for 不用 at。

Set the alarm for 6 o'clock.
把鬧鐘設定在六點鐘。

album [ˋælbəm]

名（唱片或 CD 的）專輯；相簿

用法 a photograph album　相簿
a stamp album　集郵冊

It's a song from Clara's latest album.
這是克萊拉最新專輯中的一首歌。

alike [əˋlaɪk]

形 相似的，相像的

用法 本字不可置於名詞前，只可置於 look 或 be 動詞之後。且 alike 不可被 very 修飾，只可被 much 或 very much 修飾。

The two boys are twins, but they don't **look alike**.
這兩名男孩是雙胞胎，可是看起來卻不像。

alive [əˋlaɪv]

形 活的

用法 alive 只能放 be 動詞之後，不能放在名詞之前做修飾。

Connie was still **alive** when the firemen found her.
消防隊員找到康妮時她仍活著。

all [ɔl]

形 全部的

用法 all my friends 我所有的朋友
= all of my friends

All my friends love music.
我所有的朋友都喜歡音樂。

allow [əˋlaʊ]

動 允許

用法 allow + sb + to + V
允許某人做……

Dad wouldn't **allow** me to go out at night.
老爸不**准**我晚上外出。

almost [ˋɔl͵most]

副 幾乎

用法 almost 常與 every 或 all 並用。
almost every word　幾乎每個字
= almost all the words　幾乎所有的字

Gerald could understand **almost** every word the foreigner said.　這外國人說的每個字傑拉德**幾乎**都聽得懂。

alone [əˋlon]

形 單獨的　副 獨自

用法 alone 當形容詞用時，只能放 be 動詞之後，不能放在名詞之前做修飾。

Sam enjoys living **alone**.
山姆喜歡**獨自**生活。

along [əˋlɔŋ]

介 **沿著**

用法 along 表示「沿著」時，
如 Let’s walk along the river.
（咱們沿著河走下去吧。）

How’re you getting along?
你好嗎？（= How are you?）

aloud [əˋlaʊd]

副 **大聲地**

用法 aloud 主要強調「出聲地；大聲地」，常與 read、cry、shout 等字連用。

Read it aloud, please.
請大聲唸。

alphabet [ˋælfə͵bɛt]

名 **字母（總稱）**

Aa Bb Cc Dd Ee Ff Gg
Hh Ii Jj Kk Ll Mm Nn
Oo Pp Qq Rr Ss Tt
Uu Vv Ww Xx Yy Zz

用法 the Roman alphabet
羅馬字母表

There are 26 letters in the English alphabet.
英文字母表共有二十六個字母。

already [ɔlˋrɛdɪ]

副 已經

用法 already 常與助動詞 have、has、had 並用。
如 Tim has already left.
（提姆已經離開了。）

Troy has **already** finished his homework. 特洛伊已經把家庭作業做完了。

also [ˋɔlso]

副 也

用法
ⓐ also 與 too 均表示「也」，
also 多放在句中，too 則放在句尾。
ⓑ also 也有放句尾用法。

I can sing, and Toby can **also** sing.
我會唱歌，托比**也**會唱歌。

although [ɔlˋðo]

連 雖然

用法 although 與 but 不能並存。
如 Although Steve is rich, he is not happy.
→ Steve is rich, but he is not happy.
（史蒂夫雖有錢，但並不快樂。）

Although Norman is nice, I don't like him.
諾曼人**雖然**很好，但我不喜歡他。

altogether [ˌɔltəˋgɛðɚ]

副 完全地；總共（與數字並用）

用法 altogether 當「完全地」解釋時，也可以等於 completely。

Jack owed me NT$2,050 **altogether**.
傑克總共欠我新臺幣兩千零五十元。

always [ˋɔlwez]

副 總是，始終

用法 依頻繁程度分類如下：

always	始終	usually	通常
often	經常	seldom	很少

Why is Johnny **always** late for class?
強尼為何上課**老是**遲到？

a.m. [ˌeˋɛm]

副 上午

用法 a.m. 也可以寫成 am、A.M. 或 AM。這些字要放在表示時刻的名詞之後。

Keith will meet you in the office at nine **a.m.**
上午九點凱斯會在辦公室跟你會面。

Aa

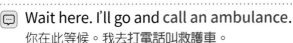

ambulance [ˋæmbjələns]

名 救護車

用法
call an ambulance 叫救護車
an ambulance driver 救護車司機
an ambulance crew 救護人員（集合名詞）

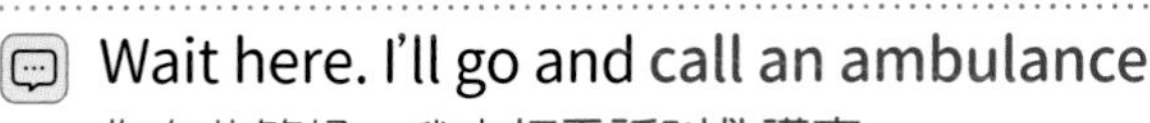

Wait here. I'll go and call an ambulance.
你在此等候。我去打電話叫救護車。

America [əˋmɛrɪkə]

名 美國

用法
America 可指美國或美洲，表示「美國」則為 the US (the United States) 或 the USA (the United States of America 美利堅合眾國)。

My friend David is from America.
我的朋友大衛來自美國。

American [əˋmɛrɪkən]

名 美國人 形 美國的；美國籍的

用法
Owen is an American.（American 為名詞）
= Owen is American.（American 為形容詞）

David is an American, and I'm a Chinese.
大衛是美國人，我則是華人。

among [əˋmʌŋ]

介 在（三者或以上）之中

用法 講「兩者之間」用介詞 between；
「三者或以上之間」則用介詞 among。

Among the three girls, which one do you like best?
這三個女孩中，你最喜歡哪一個？

amount [əˋmaʊnt]

名 量　動 計達……（與 to 並用）

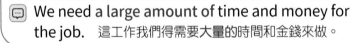

用法
ⓐ a large / small amount of + 不可數名詞
大量的…… / 少量的……
ⓑ amount to　總計……

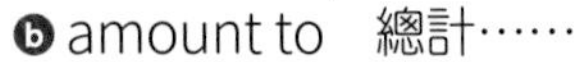

We need a large amount of time and money for the job.　這工作我們得需要大量的時間和金錢來做。

ancient [ˋenʃənt]

形 古老的

用法 ancient 也可做名詞，恆用複數，
the ancients 為「古代人」之意。

Rome is an ancient city.
羅馬是一座古城。

and [ænd]

連 和；而且

用法 and 用來連接相同的詞類。
如 Joy and I are good friends.
（喬伊和我是好朋友。）

Mary is kind and beautiful.
瑪麗心腸好又漂亮。

angel [ˋendʒəl]

名 天使

用法 angel 也可以稱呼喜愛或親密的人，
「小天使，小寶貝」的意思。

Amanda sings like an angel.
艾曼達歌唱得像天使般動聽。

anger [ˋæŋgɚ]

名 憤怒

用法 anger 為不可數名詞。

Billy tried to control his anger but failed.
比利想克制自己的憤怒但失敗了。

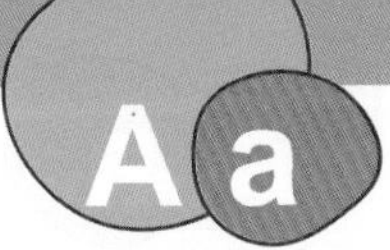

angle [ˋæŋgḷ]

名 角度；觀點

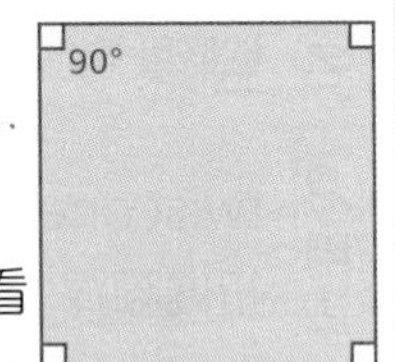

用法 a right angle 直角
from a different angle 從另一個角度來看

The interior angles of a square are right angles.
正方形的內角是直角。

angry [ˋæŋgrɪ]

形 生氣的

用法 be angry with + sb
生某人的氣

Why are you angry with Nick?
你為何生尼克的氣？

animal [ˋænəmḷ]

名 動物

用法 animal 指動物，但也可指「粗魯而無教養的人」，如 Paul is an animal.（保羅是個野蠻人。）

We can see different animals at the zoo.
我們可以在動物園看到各種動物。

ankle [ˋæŋkḷ]

名 腳踝

用法 twist one's ankle
扭傷腳踝

The child **twisted his ankle** and was sent to the hospital. 這孩子**扭傷腳踝**後被送往醫院。

another [əˋnʌðɚ]

形 另外的 代 另一個

用法 one another 彼此
如 We should love one another.
（我們應相親相愛。）

This apple tastes good. Can I have **another** one?
這顆蘋果味道不錯。我可不可以再吃一顆？

answer [ˋænsɚ]

動 回答 名 回答；答案

用法 the answer to + sth
某事物的答案

Can Lee **answer** this question?
李能回答這個問題嗎？

ant [ænt]

名 螞蟻

用法 螞蟻若跑進褲子裡，一定令我們異常難受，因此英美人士就會說 I have ants in my pants. 來表示「我現在坐立不安。」。

Is that a fire ant?
那是隻火蟻嗎？

any [ˋɛnɪ]

限 任何的　代 任何一個

用法 any 常與 not 並用，
如 Karen doesn't have any money.
（凱倫一點錢都沒有。）

Let me know if you have any questions.
你若有任何問題要讓我知道喲。

anyone [ˋɛnɪˏwʌn]

代 任何人

用法 anyone 等於 anybody，均表示「任何人」，常與 not 並用。

Larry doesn't know anyone here.
這裡的人賴瑞一個也不認識。

anything [ˋɛnɪˏθɪŋ]

代 任何事；任何東西

用法 進到一家店時，有禮貌的店員都會說：Is there anything I can do for you?（有什麼可以為您效勞的嗎？）

I don't believe anything Joe says.
喬所說的任何話我都不相信。

anywhere [ˋɛnɪˏwɛr]

副 在任何地方

用法 anywhere 沒有特別指定某個明確的地方。

It could happen anywhere in the world.
這種事情在世界任何地方都有可能會發生。

apartment [əˋpɑrtmənt]

名 公寓

用法 rent an apartment　租公寓
rent [rɛnt] 動 租用

Isaac lives in a small apartment.
艾薩克住在一間小公寓裡。

apologize [əˋpɑlə͵dʒaɪz]

動 **道歉**

apologize to sb for sth
向某人道歉某事

Kevin must **apologize to** his teacher **for** being late. 凱文遲到，因此必須向老師道歉。

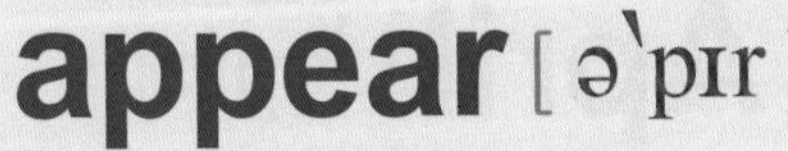

appear [əˋpɪr]

動 **似乎；出現**

appear to be + Adj
似乎……（to be 可省略）

Frank **appears (to be)** angry.
法蘭克似乎生氣了。

apple [ˋæpl̩]

名 **蘋果**

apple 有下列很好的諺語：
An apple a day keeps the doctor away.
（每日一蘋果，醫生遠離我。）

Hank doesn't like **apples**; he likes bananas.
漢克不喜歡蘋果，他喜歡香蕉。

appreciate [əˋpriʃɪˏet]

動 感激

用法 appreciate不可用「人」作受詞，只可用「幫助」或「關心」作受詞。

Thanks for your concern. I really appreciate it. 謝謝你的關心，我真的很**感激**。

April [ˋeprəl]

名 四月

用法
ⓐ 月分字首須大寫。
ⓑ 月分和年並用時，月分與年之間要有逗點。

Dora was born in April, 1995.
朵拉是一九九五年**四月**出生的。

area [ˋɛrɪə]

名 地區；範圍

用法 non-smoking area
非吸菸區

Sorry, this is the non-smoking area. You can't smoke here. 抱歉，這是**非吸菸區**。這裡不能吸菸。

argue [ˋɑrgjʊ]

動 爭論

用法 argue with + sb　與某人爭論
argue over / about + sth　爭論某事

Don't argue with your mom again.
不要再跟你媽媽爭論了。

arm [ɑrm]

名 手臂

用法 an arm and a leg　一大筆錢
The car cost me an arm and a leg.
（這輛車花了我很多錢。）

Jason broke his left arm when he fell down.　傑森跌倒時把左手臂跌斷了。

armchair [ˋɑrm͵tʃɛr]

名 有扶手單人座的大沙發

用法 chair 指有靠背或有靠背加扶手的椅子；armchair 指有扶手的椅子；bench 則指長凳；stool 指無靠背、無扶手、單人坐的凳子。

Dad likes to sit in his armchair listening to music.
爸爸喜歡坐在他的大沙發上聽音樂。

Aa

A

army [ˋɑrmɪ]

名 陸軍；軍隊

用法 army 主要指「陸軍」；navy 指「海軍」；air force 則指「空軍」。

My older brother is in the army.
我的哥哥目前在當兵。

around [əˋraʊnd]

副 附近，四處；大約 介 環繞

用法 around 表示「大約」時，等於 about，之後要接數字，如 Zora has around fifty dollars.（卓拉有大約五十元。）

A boy is running around the park.
有個男孩正繞著公園跑。

arrange [əˋrendʒ]

動 安排

用法 arrange a meeting 安排會議
arrange for + sb + to + V
安排某人做……

The secretary will arrange for you to meet the boss this morning. 今天早上祕書會安排你去見老闆。

arrive [əˋraɪv]

動 到達

用法 arrive at + 建築物（如 車站、郵局等）
arrive in + 大地方（如 城市、國家）

Vincent **arrived at** the station at four o'clock.
文森在四點時到達車站。

art [ɑrt]

名 藝術

用法 fine arts　美術（指繪畫和雕塑）
（此處的 fine 指「精緻的」）

Dance is a kind of **art**.
舞蹈是一種藝術。

artist [ˋɑrtɪst]

名 藝術家；畫家

用法 a street artist
街頭藝人

My friend is a **street artist**.
我的朋友是位街頭藝人。

as [æz]

介 當作　連 因為　副 一樣地

用法 as + Adj + as + sb　和某人一樣地……
She is as beautiful as Mary.
（她和瑪麗一樣漂亮。）

💬 **Mary works as a teacher in our school.**
瑪麗在我們學校擔任老師。

ask [æsk]

動 問；要求

用法 ask + sb + to + V　要求某人……
如 Dad asked me to help him.
（爸爸要我幫他。）

💬 **May I ask you a question?**
我可以問你一個問題嗎？

asleep [əˋslip]

形 睡著的

用法 fall asleep
睡著

💬 **Grandpa fell asleep watching TV.**
外公看電視時睡著了。

assistant [əˋsɪstənt]

名 助手，助理

用法 an assistant to...
……的助手

Vicky is an assistant to Dr. Watson.
維琪是華生醫生的助理。

assume [əˋsum]

動 假定，認為；承擔（責任）

用法 assume + that 子句　推測……
I assume that Iris doesn't know this word.
（我認為艾麗絲不懂這個字。）

Mark should assume the responsibility of raising his family.　馬克應負起養家的責任。

at [æt]

介 在……

用法 at 之後可接建築物，如 at the bank（在銀行）、at the station（在車站）；at 之後也可接時刻，如 at ten o'clock（在十點鐘）。

Will gets up at seven every morning.
威爾每天早上都在七點起床。

attack [ə\`tæk]

動 攻擊

用法 attack 也可用來表示「處理」難題，
如 attack the problem　處理問題

A bad guy **attacked** John in the park yesterday.
昨天有個壞蛋在公園裡**攻擊**約翰。

attention [ə\`tɛnʃən]

名 注意（力）

用法
ⓐ attention 為不可數。
ⓑ pay attention to...　注意……

You'll be sorry if you don't **pay attention to** your mom.　你若不**注意**聽媽媽的話，會後悔的。

August [\`ɔgəst]

名 八月

用法 下列例句中的 falls on August third（在八月三日降臨）等於 comes on August third（在八月三日到來）。

Sam's birthday falls on **August** third.
山姆的生日是**八月**三日。

A a

aunt [ænt]

名 姨媽

用法 中文的「姨媽」、「姑媽」、「伯母」、「嬸嬸」、「舅媽」，在英文中全都用 aunt 來表示。

My uncle's wife is my **aunt**.
我叔叔的太太就是我的嬸嬸。

autumn [ˋɔtəm]

名 秋天

用法 秋天時樹葉會掉落，因此美國人常用 fall 取代 autumn。如 in the fall of 2022（二〇二二年的秋天）

Leaves turn yellow in **autumn**.
入秋時，樹葉會變成枯黃色。

available [əˋveləbl̩]

形 可取得的；可買得到的；有空的

用法 available 當「有空的」時，等於 free。

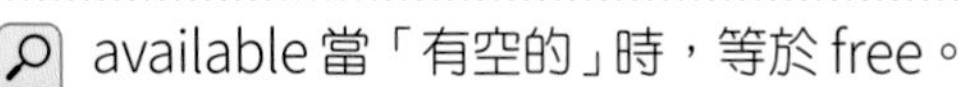

Will you be available later?（你等一下有空嗎？）

Do you have this watch **available** here?
這只錶你這裡有賣嗎？

avoid [əˋvɔɪd]

動 避開；避免

用法 avoid 後常使用動名詞做受詞使用。

Try to avoid eating too much.
設法避免吃太多東西。

away [əˋwe]

副 離開

用法 away 常與 far 及 from 並用。
如 Megan lives far away from her school.
（梅根住的地方離學校很遠。）

Go away. I don't want to see you again.
走開。我不想再見到你。

Notes

Bb

baby [ˋbebɪ]

名 嬰兒；寶貝

用法 baby 之後也可接名詞，如 a baby boy（小男嬰）、a baby girl（小女嬰）。

Be quiet. The baby is sleeping.
安靜。小寶寶還在睡覺。

babysitter [ˋbebɪˏsɪtɚ]

名（臨時幫人照顧小孩的）褓母

用法 動詞為 babysit，意思是「當臨時褓母」。

If Jamie wants to go out tonight, she has to find a babysitter first. 潔咪今晚若想外出，就須先找個褓母。

back [bæk]

副 回原處；往後　名 後面

用法 in back of...　在……後面（= behind...）
There is a garden in back of Jasmine's house.（潔絲敏家後面有一座花園。）

When will you come back, Mommy?
媽咪，妳什麼時候會回來？

backpack [ˋbæk͵pæk]

名 背包　動 背登山包徒步旅行

用法 backpacker [ˋbæk͵pækɚ] 名 背包旅行者

Mary is **backpacking** in the mountains.
瑪麗正在山中背背包徒步旅行。

backward [ˋbækwɚd]

副 向後　形 落後的

用法 backward 當副詞時，等於 backwards。
Julie can say the English alphabet backward(s).（茱莉可以倒背英文字母。）

That is a **backward** country.
那是一個落後的國家。

bad [bæd]

形 壞的；不良的

用法 go bad （食物）餿掉
（= spoil [spɔɪl]）

The food has gone **bad**. It cannot be eaten.
這食物餿掉了，不能吃了。

badminton [ˋbædmɪntən]

名 羽毛球（不可數）

用法 play badminton with a racket
用球拍打羽毛球
（racket [ˋrækɪt] 名 球拍）

Would you like to play badminton with Lauren?
你想不想跟蘿倫打羽毛球？

bag [bæg]

名 袋子

用法 Don't let the cat out of the bag.
（不要洩露祕密。）

What's in the bag?
袋子裡有什麼東西？

bake [bek]

動 烘焙

用法 bake a cake
烘焙蛋糕

Mom is baking a cake for my birthday.
媽媽正在為我的生日烘焙蛋糕。

bakery [ˋbekərɪ]

名 麵包店

用法 在麵包店內工作的麵包師父稱為 baker [ˋbekɚ]。

Candy always buys bread at that bakery.
坎蒂一向在那家麵包店買麵包。

balcony [ˋbælkənɪ]

名 陽臺

用法 電影院內二樓的「包廂」座位也叫做 balcony。

Duke likes to sit on the balcony and read.
杜克喜歡坐在陽臺上看書。

ball [bɔl]

名 球

用法 on the ball 表示某人很「機敏」、「靈光」。
如 John is really on the ball.
（約翰實在很機敏。）

Pass the ball to me, Peter.
把球傳給我，彼得。

Bb

balloon [bəˋlun]

名 氣球

用法 a hot-air balloon
熱氣球

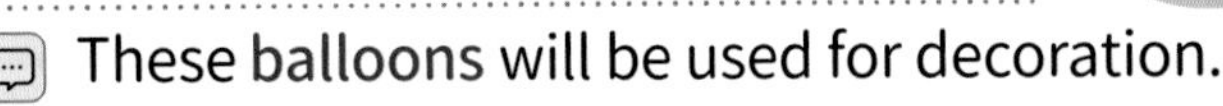

These balloons will be used for decoration.
這些氣球將用來做裝飾。

banana [bəˋnænə]

名 香蕉

用法 bananas 形 瘋狂的
如 Ryan went bananas.
（萊恩瘋了。）

Monkeys like to eat bananas.
猴子喜歡吃香蕉。

band [bænd]

名（流行音樂）樂團

用法 band 也可指圈狀物
如 a rubber band　一條橡皮筋
（rubber [ˋrʌbɚ] 名 橡膠）

The band is playing music.
樂團正在演奏音樂。

bank [bæŋk]

名 銀行

用法
keep money in the bank　把錢存在銀行
get money from the bank　從銀行提款

Evan is going to **get some money from the bank.**
伊凡要從銀行**領點錢**。

barbecue [ˋbarbɪˏkju]

名 烤肉野餐

用法
have a barbecue
舉辦烤肉野餐

My friend and I will **have a barbecue** on the balcony tonight.　我和我朋友今晚會在陽臺**烤肉**。

barber [ˋbarbɚ]

名 理髮師

用法
「理髮店」為 barber's 或 barbershop。

There are only two **barbers** at the barbershop.
這家理髮店只有兩名**理髮師**。

bark [bɑrk]

動（狗）吠叫

用法 bark 當名詞為「狗吠聲」，為可數名詞，另外也有「樹皮」的意思，為不可數名詞。

The dog kept barking at us.
那隻狗一直對我們咆哮。

base [bes]

名（棒球）壘；基礎　動 以……為根據

用法
ⓐ first / second / third / home base
一 / 二 / 三 / 本壘
ⓑ be based on...　以……為根據

The player made it to first base.
球員成功跑到了一壘。

baseball [ˋbes͵bɔl]

名 棒球

用法 play baseball
打棒球

Does Rudy like to play baseball?
魯迪喜歡打棒球嗎？

A B C D E F G H I J K L M N O P Q R S T U V W X Y Z

basement [ˋbesmənt]

名 地下室

用法 我們常說的地下一樓、地下二樓的英文常會用 B1、B2，這裡的 B 則代表 basement 的意思。

Jack used to live in the basement.
傑克有一陣子住在這地下室。

basic [ˋbesɪk]

形 基礎的

用法 basic pay / salary
基本薪資

Stan's basic problem is lack of money.
史坦的基本問題是缺乏資金。

basket [ˋbæskɪt]

名 籃子

用法
a basket of + sth　一籃的……
a basket of eggs　一籃蛋
a basket of vegetables　一籃蔬菜

Mariah can put all the fruit in the basket.
瑪麗亞可以把所有的水果都放在籃子裡。

basketball [ˋbæskɪtˏbɔl]

名 籃球

🔍用法
ⓐ play basketball　打籃球
ⓑ 注意下列例句在 team（球隊）之前的介詞是 on，而非 in。

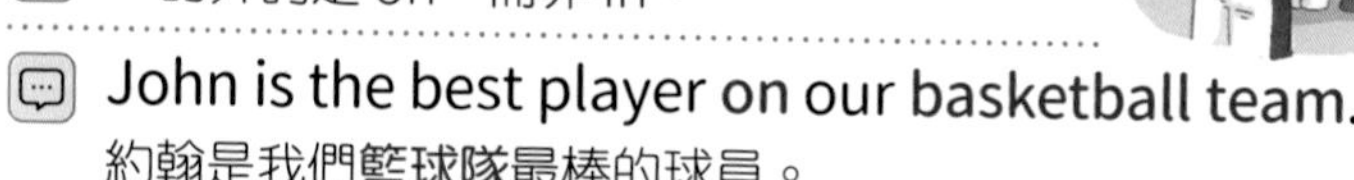

💬 John is the best player on our basketball team.
約翰是我們籃球隊最棒的球員。

bat [bæt]

名（棒球）球棒；蝙蝠

🔍用法
at bat　輪到打擊
Who is at bat now?
（現在輪到誰揮棒了？）

💬 Tim uses a bat to hit a baseball.
提姆用球棒打棒球。

bath [bæθ]

名 浴缸；沐浴

🔍用法
take a bath　泡澡
take a shower　淋浴
（shower [ˋʃaʊɚ] 名 淋浴）

💬 Gary takes a bath before going to bed.
蓋瑞睡覺前都會泡澡。

bathe [beð]

動 洗澡

用法 be bathed in... 沉浸在……
The church was bathed in sunlight.
（教堂浸浴在陽光下。）

Dan arrived just as I was bathing.
丹來的時候我正在洗澡。

bathroom [ˋbæθˏrum]

名 （帶有廁所的）浴室；廁所

用法 bathroom 多指家裡的廁所，restroom [ˋrɛstˏrum]、toilet [ˋtɔɪlɪt] 則多指公共廁所。

Debbie helps Mom clean the bathroom on Sundays.
每逢星期天黛比都會幫媽媽打掃廁所。

be [bi]

動 是；在

用法 be 動詞指的就是 is、am、are、was、were、been 的原形動詞，之後若接名詞，be 動詞譯成「是」；若接表示場所或某地方，則譯成「在」。

I am a student, and he is a teacher.
我是學生，他是老師。

beach [bitʃ]

名 海灘，沙灘

用法 on the beach
在沙灘上

Milly sees a lot of children playing on the beach.
蜜莉看到好多小朋友在海灘上玩耍。

bean [bin]

名 豆子

用法 bean 及 pea [pi] 都是豆子，但 bean 多指圓形或橢圓形較硬的豆子，如黃豆、大豆等，pea 則指扁形的豌豆。

Beans are good for your health.
豆類有益健康。

bear [bɛr]

名 熊

用法 bear 也可作動詞，表示「容忍」，
如 I can't bear the noise.
（這個噪音我受不了。）

Bears are dangerous when they get angry.
熊生氣的時候會很危險。

beard [bɪrd]

名 鬍子

用法 wear a beard
留鬍子

Adam wears a beard.
亞當留了鬍子。

beat [bit]

動 毆打；打敗

用法 三態：beat、beat、beaten [ˋbitən]

Warren beat Alex at tennis.
華倫網球打敗了艾力克斯。

beautiful [ˋbjutəfəl]

形 美麗的

用法 beautiful 與 pretty 同義，均指「美麗的」，多用來修飾女孩子或美好的事物。

All boys like beautiful girls.
所有的男生都喜歡漂亮的女生。

beauty [ˋbjutɪ]

名 **美麗（不可數）；美人（可數）**

用法 the beauty of nature
大自然之美

Mary is really a beauty.
瑪麗真是個大美人。

because [bɪˋkɔz]

連 **因為**

用法 中文的「因為……所以……」在英文中不可說：Because... so...，因為 because 跟 so 均是連接詞，只能選用其中的一個。

I don't like Victor because he is lazy.
我不喜歡維克多，因為他懶惰。

become [bɪˋkʌm]

動 **變成，成為**

用法 三態：become、became [bɪˋkem]、become。

Spring is coming, and the weather is becoming warmer and warmer. 春天來了，天氣變得愈來愈暖和了。

bed [bɛd]

名 床

用法 go to bed 去睡覺
= go to sleep

Ryan goes to bed at ten every night.
萊恩每天晚上十點睡覺。

bedroom [ˋbɛdˏrum]

名 臥室，臥房

用法 living room 客廳
kitchen 廚房

This house has three bedrooms.
這棟房子有三間臥房。

bee [bi]

名 蜜蜂

用法 beehive [ˋbiˏhaɪv] 名 蜂窩
wasp [wɑsp] 名 黃蜂
hornet [ˋhɔrnɪt] 名 虎頭蜂

Bees make honey.
蜜蜂會產蜂蜜。

beef [bif]

名 牛肉（不可數）

用法 pork [pɔrk] 名 豬肉
chicken [ˋtʃɪkən] 名 雞肉
fish [fɪʃ] 名 魚肉

Sam doesn't eat beef or pork; he eats fish.
山姆不吃牛肉或豬肉，他吃魚肉。

beer [bɪr]

名 啤酒

用法 a glass of beer
一杯啤酒

Arthur wants a glass of cold beer.
亞瑟想要一杯冰啤酒。

before [bɪˋfɔr]

介 連 在……之前　副 以前

用法 before 表示「以前」時，要放在句尾，
如 I have seen Maggie before.
（我以前曾見過瑪姬。）

Close the door before you leave.
你離開前要把門關上。

begin [bɪˋgɪn]

動 開始

用法
ⓐ 三態：begin、began [bɪˋgæn]、begun [bɪˋgʌn]
ⓑ begin + V-ing / to V　開始做……

Sean began learning English when he was six.
尚恩六歲時開始學英文。

beginner [bɪˋgɪnɚ]

名 初學者

用法
beginner's luck
新手的好運氣

The course is for beginners.
這門課是為初學者開設的。

beginning [bɪˋgɪnɪŋ]

名 開始；起點

用法
In the beginning, ...　起初，……

We missed the beginning of the movie.　我們錯過了電影的開頭。

behave [bɪˋhev]

動（言行舉止的）表現

用法 behave oneself
守規矩

Behave yourself, or I'll punish you.
守規矩，否則我會處罰你。

behind [bɪˋhaɪnd]

介 在……後面　副 後面

用法 fall behind　落後
You'll fall behind if you don't study hard.（你不努力用功就會跟不上。）

There is a big tree behind my house.
我家後面有一棵大樹。

believe [bɪˋliv]

動 相信

用法 believe it or not, ...　信不信由你，……
Believe it or not, Peter dances very well.
（信不信由你，彼得很會跳舞。）

Paula doesn't believe what Ryan says.
寶拉不相信萊恩說的話。

bell [bɛl]

名 鈴；鐘

用法 ring a bell 按字義指「搖鈴」，實際指某人名字「聽起來很耳熟」。

The bell is ringing. It's time for class again.
鈴聲響了。又是上課的時候了。

belong [bɪˋlɔŋ]

動 屬於

用法 belong 常加 to，視情況也可加 in 或 with。

This toy belongs to me.
這個玩具是我的。

below [bɪˋlo]

介 在……下面

用法 below 與 under 均表示「在……下面」，但 under 指在某物的正下面，below 則指在某物下面的任何一處。

My brother sees a few boats below the bridge.
我弟弟看到橋下有幾艘小船。

belt [bɛlt]

名 腰帶，皮帶

用法
ⓐ wear a belt　繫皮帶
ⓑ a seat belt　安全帶

John is wearing a white belt today.
約翰今天繫了一條白色的皮帶。

bench [bɛntʃ]

名 長凳

用法 bench 指公園內的長凳，也叫做 park bench；stool [stul] 則指一般的圓板凳。

An old man is sitting on the bench.
一位老先生正坐在長凳上。

beside [bɪˋsaɪd]

介 在……旁邊

用法
beside...　在旁邊
= next to...

A beautiful girl is standing beside the door.
門邊站著一位漂亮的女孩。

besides [bɪˋsaɪdz]

介 除……之外　副 再者，更何況

用法 beside 為「在……旁邊」的意思，
請不要混淆囉！

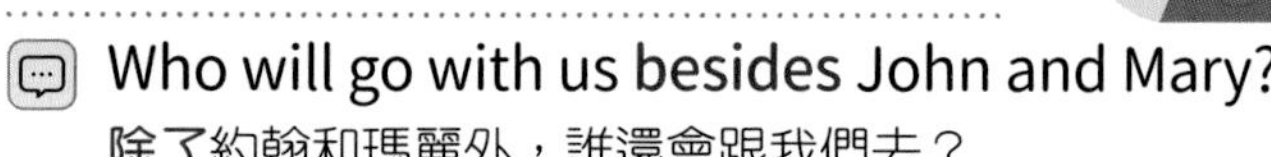

Who will go with us besides John and Mary?
除了約翰和瑪麗外，誰還會跟我們去？

between [bɪˋtwin]

介 在……之間

用法 between you and me, ...
（我要講個祕密，只有你我知道就好……）

Come and sit between Mom and Dad.
過來坐在爸媽中間。

beyond [bɪˋjand]

介 超出；超過

用法 beyond one's control
超出某人的控制

It is already beyond Tony's control.
情況已超出湯尼所能控制。

bicycle [ˋbaɪˏsɪkḷ]

名 腳踏車，自行車

用法 bicycle 常簡稱為 bike [baɪk]，也可作動詞用，如 Amanda bicycles / bikes to school every day.（亞曼達每天騎腳踏車上學。）

Billy rides his bicycle to and from school every day. 比利每天騎腳踏車上下課。

big [bɪg]

形 大的

用法 talk big　講大話，愛吹牛
Nobody believes Bruce because he likes to talk big.（沒人相信布魯斯，因為他愛吹牛。）

This ball is big, and that one is small.
這個球很大，那個球則很小。

bill [bɪl]

名 帳單

用法 pay the bill
付帳

Let me pay the bill this time.
這次由我來付帳。

biology [baɪˋɑlədʒɪ]

名 生物學

用法
ⓐ biology 為不可數。
ⓑ「生物學家」為 biologist。

Willy is very interested in biology.
威利對生物學很感興趣。

bird [bɝd]

名 鳥

用法
爸爸在週末有空時常會對我們說：
Let's go bird-watching today.
（咱們今天去賞鳥吧。）

Sid sees many birds flying in the sky.
席德看見天空有許多鳥兒在飛翔。

birthday [ˋbɝθˏde]

名 生日

用法
hold a birthday party for + sb
為某人舉行生日派對

It's my brother's birthday today.
今天是我弟弟的生日。

Bb

bite [baɪt]

動 咬　名 咬一口

用法
- ⓐ 三態：bite、bit [bɪt]、bitten [ˋbɪtən]
- ⓑ 看到某人心煩時，我們會問：What's biting Melody?（什麼事讓美樂蒂煩心？）

Be careful! That dog bites.

小心！那隻狗會咬人。

bitter [ˋbɪtɚ]

形 苦的

用法

bittersweet 則為「苦中帶甜；苦中有樂」的意思。

The tea tastes a little too bitter.

這茶的味道太苦了點。

black [blæk]

形 黑色的　名 黑色

用法
- ⓐ black tea　紅茶（非 red tea）
- ⓑ My father would like his coffee black.（我爸爸想喝不加奶精的純咖啡。）

Taylor's car is black, and Stuart's is yellow.

泰勒的車是黑色的，史都華的車是黃色的。

B b

blackboard [ˋblækˌbɔrd]

名 黑板

用法
eraser [ɪˋrezɚ / ɪˋresɚ] 名 板擦
chalk [tʃɔk] 名 粉筆
whiteboard [ˋwaɪtˌbɔrd] 名 白板

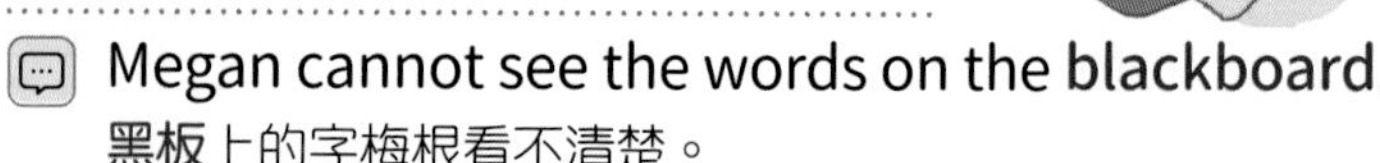

Megan cannot see the words on the blackboard.
黑板上的字梅根看不清楚。

blame [blem]

動 責備，譴責；歸咎

用法
be to blame for...　應對……負責
Who is to blame for the mistake?
（這個錯該怪誰？）

Hey, don't blame Simon for the mistake.
嘿！不要將這個錯歸咎在賽門身上。

blank [blæŋk]

名 空白；空格

用法
a blank sheet of paper
一張白紙

Fill in the blanks first, please.
請先把這些空格填好。

blanket [ˋblæŋkɪt]

名 毯子

用法 quilt [kwɪlt] 名 棉被

I feel cold. Can I have a blanket?
我覺得好冷。可以給我一條毯子嗎？

bless [blɛs]

動 （上帝）賜福於（常用被動語態）

用法
be blessed with... 有幸得到……
May God bless you! 願上帝保佑你！
= I wish God may bless you.

Thomas is blessed with good health.
湯瑪斯有幸擁有健康。

blind [blaɪnd]

形 盲的

用法
be blind to...
看不見 / 完全沒注意到……

The old man is poor and blind.
這位老伯伯又窮又盲。

block [blak]

名 街區　動 堵住

用法 Go away! Don't block my way!
（走開！不要擋我的路！）

The bank is two blocks from here.
從這裡再過兩條街就到銀行了。

blood [blʌd]

名 血液

用法 ⓐ blood 為不可數名詞。
ⓑ bleed 當動詞時，為「流血」的意思。

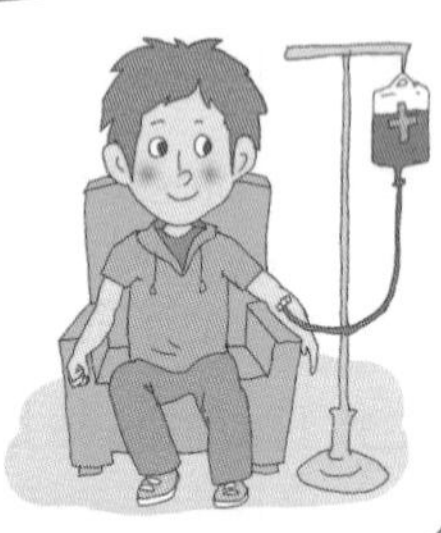

Has Troy ever given blood?
特洛依捐過血嗎？

blouse [blaʊs]

名（女用）罩衫

用法 blouse 專指女用的襯衫。

Rebecca is wearing a silk blouse.
蕾貝嘉身穿一件絲質罩衫。

blow [blo]

動 吹

用法 ⓐ 三態：blow、blew [blu]、blown [blon]
ⓑ blow up　氣炸

The wind is blowing hard.
風正猛烈地吹著。

blue [blu]

形 藍色的　名 藍色

用法 blue 也表示「憂鬱的」、「難過的」。

The blue sky looks beautiful.
藍天看起來真美。

board [bɔrd]

動 登上（飛機、火車、公車、船等）名 木板；膳食

用法 room and board　膳宿，吃住
Does the price include room and board?
（這價錢包含膳宿嗎？）

Let's board the train now.
我們現在就登上火車吧。

B

boat [bot]

名 小船

用法 We are in the same boat now.
（我們現在是同病相憐了。）

Peter and his girlfriend are rowing a boat on the lake.
彼得和他女友正在湖上划船。

body [ˋbɑdɪ]

名 身體；屍體

用法 everybody 指「每個人」、somebody 指「某個人」、nobody 指「沒有人」、anybody 指「任何人」。

Swimming is good for your body.
游泳對你身體有益。

boil [bɔɪl]

動 沸騰

用法 表示「喝開水」要說 drink boiled water。boiled 表示「已經煮開的」，boiling 則表示「正在沸騰的」。

The water is boiling.
水滾了。

bomb [bɑm]

名 炸彈

用法 bomber 為「炸彈客」的意思。

A bomb went off, killing many people.
有一枚炸彈爆炸，造成多人死亡。

bone [bon]

名 骨頭

用法 human / animal bones
人 / 動物的骨

Natasha fell and broke a bone in her foot.
娜塔莎摔斷一根腳骨頭。

book [bʊk]

名 書

用法 上課時，老師會對我們說：
“Open your books to page 10, please.”
（請把你們的書打開到第十頁。）

You can find many books in the library.
在圖書館裡你可以找到許多書。

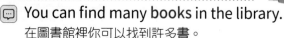

bookcase [ˋbʊk͵kes]

名 書櫃

用法 bookshelf 也是「書櫃，書架」，特別指的是像圖書館的那種開放式的書架。

My older brother put some books in my bookcase.
我哥哥放了幾本書在我的書櫃內。

bookstore [ˋbʊk͵stɔr]

名 書店

用法 bookstore 是美國人的說法，英國人則多把書店稱作 bookshop [ˋbʊk͵ʃɑp]。

There is a bookstore around the corner.
轉角附近有一家書店。

bored [bɔrd]

形 感到厭煩的

用法 be bored with...
對……感到厭倦

Charlie is bored with this job.
查理對這工作厭煩了。

boring [ˋbɔrɪŋ]

形 令人厭煩的；無聊的

用法 以 -ed 結尾的形容詞多譯成「感到……的」，如 bored。以 -ing 結尾的形容詞多譯成「令人……的」，如 boring。

This movie is boring. Earl doesn't like it.
這部電影真無聊，厄爾不喜歡。

born [bɔrn]

形 出生的

用法
be born in + 地方　在某地出生的
be born on + 日期　在某日出生的
be born in + 年分　在某年出生的

Craig was born in Taipei.
克雷格在臺北出生。

borrow [ˋbaro]

動 向……借

用法
borrow + sth + from + sb　向某人借某物
lend + sth + to + sb　把某物借給某人

Can I borrow some money from you?
我可以向你借點錢嗎？

boss [bɔs]

名 老闆；上司

用法 boss 若變成 bossy [ˋbɔsɪ]，則成了形容詞，表示「霸道的」，如 John is bossy.（約翰很霸道。）

Our boss is very nice to us.
老闆對我們很好。

both [boθ]

形 兩個的　代 兩者　副 兩者皆

用法 both 通常與 and 並用，形成固定用法：
both A and B　A 與 B 兩者皆

Both Jane and May are my friends. They both sing very well.　珍和梅兩個都是我的朋友。她們都很會唱歌。

bother [ˋbaðɚ]

動 麻煩

用法 brother 為「兄；弟」的意思，請不要混淆囉！

Don't bother your sister. She is studying.
別煩你姐姐。她在念書。

bottle [ˋbɑtḷ]

名 瓶子

用法
a bottle of...　一瓶……
a bottle of wine　一瓶酒
a bottle of soda　一瓶汽水

What is in the bottle?
瓶子裡裝的是什麼？

bottom [ˋbɑtəm]

名 底部

用法
大人們喝酒時，常說：Bottoms up!（乾杯！）（指彼此將酒飲盡，使酒杯杯底朝上。）

You can see the price on the bottom of the box.
你在盒子底部可以看到價格。

bow [baʊ]

動 鞠躬

用法
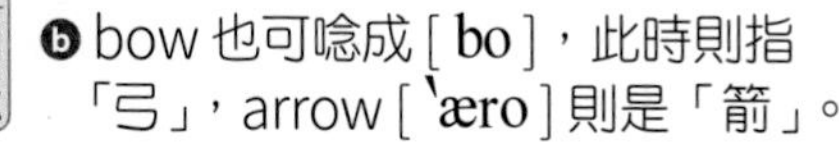
ⓐ bow to + sb　向某人鞠躬
ⓑ bow 也可唸成 [bo]，此時則指「弓」，arrow [ˋæro] 則是「箭」。

The students bow to their teacher when they see her.　學生們見到老師時都會向她鞠躬。

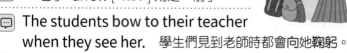

B

bowl [bol]

名 碗

用法
a bowl of 一碗……
a bowl of rice 一碗飯
a bowl of noodles 一碗麵

Can I have another bowl of rice?
我可以再來一碗飯嗎？

bowling [ˋbolɪŋ]

名 保齡球

用法
ⓐ bowling 為不可數。
ⓑ go bowling 去打保齡球

Why don’t we go bowling tonight?
我們今晚何不去打保齡球呢？

box [bɑks]

名 盒子；箱子

用法
a box of 一盒……；一箱……
a box of books 一箱書

Put all your books in the box.
把你所有的書都裝進箱子裡。

Bb

boy [bɔɪ]

名 男孩

用法 boy 亦作驚歎的用語，相當於中文的「哇塞」，如 Boy, Angel is really beautiful!（哇塞，安琪真的很美！）

Dale is a boy, and Carrie is a girl.
戴爾是男生，凱莉是女生。

branch [bræntʃ]

名 樹枝

用法 branch 也有「分店；分部」的意思。
branch manager　分店經理

The monkey jumped from branch to branch.
那隻猴子在樹枝間跳來跳去。

brave [brev]

形 勇敢的

用法 be brave to V
對做……很勇敢

Tommy is very brave for his age.
以湯米他的年齡而言，他算是很勇敢的了。

bread [brɛd]

名 麵包（不可數）

用法
a piece of bread　一塊麵包
two pieces of bread　兩塊麵包
some bread　一些麵包

Daniel had two pieces of bread for lunch yesterday.　丹尼爾昨天午餐吃了兩塊麵包。

break [brek]

動 打破　名 短暫休息

用法
ⓐ 三態：break、broke [brok]、broken [ˋbrokən]
ⓑ take a break　休息一下

Little Johnny broke the window again.
小強尼又把窗戶打破了。

breakfast [ˋbrɛkfəst]

名 早餐

用法
have＋食物＋for breakfast / lunch / dinner　早餐 / 中餐 / 晚餐吃某食物
上列的 have 表示「吃」，for 則表示「當作」。

What did Daniel have for breakfast this morning?　丹尼爾今天早上早餐吃了些什麼？

brick [brɪk]

名 磚塊

用法 a red-brick house
紅磚房

That house is made of bricks.
那棟房子是磚造的。

bridge [brɪdʒ]

名 橋梁

用法 bridge 也有「鼻梁」或是指「眼鏡的鼻梁架」的意思。

You can find my house after you cross the bridge. 你過了橋之後就可以找到我家了。

bright [braɪt]

形 明亮的

用法 bright 也可指「聰明的」，等於 clever [ˋklɛvɚ]。
如 a bright student 聰明的學生

The room is not bright. It is very dark.
房間不夠明亮。太暗了。

Bb

B

bring [brɪŋ]

動 帶來，拿來

用法 ⓐ 三態：bring、brought [brɔt]、brought
ⓑ bring 指從遠處將某物帶過來，
take 則指將某物帶到遠處。

Bring the newspaper to me, please.
請把報紙拿給我。

broad [brɔd]

形 寬的

用法 board 為「板子；董事會」等意思，
請不要混淆囉！

The room is six meters long and four meters broad.
這個房間長六公尺，寬四公尺。

broadcast [ˋbrɔdˌkæst]

動 廣播（三態同形） 名 廣播

用法 broadcaster 為「廣播員」的意思。

Evan is listening to the news broadcast.
伊凡正在收聽新聞廣播。

brother [ˋbrʌðɚ]

名 哥哥；弟弟

用法
older brother　　哥哥
younger brother　弟弟

My older brother is a teacher, and my younger brother is a soldier.　我哥哥是老師，弟弟是軍人。

brown [braʊn]

形 棕色的，褐色的　名 棕色，褐色

用法
我們吃的「紅糖」或「黑糖」就叫做 brown sugar，非 black sugar。

Wesley looks handsome in the brown coat.
衛斯理穿上那件棕色外套看起來很帥。

brunch [brʌntʃ]

名 早午餐

用法
brunch 是 breakfast 與 lunch 結合而成的合體字。

Jeff usually has brunch on Sundays.
傑夫星期天通常吃早午餐。

brush [brʌʃ]

名 刷子 動 刷

用法
brush your teeth 刷牙
brush the floor 刷地板
brush your hair 梳頭髮

Does Terry **brush** his teeth every morning? 泰瑞每天早上都刷牙嗎？

bucket [ˋbʌkɪt]

名 水桶；一桶之量

用法
a bucket of water
一桶水

We need one more **bucket** of water.
我們還需要一桶水。

buffet [bəˋfe]

名（不限量的）自助餐

用法
a buffet car
（火車上的）餐車

The price includes a **buffet** lunch.
這個價錢內含一份自助式午餐。

bug [bʌg]

名 **小蟲子**

用法 美國人常將 bug 作動詞，表示「打擾」、「煩」。如 Don't bug your sister. She is studying.（別煩你姐姐。她正在念書。）

Don't touch that bug.
別碰那隻小蟲。

build [bɪld]

動 **建造**

用法 三態：build、built [bɪlt]、built

They are building a house there.
他們正在那裡蓋房子。

building [ˋbɪldɪŋ]

名 **建築物，大樓**

用法 office building
辦公大樓

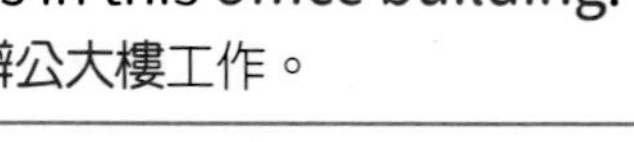

My dad works in this office building.
我爸爸在那棟辦公大樓工作。

bun [bʌn]

名 小圓麵包

用法 bun 指的就是麵包店或便利商店賣的圓麵包，可以說：a bun、two buns、three buns...。bun 屬 bread（麵包類）的一種。

The little boy is eating a bun.
小男孩正在吃一個小圓麵包。

bundle [ˋbʌndl̩]

名 捆；束

用法 a bundle of...
一捆……

There is a bundle of old newspapers on the floor.
地板上有一捆舊報紙。

burger [ˋbɝgɚ]

名 漢堡

用法 為 hamburger [ˋhæmbɝgɚ] 的簡稱。

Cheese Burger

Turkey Burger

Which do you like better, a cheese burger or a turkey burger? 你比較喜歡哪一樣，起司堡還是火雞堡？

burn [bɝn]

動 燃燒，焚燒

用法 ⓐ 三態：burn、burned / burnt [bɝnt]、burned / burnt
ⓑ burn up a letter　將信件燒掉
burn down a house　將房舍燒毀

A fire burned down Donald's house.
一場大火把唐納德的家燒毀了。

burst [bɝst]

動 爆破；（感情）爆發（三態同形）

用法 burst out crying　突然哭出來
burst out laughing　突然笑出來

Stop blowing, or the balloon will burst.
不要再吹了，否則氣球會爆開。

bus [bʌs]

名 公車

用法 by bus　搭公車
by train　搭火車
by taxi　搭計程車

Dad goes to work by bus every day.
爸爸每天搭公車上班。

business [ˈbɪznɪs]

名 生意；事情

用法 Mind your own business!
（少管閒事！）

Business is good this year.
今年生意很好。

businessman

名（男性）商人 [ˈbɪznɪsˌmæn]

用法 表示「女性商人」則使用 businesswoman [ˈbɪznɪsˌwʊmən]。

My uncle is a successful businessman.
我叔叔是個成功的生意人。

busy [ˈbɪzɪ]

形 忙碌的

用法 be busy + V-ing　忙著（從事）……
Mom is busy cooking.
（媽媽正忙著做飯。）

John is busy writing a letter.
約翰正忙著寫信。

but [bʌt]

連 但是

用法 使用 but 時，不可再使用 although / though（雖然），反之亦然。

The old man is rich, but he is not happy.
老伯伯很有錢，但是他卻不快樂。

butter [ˋbʌtɚ]

名 奶油（不可數）

用法 butter 常與 bread 並用，形成下列用語：
eat bread with butter　吃麵包夾奶油

Bella likes to eat bread with butter.
貝拉喜歡吃麵包夾奶油。

butterfly [ˋbʌtɚˏflaɪ]

名 蝴蝶

用法 butter（奶油）與 fly（蒼蠅）結合成 butterfly，表示「蝴蝶」。而 dragon（龍）與 fly 結合成 dragonfly [ˋdrægənˏflaɪ]，表示「蜻蜓」。

Most butterflies are beautiful.
大多數的蝴蝶很美麗。

button [ˋbʌtn̩]

名 鈕扣

用法 button 當動詞用時，意思為「扣上鈕扣」的意思。
button (up) you coat　把大衣扣上

A button is missing from my coat.
我外套掉了一顆鈕扣。

buy [baɪ]

動 買

用法
ⓐ 三態：buy、bought [bɔt]、bought
ⓑ buy + sth + for + sb = buy + sb + sth
買某物給某人

Could you buy me a newspaper?
你能否幫我買份報紙來？

by [baɪ]

介 被

用法 by 也可表示「在……旁邊」
如 There is a park by the lake.
（湖邊有一座公園。）

Simon was hit by a car this morning.
賽門今天早上被車子撞了。

cabbage [ˋkæbɪdʒ]

名 高麗菜

用法 spinach [ˋspɪnɪtʃ] 名 菠菜
celery [ˋsɛlərɪ] 名 芹菜
broccoli [ˋbrɑkəlɪ] 名 綠花椰菜

Mother grows some **cabbages** in the garden.
媽媽在菜園裡種了些高麗菜。

cable [ˋkebl̩]

名 電纜

用法 cable TV 有線電視
a cable car 纜車

You can **take a cable car** to the hilltop.
你可以搭纜車到山頂。

cafeteria [ˌkæfəˋtɪrɪə]

名 自助餐廳

用法 cafeteria 是自助餐廳，但不是吃到飽餐廳。自助式吃到飽的餐廳為 buffet [bəˋfe]。

May and her boyfriend will meet in the **cafeteria** for lunch. 梅和男友會在**自助餐廳**碰頭吃午餐。

cage [kedʒ]

名 籠子

用法 關鳥或其它動物的籠子一律稱作 cage。

There is a bird in the cage.
籠裡有一隻鳥。

cake [kek]

名 蛋糕

用法 a cake　一整個蛋糕
a piece of cake
一小塊蛋糕；容易做的事

Mom bought a cake for my birthday.
媽媽買了一個蛋糕慶祝我的生日。

calendar [ˋkæləndɚ]

名 日曆

用法 desk calendar　桌曆

There is a desk calendar beside the computer.　電腦旁邊有一個桌曆。

call [kɔl]

動 打電話給……；將……取名字　名 一通電話

用法 I call my dog Ben.
（我把我的狗取名為班。）

Call me when you have time.
你有空時打個電話給我。

calm [kɑm]

形 平靜的，冷靜的　動 使冷靜

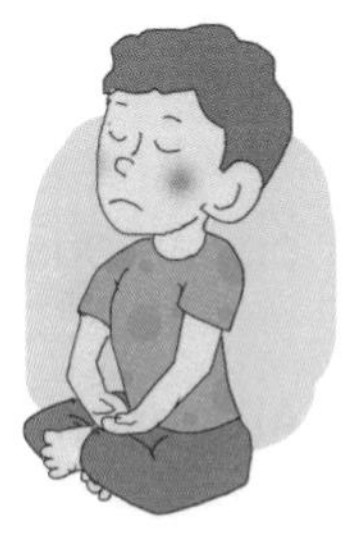

用法 stay calm　保持冷靜

Mike tried hard to **stay calm**.
麥可拼命設法保持冷靜。

camera [ˋkæmərə]

名 照相機

用法 「數位相機」的英文說法為：
digital camera [ˏdɪdʒɪtl̩ ˋkæmərə]。

We use a **camera** to take pictures.
我們用相機拍照。

camp [kæmp]

名 營地　動 露營

用法 go camping　去露營

My dad and I will **go camping** this weekend.　這個週末我和爸爸會去露營。

campus [ˋkæmpəs]

名 校園

用法 on campus　在校園內

All freshmen should live **on campus**.
所有新生都應住校。

can [kæn]

助 能；會　名 罐子

用法
ⓐ can 與 not 並用時，要寫成 cannot 或 can't，can not 可被接受，但較少使用。
ⓑ can 的過去式為 could [kʊd]。

Can you help me write the letter?
你能否幫我寫這封信？

Cc

cancel [ˋkænsḷ]

動 取消

用法 因某些名人的言行而不再支持他／她，這種現象稱之為 cancel culture（取消文化）。

The picnic was **canceled** because of the storm.
野餐活動因暴風雨被取消了。

cancer [ˋkænsɚ]

名 癌症

用法 Cancer 首字大寫的時候，為「巨蟹座」的意思。

Many people die of **cancer** every year.
每年有不少人死於癌症。

candle [ˋkændḷ]

名 蠟燭

用法 Mr. Wang is burning the candle at both ends.
（王先生蠟燭兩頭燒 —— 他過勞了。）

Let's **light the candles** on the cake to celebrate my sister's birthday. 點燃蛋糕上的蠟燭來幫妹妹慶生吧。

candy [ˋkændɪ]

名 糖果

用法 candy 指「糖果類」，同 bread（麵包類）為不可數名詞。因此要說 a piece of candy、two pieces of candy（一顆糖果、兩顆糖果）或 some candy（一些糖果）。

Eating too much **candy** is bad for your teeth. 糖果吃太多對你的牙齒不好。

cap [kæp]

名 帽子

用法 cap 指有帽尖的帽子，如棒球帽、鴨舌帽、軍官帽。hat 則多指有帽邊的帽子，如紳士帽、牛仔帽、淑女帽。

How much is this **baseball cap**?
這頂棒球帽多少錢？

captain [ˋkæptən]

名 船長；（飛機）機長；隊長

用法 captain 當動詞用時，有「率領，指揮」的意思。

John is the **captain** of our school basketball team. 約翰是我們籃球校隊隊長。

C c

car [kɑr]

名 汽車

用法
van [væn] 名 廂型車
taxi [ˋtæksɪ] 名 計程車

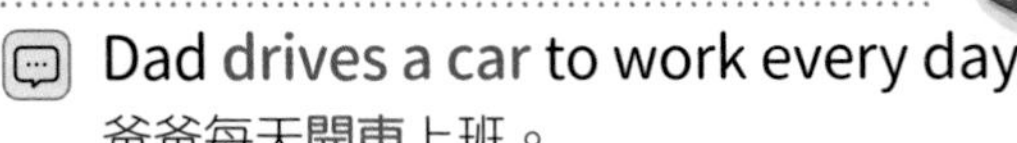

Dad **drives a car** to work every day.
爸爸每天開車上班。

card [kɑrd]

名 卡片；撲克牌

用法
play cards
玩撲克牌

Andy wrote a **card** to me for my birthday.
安迪寫了一張賀卡給我，慶祝我的生日。

care [kɛr]

名 小心　動 關切

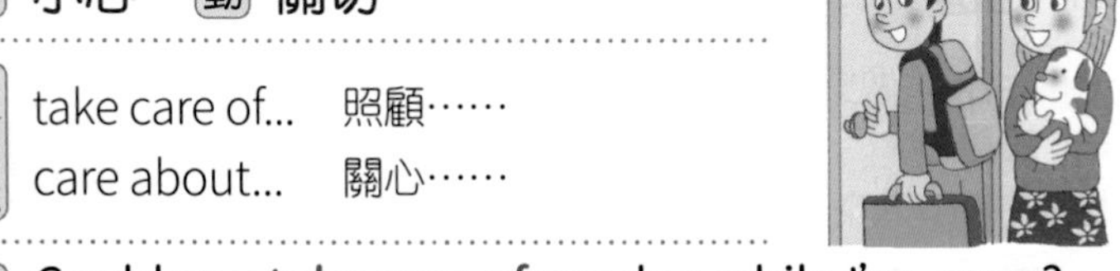

用法
take care of...　照顧……
care about...　關心……

Could you **take care of** my dog while I'm away?
我不在的時候，你能否照顧我的狗？

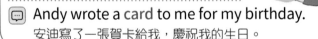

careful [ˋkɛrfəl]

形 **小心的，謹慎的**

用法 careful 的相反詞為 careless。
careless [ˋkɛrlɪs] 形 粗心的

💬 **Be careful! The water is hot.**
小心！水是燙的。

careless [ˋkɛrlɪs]

形 **粗心大意的**

用法 careless 也有「輕鬆自在，無憂無慮」的意思。

💬 **Careless driving is dangerous.**
漫不經心開車很危險。

carpet [ˋkɑrpɪt]

名 **地毯**

用法 carpet 做集合名詞時，有「一層」的意思。
a carpet of snow　一層積雪

💬 **There is a carpet in the living room.**
客廳裡有一張地毯。

carrot [ˋkærət]

名 胡蘿蔔

用法 white radish [ˏwaɪt ˋrædɪʃ]
名 白蘿蔔

Rabbits like to eat carrots.
兔子喜歡吃胡蘿蔔。

carry [ˋkærɪ]

動 攜帶

用法
ⓐ 三態：carry、carried [ˋkærɪd]、carried
ⓑ carry + sth + with + sb
某人隨身攜帶……

The bad guy is carrying a knife with him.
這個壞蛋身上帶了把刀。

cartoon [kɑrˋtun]

名 卡通

用法 a cartoon character　卡通人物

Thomas likes to watch cartoons on TV.
湯瑪斯喜歡看電視卡通節目。

case [kes]

名 箱子，盒子；案件

用法 a case of murder　謀殺案
（murder [ˋmɝdɚ] 名 謀殺）

The case is too heavy. I can't move it.
這箱子太重，我搬不動。

cash [kæʃ]

名 現金

用法
ⓐ cash 為不可數。
ⓑ pay in cash　付現

Patricia would like to pay in cash.
派翠莎想付現金。

castle [ˋkæsl̩]

名 城堡

用法 見到 castle（城堡）就會聯想到 palace [ˋpælɪs]（宮殿）。在歐洲就有許多這樣的建築物。

The king and queen lived happily in the castle.
國王及王后在城堡裡過著幸福的日子。

cat [kæt]

名 貓

用法 keep a cat / dog as a pet
養一隻貓 / 狗當寵物

Alicia keeps a cat as a pet.
艾莉西亞養了一隻貓當寵物。

catch [kætʃ]

動 抓住；接住

用法 ⓐ 三態：catch、caught [kɔt]、caught
ⓑ catch 亦可表示「趕搭」交通工具。
catch the bus / train　趕搭公車 / 火車

Catch the ball. Don't miss it.
接住球。別失手。

cause [kɔz]

動 造成　名 原因

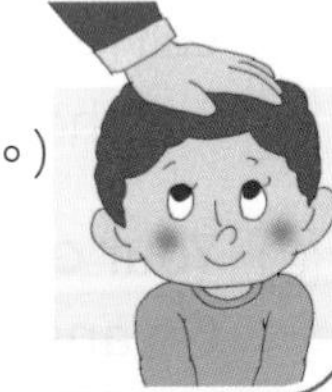

用法 the cause of...　……的原因
My carelessness was the cause of the car accident. （我的粗心是這起車禍的原因。）

Be good. Don't cause any trouble.
要乖。別惹麻煩。

C c

ceiling [ˋsilɪŋ]

名 天花板

用法
ceiling light　天花板燈
ceiling lamp　吊燈

All the rooms have high **ceilings**.
所有房間的天花板都很高。

celebrate [ˋsɛlə͵bret]

動 慶祝

用法
celebrate someone's birthday
慶祝某人生日
celebrate the National Day　慶祝國慶

We **celebrated** Taylor's **birthday** by holding a party.　我們舉行派對慶祝泰勒的生日。

cellphone [ˋsɛl͵fon]

名 手機

用法
cell [sɛl] 原指「細胞」，
cellphone 一詞即由此衍生而來。

Your **cellphone** is ringing.
Go answer it.　你的手機響了。去接吧。

cent [sɛnt]

名（美金）一分

用法 dime [daɪm] 名（美金）一角
quarter [ˋkwɔrtɚ] 名（美金）二十五分

Terry needs a few **cents** to make a phone call.
泰瑞需要幾分錢打電話。

center [ˋsɛntɚ]

名 中心

用法 in the center of...
在……中心點

Tony lives **in the center of the city**.
湯尼住在市中心。

centimeter [ˋsɛntəˌmitɚ]

名 公分（= cm）

用法 meter [ˋmitɚ] 名 公尺，米（= m）
kilometer [kɪˋlɑmətɚ] 名 公里（= km）

Tom is one hundred twenty **centimeters** tall. 湯姆身高一百二十公分。

central [ˋsɛntrəl]

形 中心的，中央的

用法 central 也有「主要的；重要的」等意思。
a central role　主要角色

Natasha and Vic live in **central** Boston.
娜塔莎和維克住在波士頓市中心。

century [ˋsɛntʃərɪ]

名 世紀，百年

用法 a century egg　皮蛋

The church was built in the fifteenth **century**.
這座教堂興建於十五世紀。

cereal [ˋsɪrɪəl]

名 穀類食品（如麥片、玉米片等）

用法 cereal crops　穀類作物

Paula usually has **cereal** and milk for breakfast.
寶拉早餐通常吃麥片加牛奶。

certain [ˋsɝtn̩]

形 肯定的，確定的（= sure）

用法 be certain about / of...　對……很確定
= be sure about / of...

Are you **certain about** that?
那件事你確定嗎？

chair [tʃɛr]

名 椅子

用法 chair 也可表示「主持」，此時當動詞用。
chair the meeting　主持會議

Sit on the **chair** and take a rest.
坐在椅子上休息一下吧。

chalk [tʃɔk]

名 粉筆（不可數）

用法 chalk 原指「石膏粉」，凝結成條狀時，就成粉筆。表示「一根粉筆」，應說：
a piece of chalk（非 a chalk）。

The teacher uses **chalk** to write on the blackboard.
老師用粉筆在黑板上寫字。

chance [tʃæns]

名 機會

用法 chance 也可表示「冒險」，常用複數。
take chances　冒險

I hope I have a **chance** to see Mr. Wang again.
我希望有機會與王先生再次見面。

change [tʃendʒ]

名 動 改變

用法 for a change　變換一下
Let's eat out tonight for a change.
（我們今晚到外面用餐換換口味。）

I'm afraid we'll have to **change the plan.**
恐怕我們得改變計畫了。

channel [ˋtʃænl̩]

名（電視）頻道

用法 channel 與 on 並用。

There is a good movie **on Channel** 56 now.
第五十六頻道正在播映一部好電影。

character [ˋkærɪktɚ]

名 品格（不可數）；人物，角色（可數）

用法 a man of great character　品格高尚的人
Your husband is a man of great character.（妳老公是個品格高尚的人。）

Most children like those **cartoon characters.**
大多數的孩子都喜歡那些卡通人物。

charge [tʃardʒ]

名 費用　動 索取費用

用法 be free of charge　免費
= be free
Is this free of charge?（這是免費的嗎？）

How much do you **charge** for a double room?
雙人房你們收費多少？

chart [tʃart]

名 圖表

用法 a weather chart　天氣圖

Let's take a look at the **weather chart.**
我們來看一下這張天氣圖。

chase [tʃes]

動 **追捕；追求**

用法 chase (after)...　追捕……；追趕……
I saw a cat chasing (after) a mouse.
我看到一隻貓在追老鼠。

I can tell John is **chasing** Mary.
我看得出約翰正在追求瑪麗。

cheap [tʃip]

形 **便宜的**

用法 表示東西「便宜的 / 昂貴的」，應使用 cheap / expensive；表示價格「便宜的 / 昂貴的」，應使用 low / high。

The rich woman never buys **cheap** things.
這位貴婦從不買便宜貨。

cheat [tʃit]

動 **欺騙；作弊**

用法 「考試作弊」指在考試卷「上面」作弊，故應說 cheat on the test / examination；不可說 cheat in the test / examination。

Don't **cheat on tests.**
考試別作弊。

check [tʃɛk]

動 名 檢查

用法 check 除表示「檢查」外，也有下列用法：
check in at the hotel　在飯店辦理住房手續
check in at the airport　在機場辦理登機手續

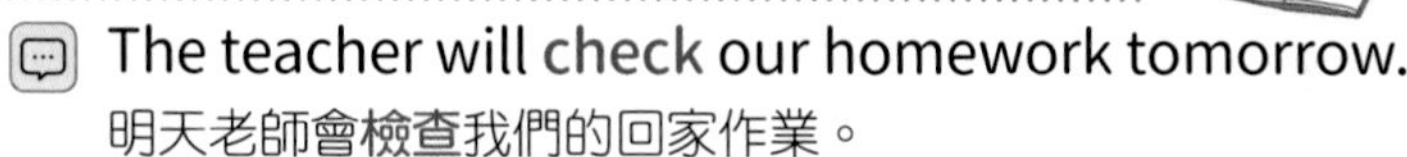

The teacher will **check** our homework tomorrow.
明天老師會檢查我們的回家作業。

cheer [tʃɪr]

動 歡呼；振作

用法
ⓐ cheer 也可作名詞，為「歡呼聲」之意。
ⓑ cheer 常與 up 並用，表示「振作起來」。

Cheer up! Don't be so sad.
振作起來！別這麼難過嘛。

cheese [tʃiz]

名 乳酪，起司

用法 我們唸 cheese 時，會自然呈露齒微笑狀。故拍照時常會希望對方說 Cheese! 即表示要對方作出露齒微笑狀。

Anita loves **cheese cake** very much.
艾妮塔很喜歡起司蛋糕。

chemistry [ˋkɛmɪstrɪ]

名 化學

用法
- a chemistry 為不可數。
- b chemist [ˋkɛmɪst] 名 化學家

Tom failed the **chemistry** test again.
湯姆化學又考不及格。

chess [tʃɛs]

名 西洋棋（不可數）

用法
中國的象棋稱 Chinese chess，表示「下」棋，均使用 play 一字。

Can you **play chess**?
你會下西洋棋嗎？

chicken [ˋtʃɪkən]

名 雞（可數）；雞肉（不可數）

用法
- a a chicken（一隻雞）、
  two chickens（兩隻雞）
- b eat chicken　吃雞肉（非 eat a chicken）

Fried chicken is not good for your health.
炸雞對你的健康不好。

child [tʃaɪld]

名 小孩，孩子

用法 child 是單數，children [ˋtʃɪldrən] 則是複數。即 one child、two children、many children。

Mr. Wang has one **child**, and Mr. Li has five **children**.
王先生有一個孩子，李先生則有五個孩子。

childhood [ˋtʃaɪld͵hʊd]

名 童年

用法 childhood memories　童年回憶

George spent his **childhood** in the mountains.
喬治的童年是在山上度過的。

childish [ˋtʃaɪldɪʃ]

形 幼稚的

用法 childish 指某人很幼稚、不成熟的意思；childlike 則指像小孩般單純、純真的意思。

Ronald cannot stand her **childish** behavior.
羅納德無法忍受她那種幼稚的行為。

C

childlike [ˋtʃaɪld͵laɪk]

形 天真的

用法 a childlike quality
像孩子般天真的氣質

Even though Samuel is 20, he is childlike.
雖然薩姆爾已二十歲了，卻仍像孩子般純真。

chin [tʃɪn]

名 下巴

用法 Chin up!　振作起來！

Peter has a long chin.
彼得的下巴很長。

China [ˋtʃaɪnə]

名 中國

用法 China 改成小寫的 china 時，則指「陶瓷品」（不可數）。

Mr. Wei was born in China, but his wife was born in Taiwan.　魏先生在中國出生，但他太太是在臺灣出生。

Chinese [tʃaɪˋniz]

名 中國人；中文　形 中國籍的

用法 表示「他是個中國人」時，可說：
He is a Chinese.（名詞，指「中國人」）
He is Chinese.（形容詞，指「中國籍的」）

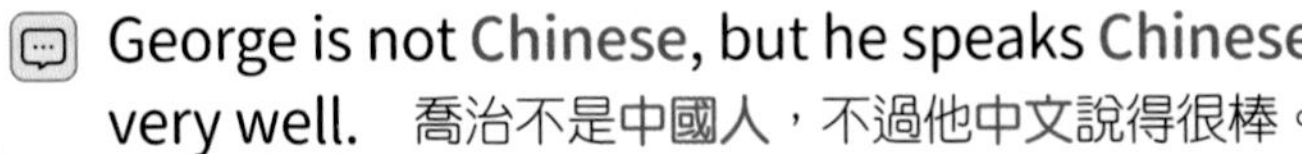

George is not **Chinese**, but he speaks **Chinese** very well.　喬治不是中國人，不過他中文說得很棒。

chocolate [ˋtʃɔklɪt]

名 巧克力

用法
ⓐ chocolate 為不可數。
ⓑ a piece of chocolate（一塊 / 一條巧克力）、two pieces of chocolate（兩塊 / 兩條巧克力）

Chelsea likes **chocolate ice cream**.
雀兒喜喜歡巧克力冰淇淋。

choice [tʃɔɪs]

名 選擇

用法 make choices　做選擇

You can **make your own choice**.
你可以自己做選擇。

choose [tʃuz]

動 選擇

用法 三態：choose、chose [tʃoz]、chosen [ˋtʃozən]

There are so many toys here. My son doesn't know which to **choose**. 這裡有很多玩具。我兒子不知該選哪個。

chopstick [ˋtʃɑpˏstɪk]

名 筷子

用法 chopstick 常用複數，表示「一雙筷子」要說：a pair of chopsticks。

Dolly is teaching that foreigner how to use **chopsticks**. 朵莉正在教那個外國人如何使用筷子。

Christmas [ˋkrɪsməs]

名 聖誕節

用法 on Christmas Day
聖誕節當天（十二月二十五日）

Christmas falls on December 25th.
聖誕節是十二月二十五日。

chubby [ˋtʃʌbɪ]

形 （尤指小孩）胖嘟嘟的

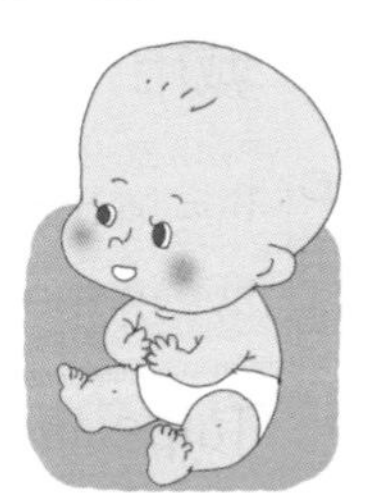

用法 chubby legs / cheeks
胖嘟嘟的腿 / 臉頰

Look at the baby's **chubby** cheeks.
看看這個嬰兒**胖嘟嘟的**臉頰。

church [tʃɝtʃ]

名 教堂，教會

用法 go to church　到教會做禮拜
go to the church
到教會去（未必做禮拜）

Jason **goes to church** every Sunday.
傑森每個星期天都會**到教會做禮拜**。

circle [ˋsɝkḷ]

名 圓圈

用法 circle 也可作動詞用，表示「圈出」。
circle the answer　把答案圈出來

The little boy is drawing **circles** on the wall.
小男孩正在牆上畫**圓圈**。

city [ˋsɪtɪ]

名 城市

用法
live in the city　住在城市裡
live in the country　住在鄉下

Taipei is a big city.
臺北是一座大城市。

clap [klæp]

動 鼓掌

用法
ⓐ 三態：clap、clapped [klæpt]、clapped
ⓑ Let's clap (our hands) for her.
（我們為她鼓掌吧。）

The girl sang so well. Let's clap our hands for her. 這女孩唱得真好。我們為她鼓掌吧。

class [klæs]

名 班級；課

用法
go to class　上課
cut class　逃課，逃學

Peter is sick, so he didn't go to class today. 彼得生病了，所以他今天沒去上課。

classical [ˋklæsɪkḷ]

形 古典的

用法 classical music　古典樂

Does Tom like **classical music** or pop music?　湯姆喜歡古典樂還是流行樂？

classmate [ˋklæs͵met]

名 同學

用法 classmate 指「同班同學」，schoolmate 則指同校同學。

Johnny invited all his **classmates** to his birthday party yesterday.　強尼昨天邀請同學參加生日派對。

classroom [ˋklæs͵rum]

名 教室

用法 我們放學時，老師會要求我們打掃教室，英文的說法就是：clean up the classroom。

We should be quiet when we are in the **classroom**.
我們在教室裡的時候應該保持安靜。

clean [klin]

形 **乾淨的**

用法 clean 也可作動詞，常與 up 並用，表示「將……清理乾淨」。

clean up the table　把餐桌整理乾淨

Your room is not **clean**. Please **clean it up**.

你的房間不整潔。請把它整理乾淨。

clear [klɪr]

形 **清澈的；清晰的**

用法 clear water　清澈（可見底）的水

a clear voice　清晰的聲音

a clear picture　清晰的照片

The river is **clear**. I can see many fish in it.

河水很清澈，我可以看到河中有許多魚。

clerk [klɝk]

名 **職員；店員**

用法 clerk 可指辦公室的一般行政人員、銀行內的職員或一般商店的店員。

My sister is a **clerk** in a big bank.

我姊姊在某大銀行擔任職員。

clever [ˋklɛvɚ]

形 聰明的，機靈的

用法 a clever idea / plan
聰明的點子 / 妙計

What **a clever idea** it is!
這真是**聰明的點子**！

climate [ˋklaɪmɪt]

名（某地區的）氣候

用法 weather [ˋwɛðɚ] 名（一天的）天氣
What's the weather like today?
（今天天氣怎麼樣？）

We have a warm **climate** here.
我們這裡的**氣候**很暖和。

climb [klaɪm]

動 攀爬，攀登

用法 climb 也可作名詞，意思為「攀登」。
It's quite a climb to the tenth floor!
（十樓真難爬！）

The cat **climbed up the tree** when it saw the dog. 貓在看到狗時便**爬到樹上**去了。

clock [klɑk]

名 **鐘，時鐘**

用法 alarm clock 指「鬧鐘」。
set the alarm clock for nine
把鬧鐘設定在九點

There is a clock on the wall.
牆上有一個時鐘。

close [kloz]

動 **關閉**

用法 close 也可作形容詞或副詞，唸成 [klos] 表示「靠近的」，常與 to 並用。

Could you please close the window?
請您把窗戶關上好嗎？

closet [ˋklɑzɪt]

名 **衣櫥**

用法 a storage closet　儲藏室

Jane has a closet full of clothes.
珍有一整櫥的衣服。

clothes [kloz]

名 衣服

用法 clothes 通稱穿在身上的衣物，恆為複數形。故要說：some clothes、many clothes、a lot of clothes。

Dad bought me a lot of new **clothes** for my birthday. 爸爸買了許多新衣服為我慶生。

cloud [klaʊd]

名 雲

用法 be on cloud nine 高興極了

There are a few **clouds** in the sky.
天空有幾朵雲。

cloudy [ˋklaʊdɪ]

形 多雲的，陰天

用法 cloudy 源自名詞 cloud [klaʊd]（雲）。
There are many clouds in the sky.
（天上有許多雲。）

It was **cloudy** yesterday, but it's sunny today. 昨天是陰天，不過今天就放晴了。

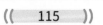

club [klʌb]

名 俱樂部

用法 學校內社團亦稱 club，
如 the Chinese chess club（象棋社）、the English club（英語社）等。

Trevor is a member of the **Chinese chess club** in his school. 崔佛是學校**象棋社**的社員。

coach [kotʃ]

名 長途巴士；（運動）教練

用法 by coach　搭長途巴士
They went to Kenting by coach.
（他們搭長途巴士到墾丁。）

When did Paul become **a baseball coach**? 保羅何時當起**棒球教練**的？

coast [kost]

名 海岸；海濱

用法 coast 與 on 並用。

There is a hotel **on the coast**.
海濱有一家旅館。

coat [kot]

名 外套

用法
put on one's coat　穿上外套
take off one's coat　脫下外套

Put on your coat. It's very cold today.
把你的外套穿上，今天天氣很冷。

cockroach [ˋkɑkˏrotʃ]

名 蟑螂

用法
也可以說 roach。

Is Natasha afraid of cockroaches?
娜塔莎怕蟑螂嗎？

coffee [ˋkɔfɪ]

名 咖啡

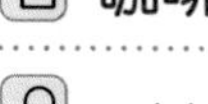

用法
ⓐ black coffee　不加牛奶的咖啡（黑咖啡）
ⓑ a cup of coffee　一杯咖啡

Steven can't sleep if he drinks coffee.
史蒂芬若喝咖啡就睡不著。

coin [kɔɪn]

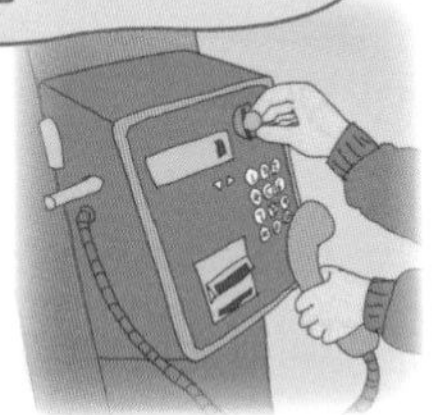

名 硬幣

用法 gold coins　金幣

Lauren needs some **coins** to make a phone call.
蘿倫需要幾枚硬幣來打電話。

coke [kok]

名 可樂

用法 coke 統稱各廠商所生產的可樂飲料，
也可寫成大寫 Coke，源自可口可樂的
商標 Coca-Cola [ˌkokəˋkolə]

Can I have a hamburger and a **coke**, please?　請給我一份漢堡及一杯可樂好嗎？

cold [kold]

形 冷的　名 感冒

用法
ⓐ It's very cold today.
（今天天氣很冷。）
ⓑ catch a cold　得感冒

Put on your coat, or you'll **catch a cold**.
穿上你的外套，否則你會感冒的。

collect [kəˋlɛkt]

動 **收集，蒐集**

用法 collection [kəˋlɛkʃən] 名 收藏
John has a large collection of foreign stamps. （約翰收藏了許多外國郵票。）

Ron **collects stamps.**
榮恩蒐集郵票。

college [ˋkalɪdʒ]

名 **學院，大學**

用法 go to college　上大學

When will your son **go to college**?
你兒子何時上大學？

color [ˋkʌlɚ]

名 **顏色**

用法 sth + come in + 顏色　某物有某種顏色
This car comes in two colors: blue and black. （這款車有兩種顏色：藍色和黑色。）

What **color** does Amy like best?
艾咪最喜歡什麼顏色？

colorful [ˋkʌlɚfəl]

形 顏色鮮豔的

用法 a colorful life　多采多姿的生活

The old man enjoys wearing **colorful** clothes.　這位老伯伯喜歡穿顏色鮮豔的衣服。

comb [kom]

名 梳子　動 用梳子梳

用法 comb 還有「認真搜尋」的意思：
comb the beach for seashells
在沙灘搜尋貝殼 / 在沙灘找貝殼

Give me the **comb**. I want to **comb** my hair.
把梳子給我。我要梳頭髮。

come [kʌm]

動 來

用法
ⓐ 三態：come、came [kem]、come
ⓑ come up with a good idea
想出一個好點子

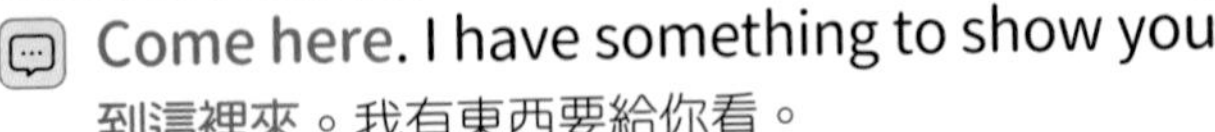

Come here. I have something to show you.
到這裡來。我有東西要給你看。

comfortable

形 舒適的 [ˋkʌmfɚtəbl̩]

用法 美語人士常將這個字唸成 [ˋkʌmftəbl̩]，以求發音的簡化。

Are you feeling **comfortable** now?
你現在覺得舒服了嗎？

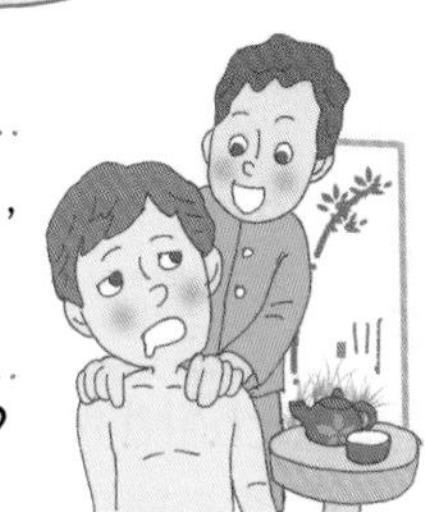

comic [ˋkamɪk]

名 漫畫　形 漫畫的；滑稽好笑的

用法 comic book = comic　漫畫書
Milly likes to read comic books.
（蜜莉喜歡看漫畫書。）

John has many **comic books**.
約翰有許多漫畫書。

command [kəˋmænd]

動 命令，指揮　名（語言）掌控（能力）

用法 have a good command of + 語言
對某種語言有良好的造詣
Rachel has a good command of Japanese.
（瑞秋精通日語。）

Do as I **command**.　照我的命令去做。

comment [ˋkamɛnt]

名 動 評論（均與 on 並用）

用法 No comment!
（不予置評！/無可奉告！）

Richard refused to **comment on** the plan.
理查拒絕評論此計畫。

common [ˋkamən]

形 普通的；共同的

用法 have many things in common　有許多共同點
John and I have many things in common.
（約翰和我有許多共同點。）

It's **common** to marry foreigners in Taiwan.　在臺灣跟外國人通婚很普遍。

company [ˋkʌmpənɪ]

名 公司（可數）；陪伴（不可數）

用法 keep + sb + company　陪某人
I'll stay and keep you company.
（我留下來陪你好了。）

Sean works for a computer **company**.　尚恩在一家電腦公司任職。

compare [kəmˋpɛr]

動 比較

用法 compare with...　與……相比

No one can **compare with** John. He is just too good.
誰都無法與約翰相比。他太棒了。

complain [kəmˋplen]

動 抱怨

用法 complain 與 about 並用。
complain about...　抱怨……

What is Rick **complaining about**?
瑞克在抱怨什麼？

complete [kəmˋplit]

形 全部的，完整的　動 完成

用法 當形容詞有「完整的；完美的」之意。
The party wouldn't be complete without Sid.（這個派對沒有席德就不完美。）

The report took eight months to **complete**.　這份報告花了八個月才完成。

C

computer [kəmˋpjutɚ]

名 電腦

用法
desktop computer　桌上型電腦
laptop computer　筆記型電腦

Computers can help us do many things.
電腦可以幫我們做許多事。

concern [kənˋsɝn]

名 關心的事　動 關係到

用法
concerned [**kənˋsɝnd**] 形 關切的，憂慮的
Your teacher is concerned about your future.（你的老師很擔心你的前途。）

It **concerns** everyone's safety.
這可是關係到大家的安全問題。

confident [ˋkɑnfədənt]

形 有信心的

用法
be confident of / about...
對……有信心

Your boss **is confident of** your ability.
你的老闆對你的能力有信心。

confuse [kənˋfjuz]

動 使迷惑，使混淆

用法 confused [kənˋfjuzd] 形 感到迷惑的

be confused about... 對……感到迷惑

If Zora doesn't explain clearly, she'll only **confuse** me. 如果卓拉不解釋清楚，她只會把我搞糊塗。

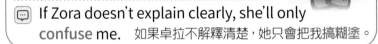

congratulation

[kənˌgrætʃʊˋleʃən]

名 恭喜；道賀

用法 恆用複數，與 on 並用。

Congratulations on your success! 恭喜你成功了！

consider [kənˋsɪdɚ]

動 考慮

用法 consider + V-ing

考慮做……（以動名詞作受詞）

Ted's **considering** buying a used car.

泰德在考慮買臺二手車。

considerate [kən`sɪdərɪt]

形 **體貼的**

用法 It was considerate of Tracy to say so.
（崔西這樣說很體貼。）

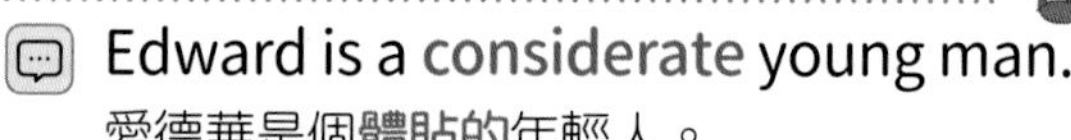

Edward is a **considerate** young man.
愛德華是個**體貼的**年輕人。

contact lens

[`kɑntækt ˏlɛnz]

名 **隱形眼鏡**

用法 複數為 contact lenses

Tommy used to wear **contact lenses.**
湯米有一陣子戴**隱形眼鏡**。

continue [kən`tɪnju]

動 **繼續**

用法 continue to + V
= continue + V-ing

Gina will **continue to** learn English after she graduates.　畢業後吉娜會**繼續**學英文。

contract [ˋkɑntrækt]

名 契約，合同

用法 sign a contract 簽合約

We've signed a contract with them.
我方已跟他們簽好契約。

control [kənˋtrol]

動 控制，克制 名 控制

用法 be under control 在掌控中
be out of control 失控

Try to control yourself.
你要設法克制一下自己。

convenience store

名 便利商店

用法 convenience [kənˋvinjəns]
名 方便，便利
store [stɔr] 名 商店

There is a convenience store at the corner. 轉角處有一家便利商店。

convenient [kən`vinjənt]

形 方便的

用法 convenient 指時間、交通、生活的方便，不可修飾人。

The MRT has made life much more **convenient**.
捷運使生活方便多了。

conversation

名 交談，會話 [ˌkɑnvɚ`seʃən]

用法 have a conversation with sb
和某人交談

Joshua and Grace are **having a conversation**. 約書亞和葛瑞絲正在交談。

cook [kʊk]

動 烹飪，做菜　名 做菜者，廚師

用法 It's time to cook / make / prepare dinner.
（該是準備晚飯的時候了。）

Mom is good at **cooking**.
媽媽很會做菜。

cookie [ˋkʊkɪ]

名 餅乾

用法 cookie 指「甜而酥的小餅乾」，而 cracker [ˋkrækɚ] 則指「脆硬的薄餅乾」。

My little brother likes to eat cookies.
我小弟喜歡吃餅乾。

cool [kul]

形 涼爽的；棒的（俚語，= great）

用法 That's a cool car.
= That's a great car.（那臺車好酷。）

It's cool today.
今天天氣很涼爽。

copy [ˋkɑpɪ]

動 影印，拷貝　名 影印本，拷貝

用法
ⓐ 三態：copy、copied [ˋkɑpɪd]、copied
ⓑ copycat [ˋkɑpɪˏkæt] 名 模仿者
You are a copycat.（妳是個學人精。）

Please copy this page for me. I need five copies.
請把這一頁影印給我，我需要五份。

corn [kɔrn]

名 玉米

用法
❶ corn 為不可數。
❷ popcorn [ˋpɑpˏkɔrn] 名 爆米花

Irene loves to eats **corn soup.**
艾琳喜歡喝玉米湯。

corner [ˋkɔrnɚ]

名 角落

用法
in the corner　在（室內的）角落處
on the corner　在（室外的）角落處

David sees a cat **in the corner of** the room.
大衛看到房間角落裡有隻貓。

correct [kəˋrɛkt]

形 正確的　動 修正

用法
correct 作動詞時，表示「修正；改正」。
Thank you for correcting Martha's mistakes.（謝謝你糾正了瑪莎的錯誤。）

Teddy's answer is not **correct**. It's wrong.
泰迪的答案不正確，是錯的。

cost [kɔst]

動 花費　名 費用

用法 ⓐ cost 三態同形。
ⓑ 使用 cost 時，主詞一定是「東西」，而非「人」。

This watch **cost** Tommy a lot of money.
這只錶花了湯米好多錢。

cotton [ˋkatn̩]

名 棉布，棉花

用法 ⓐ cotton 為不可數。
ⓑ cotton candy　棉花糖

Cotton is more comfortable to wear.
棉布料穿起來比較舒適。

cough [kɔf]

動 名 咳嗽

用法 have a bad cough　咳得很厲害
Elva had a bad cough last week.
（艾娃上週咳得很厲害。）

Jeremy **coughed** a lot last night.
昨晚傑瑞米咳得很厲害。

count [kaʊnt]

動 計算

用法 count 與 on 並用時，表示「依賴」。
You can count on Nelly to help you.
（你可以指望娜莉幫助你。）

Dad asked me to **count** the money for him.
爸爸要我幫他數錢。

country [ˋkʌntrɪ]

名 國家；鄉下

用法 country 指「鄉下」時，無複數形，且之前要有 the。Nora likes to live in the country.（諾拉喜歡住在鄉下。）

America is a big **country**.
美國是大國。

couple [ˋkʌpl̩]

名 兩（三）個；一對夫婦，情侶

用法 a couple of... 幾個……
Milly will invite a couple of friends over.
（蜜莉會邀請幾個朋友過來。）

A young **couple** just moved in.
一對年輕的夫婦剛搬進去。

courage [ˋkɝɪdʒ]

名 勇氣

用法 have the courage to... 有……的勇氣

Do you **have the courage to** apologize?
你有道歉的勇氣嗎？

course [kɔrs]

名 課程

用法
ⓐ take a course 修一門課
ⓑ of course 當然

Stan is **taking a course** in English.
史坦正在修一門英文課。

court [kɔrt]

名 法庭，法院；球場

用法
ⓐ tennis court 網球場
ⓑ take + sb + to court 告發某人

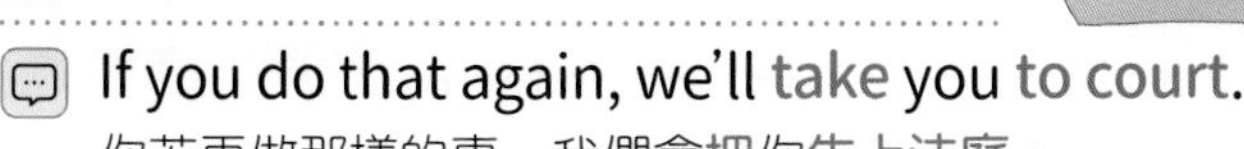

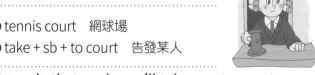

If you do that again, we'll **take** you **to court**.
你若再做那樣的事，我們會把你告上法庭。

cousin [ˋkʌzn̩]

名 堂兄 / 姊；堂弟 / 妹；表兄 / 姊；表弟 / 妹

用法 cousin 可指男性或女性的堂 / 表兄弟姊妹其中的任何一位。

My uncle's children are my cousins.
我叔叔的孩子就是我的堂兄弟姊妹。

cover [ˋkʌvɚ]

動 覆蓋　名（書或雜誌）封面，封皮；蓋子

用法 be covered with...　被……覆蓋
= be covered in...

The mountaintop is covered with snow.　山頂已被白雪覆蓋。

cow [kaʊ]

名 牛，乳牛

用法 公牛稱 bull [bʊl]，水牛則稱 water buffalo [ˋwɑtɚ ˌbʌfl̩o]。

There are many cows on the farm.
農場上有許多乳牛。

cowboy [ˋkaʊˏbɔɪ]

名 牛仔

用法 a cowboy hat　牛仔帽
cowboy boots　牛仔靴

A **cowboy**'s job is to look after cattle.
牛仔的工作就是照顧牛群。

crab [kræb]

名 螃蟹

用法 crab meat / salad
蟹肉 / 蟹肉沙拉

Crabs walk sideways.
螃蟹橫著走。

crayon [ˋkreən]

名 蠟筆

用法 crayon 當動詞用時，意思為「用蠟筆畫畫」。

The child is using a few **crayons** to draw a picture.
這個孩子正用幾隻**蠟筆**在畫畫。

A B C D E F G H I J K L M N O P Q R S T U V W X Y Z

crazy [ˋkrezɪ]

形 瘋狂的

用法
ⓐ go crazy　發瘋
ⓑ be crazy about...　瘋狂喜愛……

The old man **went crazy** when he heard the bad news.　老伯伯聽到這個壞消息時便瘋了。

cream [krim]

名 鮮奶油

用法
cream 指的是「鮮奶油」；
butter 則是指「固態奶油」。

Add some **cream** to your coffee.
加點鮮奶油在你的咖啡裡。

create [krɪˋet]

動 創造

用法
creative [krɪˋetɪv] 形 有創意的
creation [krɪˋeʃən] 名 創造，創作

The plan will **create** more than 2,000 jobs.
該計畫將創造兩千多個工作機會。

credit card

名 信用卡 [ˋkrɛdɪt ˏkɑrd]

用法 credit 是名詞，原指「賒帳」或「先欠帳再付款」。

Can I use a **credit card** there?
那裡我可以使用信用卡嗎？

crime [kraɪm]

名 罪行

用法 commit a crime　犯罪

Vic has **committed a crime**.
維克已經犯罪了。

cross [krɔs]

動 穿越

用法 cross the road / street / river
過馬路 / 街道 / 河

Be careful when you **cross the street**.　你過街時要小心。

crowd [kraʊd]

名 群眾

用法 crowded [ˋkraʊdɪd] 形 擁擠的
be crowded with... 擠滿了……
The station is crowded with people. （車站擠滿了人。）

A **crowd** gathered in the train station.
大批的人聚集在車站。

cruel [ˋkrʊəl]

形 殘忍的

用法 be cruel to be kind
忠言逆耳，良藥苦口

How can you **be so cruel to** Nicole?
你怎能對妮可如此殘忍呢？

cry [kraɪ]

動 哭

用法 ⓐ 三態：cry、cried [kraɪd]、cried
ⓑ cry 也可表示「大叫」，常與 out 並用。
"Don't touch me!" Amy cried out.（「不要碰我！」艾咪大叫。）

The sad story **made** Sara **cry**.
這個悲傷的故事讓莎拉哭了。

culture [ˋkʌltʃɚ]

名 文化

用法 culture shock　文化衝擊
（指身處不同國家的文化所產生的困惑感）

Monica likes meeting people from different **cultures**.
莫妮卡喜歡認識一些來自不同文化的人。

cup [kʌp]

名 杯子

用法 cup 多指瓷杯或塑膠杯，用來裝熱飲（如 茶、咖啡）；而 glass 則指玻璃杯，用來裝冷飲。

Would you like **a cup of** coffee?
你要不要來一杯咖啡呀？

cure [kjʊr]

動 治療，治癒　名 療法

用法 cure for + 疾病　（某疾病的）療法
There is no cure for AIDS.
目前沒有療法可治好愛滋病。

Tommy's bad cold was finally **cured**.
湯米的重感冒終於痊癒了。

curious [ˋkjʊrɪəs]

形 好奇的

用法 be curious about... 對……好奇

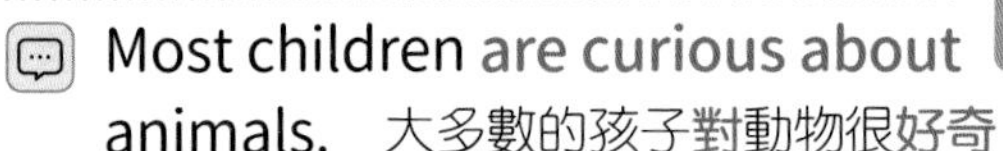

Most children **are curious about** animals. 大多數的孩子對動物很好奇。

current [ˋkɝənt]

名 水流

用法 current 當形容詞時，為「當前的，現行的」之意。
current affairs 時事

Strong **currents** in the river can be dangerous for swimmers. 河中強勁的**水流**可能對泳客造成危險。

curtain [ˋkɝtn̩]

名 窗簾，（舞臺上的）布幕

用法 curtain call 謝幕

Open the **curtain** and let sunlight in.
打開窗簾讓陽光進來。

curve [kɝv]

名 彎曲；彎道　動 彎曲

用法 There is a curve on the road.
（這條路上有一處彎道。）

The road **curves** to the left.
馬路向左彎。

custom [ˋkʌstəm]

名 風俗，習慣

用法 a local custom　當地的風俗
an ancient custom　古老的習俗

We should respect the **local customs**.
我們應該尊重當地的風俗。

customer [ˋkʌstəmɚ]

名 顧客

用法 a regular customer　老主顧

The good food of that restaurant has attracted a lot of **customers**.　那家餐廳的美食吸引了不少顧客前來。

cut [kʌt]

動 切，割

用法 ⓐ cut 三態同形。
ⓑ cut 當名詞用時，為「傷口」的意思。

Nora used a knife to **cut** the cake.
諾拉用刀子切蛋糕。

cute [kjut]

形 可愛的

用法 cute 常與 little 並用。
a cute little baby / dog
可愛的小寶寶 / 小狗狗

My little sister is **cute** and beautiful.
我的小妹既可愛又美麗。

Notes

daily [ˋdelɪ]

副 每天　形 每天的　名 日報

用法 當副詞時等於 every day（每天）。
當形容詞時等於 everyday（每天的）。
當名詞時等於 daily newspaper（日報）。

The restaurant is open daily, from 11 a.m. to 9 p.m.
這家餐廳每天都營業，上午十一點開張，晚上九點打烊。

damage [ˋdæmɪdʒ]

名 動 損害，損失

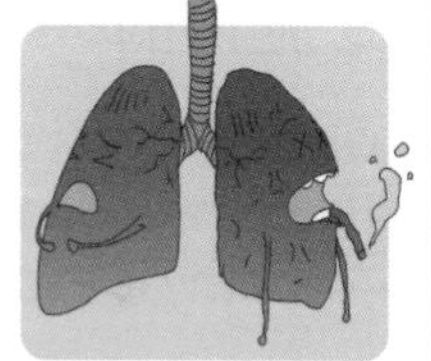

用法 do damage to...　對……造成損害

Smoking does damage to your health.
抽菸有損健康。

dance [dæns]

動 舞蹈　名 舞會

用法 dance to + 音樂　隨音樂起舞
dance with + sb　與某人共舞

May I dance with you?
我可以跟你跳舞嗎？

A B C D E F G H I J K L M N O P Q R S T U V W X Y Z

danger [ˋdendʒɚ]

名 危險

用法 be in danger　有危險，處於險境

You'll **be in danger** if you don't stay away from Derek.　你若不和德瑞克保持距離，就會有危險。

dangerous [ˋdendʒərəs]

形 危險的

用法 注意下列兩句意思的不同：
Cathy is dangerous.（凱西是危險人物。）
Cathy is in danger.（凱西有危險。）

It is **dangerous** to go swimming in the river.　在河裡游泳很危險。

dark [dark]

形 陰暗的；天色暗的　名 陰暗

用法 before / after dark　天黑前 / 後
Do not go out after dark.
（天黑後不要外出。）

It's so **dark** in here; I can't see anything.
這裡面很暗，我什麼都看不見。

date [det]

名 日期；約會　動 約（某異性朋友）

用法 Roy will go out on a date with Mary tonight.
（羅伊今晚要跟瑪麗約會。）

What's the **date** today?
今天是幾月幾號？

daughter [ˋdɔtɚ]

名 女兒

用法 「女兒」稱 daughter，「兒子」稱 son。

Mr. Johnson has two sons and three **daughters**.　強森先生有兩個兒子和三個女兒。

dawn [dɔn]

名 黎明

用法 at dawn　在黎明時

The team set out **at dawn**.
這支團隊於黎明出發。

day [de]

名 日子

用法 注意下列兩個問句的不同：
What's the date today?（問日期）
What day is it today?（問星期）

What day is it today?
今天是星期幾？

dead [dɛd]

形 死亡的，死去的

用法 電池（battery [ˋbætərɪ]）沒電時，可說：
The battery is dead.（電池沒電了。）

There is a dead dog on the road.
路上有一隻死掉的狗。

deaf [dɛf]

形 耳聾的

用法 Sam is deaf to my advice.
（山姆對我的忠告充耳不聞。）

Deaf people communicate in sign language.
聾人用手語溝通。

deal [dil]

動 處理；交往　名 量

用法 ⓐ deal 表示「處理」或「交往」時要與 with 並用。
ⓑ a great deal of money　大量的金錢

David doesn't know how to **deal with** this problem.　大衛不知道要如何處理這個問題。

dear [dɪr]

形 親愛的

用法 dear 多用作信的開頭稱呼語，要大寫，之後再置某人的姓名。
Dear Mr. Lai, ...（親愛的賴先生，……）

Dear Peter, will you marry me?
親愛的彼得，你會娶我嗎？

debate [dɪˋbet]

動 名 辯論

用法 Warren and Regina are still debating on that matter.
（華倫和瑞吉娜仍舊針對那件事情在辯論。）

It was a heated **debate**.
這是一場激烈的辯論。

December [dɪˋsɛmbɚ]

名 十二月

用法
in December　十二月期間
on December 10　十二月十日那一天

It's cold in **December**.
十二月的天氣很冷。

decide [dɪˋsaɪd]

動 決定

用法
decide to + V　決定要……

Ian has **decided to** go fishing this weekend.　伊恩已經決定這個週末要去釣魚。

decision [dɪˋsɪʒən]

名 決定

用法
make a decision　做決定
It's time to make a decision now.
（現在是做決定的時候了。）

Britney has **made a decision** to see Andy tomorrow.
布蘭妮已決定明天去見安迪。

decorate [ˋdɛkəret]

動 裝飾

用法 be decorated with... 被裝飾著……
The whole room was decorated with roses. （整個房間都裝飾著玫瑰。）

My brothers are **decorating** our Christmas tree.
我弟弟們正在**裝飾**聖誕樹。

decrease

[dɪˋkris] 動 減少　[ˋdikris] 名 減少

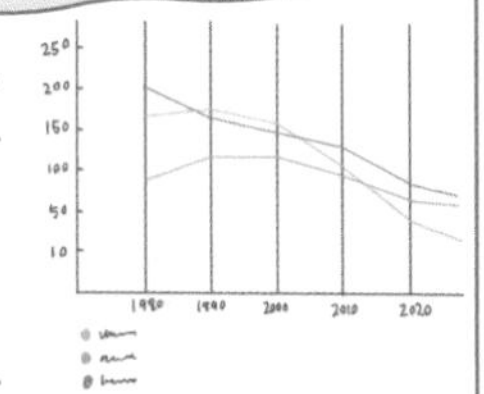

用法 請見上述音標，decrease 當動詞與名詞時的重音分別在不同位置。

There has been a **decrease** in the number of violent crimes.　暴力犯罪一直有**減少**的趨勢。

deep [dip]

形 深的

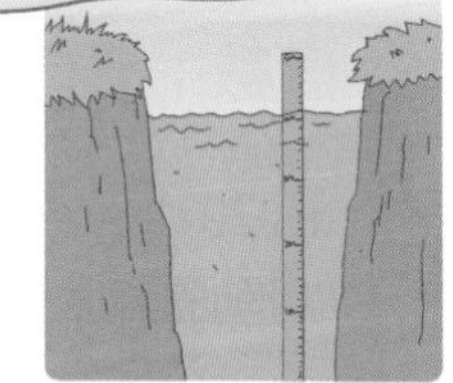

用法 deep river / sea　很深的河 / 海

The river is **deep**, so it's dangerous to swim in there.
那條河很**深**，因此在裡面游泳很危險。

deer [dɪr]

名 **鹿**

用法 deer 單複數同形。

Renee sees a few deer in the park.

芮妮看到公園裡有幾隻鹿。

define [dɪˋfaɪn]

動 **下定義，解釋**

用法 define A as B　將 A 定義為 B
The dictionary defines this word as a vulgar word.（字典把這個字定義為不雅的字。）

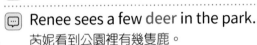

It is difficult to define the word "love."

要為「愛」這個字去下定義是很困難的。

degree [dɪˋgri]

名 **度數；學位**

用法 It's 20 degrees Celsius now.
（目前的溫度是攝氏二十度。）

Caroline has a doctor's degree.

卡洛琳擁有博士學位。

delicious [dɪˋlɪʃəs]

形 好吃的，美味的

用法 食物好吃時，我們可用 delicious 或 tasty [ˋtestɪ] 表示。
The food is tasty. （這道食物真好吃。）

The food is delicious. Can I have some more?
這道菜很好吃，我可不可以再來一點？

deliver [dɪˋlɪvɚ]

動 遞送（信件，貨物）；發表（演說）

用法 deliver / make a speech　發表演說
Doug will deliver / make a speech today.
（道格今天會發表演說。）

The TV set will be delivered to Tim's house.　這臺電視機將會送到提姆家。

dentist [ˋdɛntɪst]

名 牙醫

用法 go to the dentist　去看牙醫
My son needs to go to the dentist now. （我兒子必須現在就去看牙醫。）

The dentist is checking my teeth.
牙醫正在檢查我的牙齒。

department store

名 百貨公司 [dɪˋpartmənt ˏstɔr]

用法 department 指部門，store 指商店。建築物各樓層均有各部門販售的東西，這類綜合性商店就稱為 department store。

There is a big **department store** near Edna's house. 伊德娜的家附近有一家大型百貨公司。

depend [dɪˋpɛnd]

動 依賴，信賴

用法 depend on... 依賴……

You can **depend on** Nora when you need help. 需要幫忙時你可以依靠諾拉。

describe [dɪˋskraɪb]

動 描述，形容

用法 describe sb/sth as...
把某人 / 某事描述成……

Could you **describe** what happened?
你能否描述事情的經過？

desert [ˋdɛzɚt]

名 沙漠

用法 相似字為 dessert [dɪˋzɝt]（甜點），請不要混淆囉！

Life in the **desert** is hard.
沙漠生活很艱苦。

design [dɪˋzaɪn]

動 名 設計

用法 The room will be designed as a study. （這個房間將被設計為書房。）

Elva likes the **design** of the car.
艾娃喜歡這輛車的設計。

desire [dɪˋzaɪr]

名 欲望，願望　動 想要

用法 have no desire to...　沒有……的欲望
Max has no desire to cause trouble.
（麥克斯並不想造成困擾。）

Hannah **desires to** meet Larry this morning.
漢娜想在今天早上跟賴瑞見面。

desk [dɛsk]

名 書桌

用法 table [ˋtebḷ] 與 desk 均表示「桌子」。table 多指「餐桌」，而 desk 則指「書桌」。

Put your book **on the desk.**
把你的書放在書桌上。

dessert [dɪˋzɝt]

名（餐後的）甜點

用法 have... for dessert　吃……當甜點

What are we **having for dessert?**
我們吃什麼甜點？

detect [dɪˋtɛkt]

動 查出，發覺

用法 detective [dɪˋtɛktɪv] 名 偵探

Janice **detected** something strange about Paul.
珍妮絲發覺保羅有點怪怪的。

develop [dɪˋvɛləp]

動 發展

用法 develop into... 發展成為……

My friends are waiting to see how things **develop**. 我朋友正在靜觀事情的發展。

dial [ˋdaɪəl]

動 按號碼，撥（電話）

用法 Dial 9 for the switchboard.
（總機請按 9。）

Dial 119 in an emergency.
有緊急事件時打 119。

diamond [ˋdaɪmənd]

名 鑽石

用法 a diamond ring / necklace
鑽戒 / 鑽石項鍊

Rick bought **a diamond ring** for Leah.
瑞克買了一枚鑽戒給莉亞。

diary [ˋdaɪərɪ]

名 日記

用法 keep a diary　寫日記

Lucy has **kept a diary** since she was ten.　露西從十歲開始寫日記至今。

dictionary [ˋdɪkʃənˏɛrɪ]

名 字典

用法 查字典：consult the dictionary
consult [kənˋsʌlt] 動 查閱
查單字：look up the word

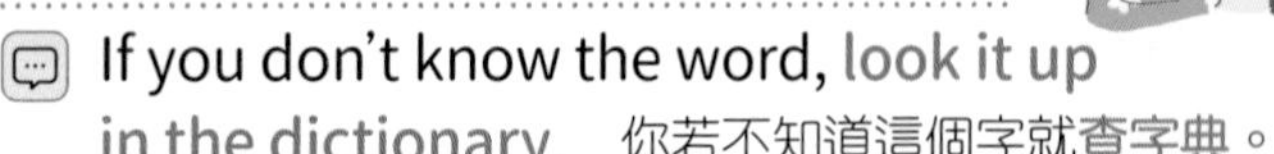
If you don't know the word, **look it up in the dictionary**.　你若不知道這個字就查字典。

die [daɪ]

動 死亡

用法 die 在 is / are / am / was / were 之後要改成 dying。dying 表示「垂死的」、「即將死亡的」。

I feel sad because my dog **died** yesterday.
我的狗昨天死了，因此我感到很難過。

diet [ˋdaɪət]

名 節食（為減肥而設計的飲食）

用法
go on a diet　節食
be on a diet　在節食中

No sugar! I'm on a diet.
不要加糖！我在減肥。

difference [ˋdɪf(ə)rəns]

名 不同，差異

用法
tell the difference between A and B
分辨 A 與 B 的差異

How do you tell the difference between the two cars?　你如何看出這兩臺車的差異？

different [ˋdɪfrənt]

形 不同的

用法
be different from...　與……不同

Eugene's watch is different from mine.
尤金的手錶跟我的不一樣。

A B C D E F G H I J K L M N O P Q R S T U V W X Y Z

Dd

difficult [ˋdɪfə͵kʌlt]

形 困難的

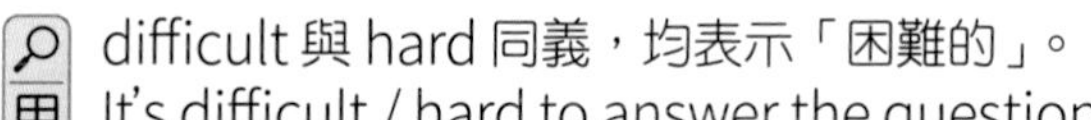

用法 difficult 與 hard 同義，均表示「困難的」。
It's difficult / hard to answer the question.
（這個問題很難回答。）

The test this morning was very **difficult**.
今天早上的考試很難。

difficulty [ˋdɪfə͵kʌltɪ]

名 困難

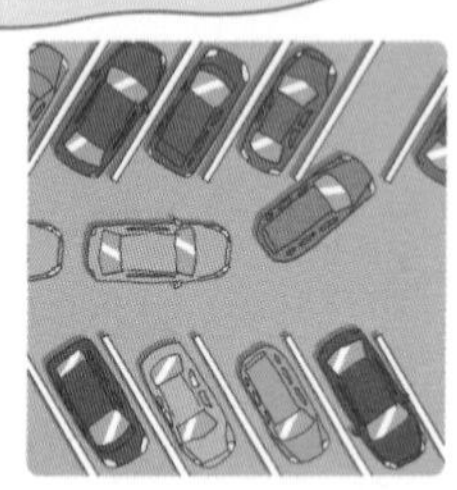

用法 have difficulty + V-ing
（從事）……很困難

Melvin **had difficulty** finding a parking space.　馬文很難找到停車位。

dig [dɪg]

動 挖掘

用法 三態：dig、dug [dʌg]、dug

The dog is **digging a hole**.
這隻狗正在挖洞。

diligent [ˋdɪlɪdʒənt]

形 勤勉的，用功的

用法 be diligent in / about
做……很勤奮

All teachers like diligent students.
所有的老師都喜歡用功的學生。

dining room

名 餐廳 [ˋdaɪnɪŋ ˏrum]

用法 living room [ˋlɪvɪŋ ˏrum] 名 客廳
kitchen [ˋkɪtʃɪn] 名 廚房
bedroom [ˋbɛdˏrum] 名 臥室

Henry helped Mom set the table in the dining room. 亨利幫媽媽在餐廳擺餐具準備吃飯。

dinner [ˋdɪnɚ]

名 晚餐

用法 breakfast [ˋbrɛkfəst] 名 早餐
lunch [lʌntʃ] 名 午餐

It's time to have dinner now.
現在該是吃晚餐的時候了。

dinosaur [ˋdaɪnəˏsɔr]

名 恐龍

用法 dinosaur 也可以指「過時的人或物」。

We can't see living **dinosaurs** today. 我們現在看不到活**恐龍**了。

diplomat [ˋdɪpləˏmæt]

名 外交官

用法 diplomat 也可以表示「善於與人打交道的人」。

Ron has dreamed of becoming a **diplomat**. 榮恩一直夢想要當**外交官**。

direct [dəˋrɛkt]

形 直接的　動 指揮

用法 a direct flight　直飛
There is a direct flight from London to Los Angeles.（有一架班機從倫敦直飛洛杉磯。）

A policeman is **directing** traffic there.
有一位警察在那裡**指揮**交通。

direction [dəˋrɛkʃən]

名 方向

用法 sense of direction　方向感

A man ran away in that **direction**.
有一名男子朝那個方向跑掉了。

dirty [ˋdɝtɪ]

形 骯髒的

用法 clean [klin] 形 乾淨的

Your hands are too **dirty**. Go wash them.
你的手很髒，去洗手。

disappear [ˏdɪsəˋpɪr]

動 消失，不見

用法 disappear into thin air
消失得無影無蹤

The moon **disappeared** behind a cloud.　月亮消失在一朵雲後面。

discover [dɪˋskʌvɚ]

動 發現

用法 discovery [dɪˋskʌvərɪ] 名 發現

Columbus discovered America in 1492.
哥倫布於一四九二年發現美洲。

discuss [dɪˋskʌs]

動 討論

用法 discuss with sb 與某人討論

You should discuss this problem with your doctor.
你應該跟你的醫生討論這個問題。

discussion [dɪˋskʌʃən]

名 討論

用法 be under discussion 在討論中
Your idea is under discussion now.
(你的想法正在討論中。)

Our team needs to have a discussion about the matter. 我們團隊需要針對這件事情進行討論。

dishonest [dɪsˋɑnɪst]

形 不誠實的

用法 honest [ˋɑnɪst] 形 誠實的

Nina doesn't want to deal with **dishonest** people.
妮娜不想跟**不誠實的**人來往。

dish [dɪʃ]

名 一道菜；菜盤

用法
ⓐ do / wash the dishes 洗碗盤
ⓑ This dish is delicious.
（這道菜很好吃。）

Do the dishes after dinner, Johnny.
強尼，吃完晚飯後要**洗碗盤**。

distance [ˋdɪstəns]

名 距離

用法 keep sb at a distance 與某人保持距離
Keep that guy at a distance.
（跟那傢伙保持距離。）

Nicole sees a train **in the distance.**
妮可看到**遠處**有一輛火車。

distant [ˋdɪstənt]

形 遙遠的

用法 a distant relative　遠房親戚

Vic is **a distant relative** of mine.
維克是我的一位遠親。

divide [dəˋvaɪd]

動 分開；分配

用法 be divided into...　被分成……
The book is divided into three parts.
（這本書分成三部分。）

Martha **divided** all the money among her children.
瑪莎把所有的錢分配給孩子。

dizzy [ˋdɪzɪ]

形 暈眩的

用法 feel dizzy　覺得暈眩

Jack **felt dizzy** all day yesterday.
傑克昨天一整天都覺得暈眩。

Dd

do (does, did, done)

動 助 做

用法 do、does、did 可作助動詞，用以形成問句，在其後的動詞一律改用原形。
Does he study hard? （他用功嗎？）

What can I do for you, sir?
先生，有什麼我能為您效勞的嗎？

doctor [ˋdaktɚ]

名 醫生

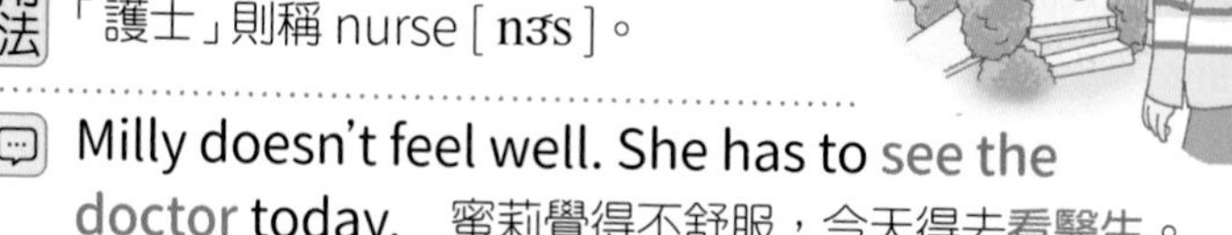

用法 「病人」則稱 patient [ˋpeʃənt]；
「護士」則稱 nurse [nɝs]。

Milly doesn't feel well. She has to see the doctor today. 蜜莉覺得不舒服，今天得去看醫生。

dodge ball [ˋdadʒ ˏbɔl]

名 躲避球

用法 play dodge ball 打躲避球
（非 play the dodge ball）

Many boys like to play dodge ball.
許多男孩子喜歡玩躲避球。

Dd

dog [dɔg]

名 狗

用法 表示「狗在對我吠叫」可說：
The dog is barking at me.
（bark [bɑrk] 吠叫）

Dogs are man's best friends.
狗是人類最好的朋友。

D

doll [dɑl]

名 洋娃娃

用法 play with a doll　玩洋娃娃

The little girl is playing with a doll.
小女孩正在玩洋娃娃。

dollar [ˋdɑlɚ]

名（美金）元

用法 a dollar　美金一元
an NT dollar　新臺幣一元
（是 a New Taiwan Dollar 的縮寫）

That dictionary cost Phil five hundred NT dollars.　那本字典花了菲爾新臺幣五百元。

Dd

dolphin [ˋdalfɪn]

名 海豚

用法 a dolphin show　海豚表演

Let's go to see the **dolphin show**.
咱們去看海豚表演吧。

donkey [ˋdaŋkɪ]

名 驢子

用法 do the donkey work
做枯燥乏味的工作

A **donkey** is smaller than a horse.
驢子的體型要比馬來得小。

door [dɔr]

名 門

用法 open the door　開門
close the door　關門
= shut the door（shut [ʃʌt] 動 關閉）

Close the door when you leave.
你離開時把門關上。

dot [dɑt]

名 點

用法 某幾點鐘 + on the dot　某幾點整
It's eight o'clock on the dot.
= It's eight o'clock sharp.（現在時刻八點整。）

It's ten o'clock **on the dot.**
現在時刻十點整。

double [ˋdʌbḷ]

形 雙倍，雙份的　動 將……變成雙倍

用法 a double room　雙人房
I need a double room, not a single room.
（我需要一間雙人房，而非單人房。）

I'll **double** your pay if you work hard.
你若努力，我就會把你的待遇加倍。

doubt [daʊt]

動 懷疑　名 疑問，疑慮

用法 be in doubt about...　對……存疑
Molly is still in doubt about that.
（莫莉對於那件事仍有疑慮。）

David **doubts** if his parents will agree.
大衛懷疑他父母是否會同意。

doughnut [ˋdo͵nʌt]

名 甜甜圈

用法 也作 donut。

Amy sells doughnuts for a living.
艾咪賣甜甜圈維生。

down [daʊn]

副 往下

用法 down 也可作形容詞，表示「沮喪的」、「消沈的」。
Don't feel down. Cheer up.
（不要沮喪，振作起來。）

Sit down, please.　請坐。

download [ˋdaʊn͵lod]

動 (電腦) 下載

用法 upload [ˋʌp͵lod] 動 上傳

First, download these files and save them on the hard disk.　首先，下載這些檔案並將它們存在硬碟裡。

downstairs [ˌdaʊnˋstɛrz]

副 在樓下；到樓下

用法 upstairs [ˌʌpˋstɛrz] 副 在樓上；上樓

Pamela and her sister were both **downstairs**. 潘蜜拉和她妹妹都在樓下。

downtown [ˌdaʊnˋtaʊn]

副 到鬧區

用法 uptown [ˌʌpˋtaʊn] 副 到市郊

When will Patricia go **downtown**?
派翠莎什麼時候要去鬧區？

dozen [ˋdʌzn̩]

名 打

用法
a dozen eggs 一打蛋
two dozen eggs 兩打蛋
dozens of eggs 好幾打蛋

Gail bought **two dozen** eggs at the supermarket. 蓋兒在超市買了兩打蛋。

dragon [ˋdrægən]

名 龍

用法 dragon 與 fly 合在一起就成 dragonfly [ˋdrægən͵flaɪ]，表示「蜻蜓」。

Are there **dragons** in the world?
世上真有龍嗎？

drama [ˋdrɑmə]

名 戲劇

用法 a TV drama　電視劇

My husband teaches **drama** at a university.　我老公在某大學教戲劇。

draw [drɔ]

動 畫；吸引

用法
ⓐ 三態：draw、drew [dru]、drawn [drɔn]
ⓑ The movie drew many people.
（這部電影吸引很多人去看。）

Can you **draw** pictures?
你會畫畫嗎？

drawer [ˋdrɔɚ]

名 抽屜

用法
open the drawer　打開抽屜
close / shut the drawer　把抽屜關起來

Joanna puts her pens in the **drawer**.
瓊安娜把她的筆放在抽屜裡。

dream [drim]

名 夢　動 做夢

用法
have a sweet dream　做了一個甜蜜的夢
have a bad dream　做了一個惡夢

Mark **had a sweet dream** last night.
馬克昨晚做了一個甜蜜的夢。

dress [drɛs]

名 洋裝　動 穿衣服

用法
get dressed　穿好衣服
We'll be leaving. Get dressed now.
(我們就要動身了，現在就把衣服穿好。)

Joy looks beautiful in that **dress**.
喬伊穿上那件洋裝模樣真美。

dresser [ˋdrɛsɚ]

名 梳妝臺

用法 dresser 也可以指「穿著……的人」。
a very stylish dresser　穿著時髦的人

Natasha sat in front of the dresser crying.
娜塔莎坐在梳妝臺前哭泣。

drink [drɪŋk]

動 喝　名 飲料

用法
ⓐ 三態：drink、drank [dræŋk]、drunk [drʌŋk]
ⓑ get drunk　喝醉了

What would you like to drink, Mary?　瑪麗，妳想喝什麼？

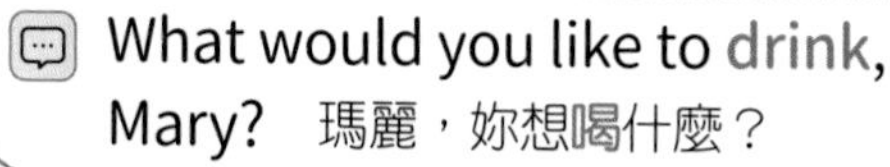

drive [draɪv]

動 駕駛

用法
ⓐ 三態：drive、drove [drov]、driven [drɪvən]
ⓑ Can you drive (a car)?（你會開車嗎？）

We cannot drive cars until we are eighteen.　我們要在十八歲以後才能開車。

D

driver [ˋdraɪvɚ]

名 駕駛人，司機

用法
a taxi driver 計程車司機
a truck driver 卡車司機
a bus driver 公車司機

My father is a taxi driver.
我爸爸是計程車司機。

drop [drɑp]

動 （使）掉落

用法
drop in on + sb 順道探訪某人
Drop in on me on your way to the station.（你到車站途中順便來看我。）

Be careful! Don't drop it.
小心！別讓它掉落下來。

drugstore [ˋdrʌgˏstɔr]

名 藥房

用法
drugstore 除了賣藥之外，還有賣化妝品、零食等雜貨。

Sandra bought beauty products at the drugstore. 珊卓在那間藥房買了些美容用品。

drum [drʌm]

名 鼓

用法 play the drums　打鼓
（此處 play 表示「演奏」樂器）
play the piano　彈鋼琴

My brother **plays the drums very** well.　我哥哥鼓打得很好。

dry [draɪ]

形 乾的，乾燥的　動（使）變乾

用法 ⓐ 三態：dry、dried [draɪd]、dried
ⓑ Dry your hair.
（把你的頭髮弄乾。）

The clothes aren't **dry**; they are still wet.
這些衣服沒乾，還是溼的。

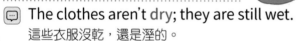

dryer [ˋdraɪɚ]

名 烘乾機

用法 a hair dryer　吹風機

Rita needs **a hair dryer** to dry her hair.
麗塔需要吹風機把頭髮吹乾。

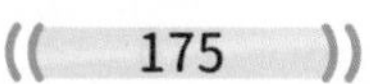

duck [dʌk]

名 鴨子

用法 duckling [ˋdʌklɪŋ] 名 小鴨

A few **ducks** are swimming around in the pond.
有幾隻鴨子在池塘裡游來游去。

dumb [dʌm]

形 啞的；笨的

用法
ⓐ 請注意 b 不發音。
ⓑ dumb show　比手勢

Tom is **deaf and dumb.**
湯姆又聾又啞。

dumpling [ˋdʌmplɪŋ]

名 水餃

用法
水餃（= boiled dumpling）
wrap dumplings　包水餃
（wrap [ræp] 名 將⋯⋯包起來）

Nick likes to eat **dumplings.**
尼克喜歡吃水餃。

during [ˋdjʊrɪŋ]

介 在……的期間

用法 during 之後要加 the、those、my、your... 等字方可再接時間。
during the night（在夜間）

What did Ned do **during** the summer vacation? 奈德暑假期間做了些什麼？

duty [ˋd(j)utɪ]

名 責任

用法 be on duty　值勤，當班
Dad is on duty today.
（老爸今天值班。）

It's William's **duty** to do the dishes.
洗碗盤是威廉的責任。

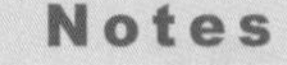

each [itʃ]

冠 代 **每個**

用法
ⓐ each other　彼此
ⓑ each of you / us / them
你們 / 我們 / 他們每個人

We should help each other.
我們彼此應**相互**幫助。

eagle [ˋigl̩]

名 **老鷹**

用法
eagle eyes　銳利的眼光

Eagles catch small animals for food.
老鷹抓小動物吃。

ear [ɪr]

名 **耳朵**

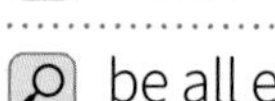

用法
be all ears　豎著耳朵聽，注意聽
Tell me the story. I'm all ears.
（把故事告訴我。我在注意聽。）

Gary's left ear is bigger than his right ear.
蓋瑞的**左耳**比**右耳**大。

early [ˋɝlɪ]

副 早地　形 提早的

用法
get up early　很早起床
arrive early　提早抵達

Debbie gets up early every morning.
黛比每天早上都很早起床。

earn [ɝn]

動 賺取

用法
earn a living　謀生

Linda earns about NT$30,000 a month.
琳達每個月賺大約新臺幣三萬元。

earring [ˋɪr͵rɪŋ]

名 耳環

用法
a pair of earrings　一副耳環

Janice is wearing a pair of earrings.
珍妮絲戴了一副耳環。

earth [ɝθ]

名 地球

用法 on earth　在世界上，世上
Daisy is the most beautiful girl on earth.
（黛西是世上最美的女孩。）

The earth is round.
地球是圓的。

ease [iz]

名 輕鬆，舒適（不可數）

用法 with ease　輕鬆地
（= easily [ˋizlɪ]）

Duke passed the test with ease.
杜克輕鬆地通過了考試。

earthquake [ˋɝθˏkwek]

名 地震

用法 等於 quake [kwek]。

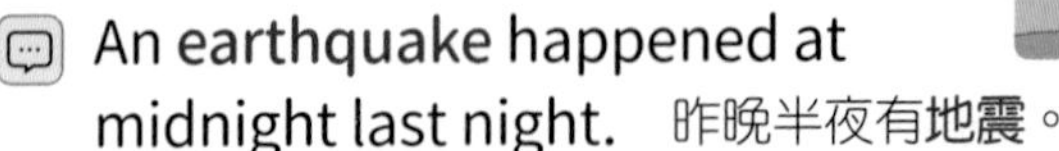

An earthquake happened at midnight last night.　昨晚半夜有地震。

east [ist]

名 東方　形 東方的　副 往東

用法
the east　東方
east wind　東方吹來的風，東風
go east　往東行

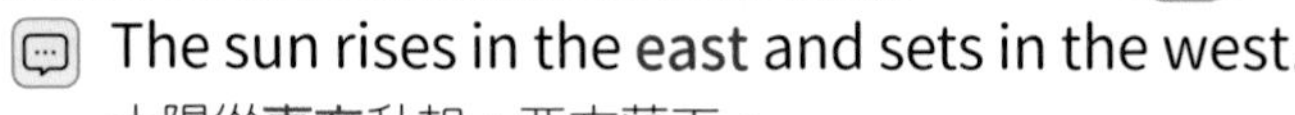

The sun rises in the **east** and sets in the west.
太陽從**東方**升起，西方落下。

Easter [ˋistɚ]

名 復活節

用法 Easter 在三月底或四月初的星期天降臨，是基督徒記念耶穌逝世後復活的日子。孩子們會穿新衣，玩找彩蛋的活動。

Very few people celebrate **Easter** in Taiwan.
在臺灣慶祝**復活節**的人少之又少。

easy [ˋizɪ]

形 容易的

用法 我們若表示某件事很容易時，可說：
It's easy as pie.（這件事容易極了——容易得就如做 pie [paɪ] 一樣。）

This question is **easy**, but that one is difficult.
這個問題很**容易**，不過那個問題卻很難。

eat [it]

動 吃

用法 三態：eat、ate [et]、eaten [ˋitn̩]

Joe is hungry. He wants something to eat.
喬很餓，想吃點東西。

edge [ɛdʒ]

名 邊緣

用法 on the edge of...　在……的邊緣

Tina is sitting on the edge of the bed.
提娜坐在床的邊緣。

education [ˏɛdʒʊˋkeʃən]

名 教育

用法 educate [ˋɛdʒʊˏket] 動 教育
How do you educate your children?
（你怎麼教育孩子？）

Carrie wants her children to have a good education.　凱莉要她的孩子受良好的教育。

effort [ˋɛfɚt]

名 努力

用法 make an effort to + V
努力要⋯⋯；設法要⋯⋯

Make an effort to drink less coffee.
設法少喝點咖啡。

egg [ɛg]

名 蛋；卵

用法 lay an egg　生一顆蛋
The hen lays an egg a day.
（這隻母雞每天生一顆蛋。）

The students need eggs to make a cake.
學生們做蛋糕需要蛋。

eight [et]

名 八　形 八個的

用法 eight 之後要加複數名詞
（如 boys、books 等）。

There are eight eggs in the basket.
籃子裡有八顆蛋。

eighteen [eˋtin]

名 十八　形 十八個的

用法 eighteen 之後要加複數名詞（如 boys、books 等）。

When Norman is **eighteen** years old, he will study abroad.　諾曼十八歲時會出國念書。

eighty [ˋetɪ]

名 八十　形 八十個的

用法 eighty 之後要加複數名詞（如 boys、books 等）。

My grandfather is **eighty** years old.
我爺爺八十歲了。

either [ˋiðɚ]

連 兩者任何一個

用法 either... or...　不是……就是……
Either you or he is wrong.
（不是你錯就是他錯。）

Paul will call you **either** today **or** tomorrow.
保羅不是今天就是明天會打電話給妳。

Ee

elder [ˋɛldɚ]

形 年長的

用法 elder brother / sister　哥哥 / 姊姊
(= older brother / sister)
younger brother / sister　弟弟 / 妹妹

Annie has two **elder brothers** and one younger sister.　安妮有兩個**哥哥**、一個妹妹。

elect [ɪˋlɛkt]

動 以投票選出

用法 be elected + 職位　被選為……

John was **elected** class leader.
約翰**獲選**當班長。

electric [ɪˋlɛktrɪk]

形 電的

用法 electricity [ɪˋlɛktrɪsətɪ] 名 電
(不可數)

Phil wants to have an **electric** guitar.
菲爾想要一把**電**吉他。

elementary school

名 小學 [ˌɛləˋmɛntərɪ ˌskul]

用法 等於 primary school
(primary [ˋpraɪmərɪ] 形 初級的)

Julie is studying in that elementary school. 茱莉在那所小學念書。

elephant [ˋɛləfənt]

名 象

用法 an Asian elephant
亞洲象（耳朵下垂，性溫馴）
an African elephant 非洲象（耳朵較大）

The elephant has a long nose.
大象的鼻子很長。

eleven [ɪˋlɛvən]

名 十一 形 十一個的

用法 eleven 之後要加複數名詞
（如 boys、books 等）。

There are eleven players on our basketball team. 我們籃球隊有十一位球員。

else [ɛls]

副 其他的，別的

用法 else 要放在 nothing、something、anything、no one、someone、anyone 之後。

Is there anything else I can do for you?
還有什麼**別的**事我可以為您效勞的嗎？

e-mail [ˋi͵mel]

動 以電子郵件方式寄送　名 電子郵件

用法 e-mail 是由 electronic mail 化簡而成。
electronic [ɪ͵lɛkˋtrɑnɪk] 形 電子的
mail [mel] 名 郵件

Please e-mail this letter to Mr. Lin.
請把這封信**以電子郵件的方式寄給**林先生。

embarrass [ɪmˋbærəs]

動 使難堪，尷尬

用法 embarrassed [ɪmˋbærəst] 形 感到尷尬的
I felt embarrassed when Rick called my nickname.（瑞克叫我綽號時，我感到很難堪。）

Paul's jokes embarrassed his friend.
保羅的笑話讓他的朋友感到很**尷尬**。

emotion [ɪˋmoʃən]

名 情感；情緒

用法 express one's emotions
表達某人的情感

As a nurse, I have to control my **emotions**.
身為護士，我必須要控制自己的**情緒**。

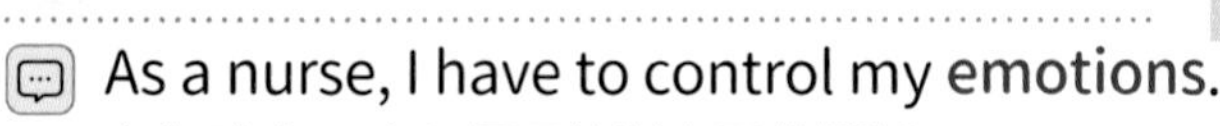

emphasize [ˋɛmfəˏsaɪz]

動 強調

用法 emphasis [ˋɛmfəsɪs] 名 強調，重視

Our teacher **emphasizes** the importance of learning English. 我們老師**強調**學習英文的重要性。

employ [ɪmˋplɔɪ]

動 僱用

用法
ⓐ employee [ˏɪmplɔɪˋi] 名 員工
ⓑ employer [ɪmˋplɔɪɚ] 名 雇主，老闆

We **employed** Jane to do all the housework. 我們**僱用**珍來做所有的家事。

Ee

empty [ˋɛmptɪ]

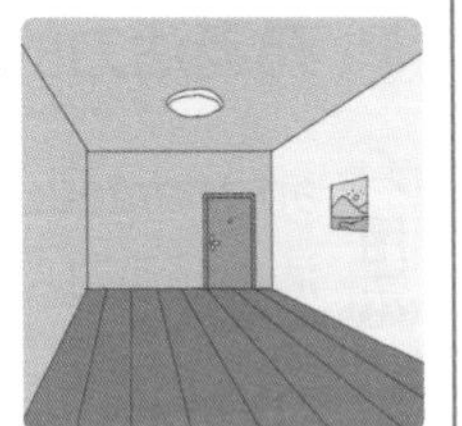

形 空的

用法 an empty house　空屋

The house is empty. There is no one in it.　房子空蕩蕩的，裡面沒有人。

end [ɛnd]

名 盡頭　動 結束

用法
ⓐ come to an end　結束
ⓑ The party ended at eight.
（派對在八點結束。）

The meeting finally came to an end.
會議終於結束了。

enemy [ˋɛnəmɪ]

名 敵人

用法 複數為 enemies。

Scott is making more and more enemies.　史考特樹立的敵人愈來愈多了。

energetic [ˌɛnəˋdʒɛtɪk]

形 充滿活力的

用法 an energetic person
活力充沛的人

Thomas was **an energetic person** in this office. 湯瑪士在辦公室裡是位**充滿活力的人**。

energy [ˋɛnədʒɪ]

名 活力（不可數）

用法 energy 也有「能源」的意思。
solar / nuclear energy 太陽能 / 核能

Ryan still has some **energy** to deal with the problem.
萊恩還有一些**精力**來處理這個問題。

engine [ˋɛndʒən]

名 引擎

用法 a car engine 汽車引擎

The **engine** of the car is broken.
汽車的**引擎**壞掉了。

engineer [ˌɛndʒəˋnɪr]

名 工程師

用法 a computer / mechanical / chemical engineer　電腦 / 機械 / 化學工程師

My brother is a computer engineer.
我哥哥是電腦工程師。

English [ˋɪŋglɪʃ]

名 英文，英語　形 英國的

用法 Jack speaks English well.
= Jack speaks good English.
(傑克英語說得很好。)

Peter speaks English well.
彼得英語說得很棒。

enjoy [ɪnˋdʒɔɪ]

動 喜歡

用法 enjoy 之後的動詞字尾要加 -ing。
enjoy singing　喜歡唱歌
enjoy dancing　喜歡跳舞

Robin enjoys hiking on Sundays.
羅賓喜歡在星期天健行。

enough [ɪˋnʌf]

形 足夠的　副 足以

用法
ⓐ enough 作形容詞時，要放在名詞前面。

ⓑ enough 作副詞用時，要放在形容詞前面。

Is Thomas good enough to do the work?
湯瑪斯是否很優秀足以做這個工作呢？

enter [ˋɛntɚ]

動 進入

用法
enter the room　進入房間
（非 enter into the room）

Take off your hat when you enter the classroom.　你進教室時要脫帽。

entrance [ˋɛntrəns]

名 入口

用法
exit [ˋɛgzɪt / ˋɛgsɪt] 名 出口

I'll meet Lydia at the entrance.
我會和莉迪亞在入口見面。

envelope [ˋɛnvə͵lop]

名 信封

用法 stick a stamp onto the envelope
把郵票貼在信封上

Put the letter in an envelope and mail it to Mary. 把信放到信封裡寄給瑪麗。

environment

名 環境 [ɪnˋvaɪrənmənt]

用法 environmental [ɪnˋvaɪrənmənt!]
形 有關環境的
environmental protection 環保

The workers need a safe working environment. 員工們需要一個安全的工作環境。

envy [ˋɛnvɪ]

動 名 嫉妒；羨慕

用法 ⓐ 三態：envy、envied [ˋɛnvɪd]、envied
ⓑ be green with envy 感到嫉妒，眼紅

We all envy Mary for her beautiful looks.
瑪麗長相很美，因此我們都很羨慕她。

A B C D E F G H I J K L M N O P Q R S T U V W X Y Z

equal [ˋikwəl]

形 相等的

用法 be equal to... 相等於……

One inch is equal to 2.54 centimeters.
（一英寸相當於 2.54 公分。）

The two boys are **equal** in height.
這兩個男孩**一樣**高。

eraser [ɪˋresɚ]

名 橡皮擦；黑板擦

用法 erase [ɪˋrez] 動 擦掉

Erase the word with an eraser.
（用橡皮擦把這個字擦掉。）

Can you lend me your **eraser**?
你能把你的**橡皮擦**借給我嗎？

error [ˋɛrɚ]

名 錯誤

用法 make an error 犯一個錯

Taylor made two **errors** in that sentence.
那個句子泰勒犯了兩個**錯**。

especially [əˋspɛʃəlɪ]

副 特別地

用法 especially 等於 particularly [pəˋtɪkjələlɪ]。

Ted hates insects, especially cockroaches. 泰德討厭昆蟲，尤其是蟑螂。

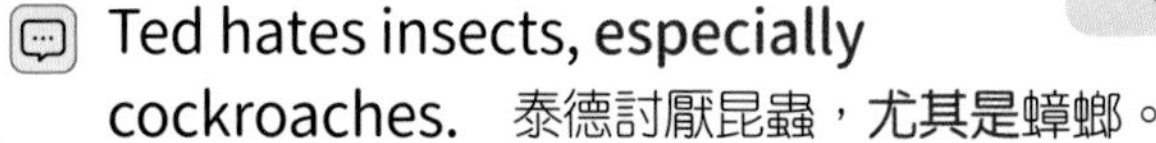

eve [iv]

名 前夕

用法 eve 要與 on 並用。
on Chinese New Year's Eve
在農曆年除夕

My family will have a party on Christmas Eve. 聖誕夜我們家將舉行派對。

even [ˋivən]

副 甚至　形 偶數的

用法
an even number　偶數
an odd number　奇數

This question is easy. Even my little brother can answer it. 這個問題很容易。甚至我小弟都會回答。

evening [ˋivnɪŋ]

名 傍晚；晚上

用法
ⓐ in the evening　晚上
ⓑ Good evening!　晚安！（晚上見面時的問候語）
ⓒ Good night!　晚安！（晚上道別時的用語）

Danny will play basketball with his friends this evening.　今天晚上丹尼會跟他朋友打籃球。

event [ɪˋvɛnt]

名 事件

用法
a big event　大事，重要的事

Getting married is a big event in one's life.　結婚是人一生中的大事。

ever [ˋɛvɚ]

副 曾經

用法
ever 不能用在肯定句中。
I have ever seen Bella. (×)
→ I have seen Bella before. (○)

Have you ever been to Tokyo?
你曾經去過東京嗎？

every [ˋɛvrɪ]

限 每個

用法 every day / month / year
每天 / 每月 / 每年

My father jogs **every** morning.
我爸爸**每天**早上都會慢跑。

everyone [ˋɛvrɪˏwʌn]

代 每個人

用法 everyone = everybody
Everyone should study hard.
(每個人都應用功讀書。)

Everyone in my class loves music.
我班上**每個人**都喜歡音樂。

everything [ˋɛvrɪˏθɪŋ]

代 每個東西；每件事

用法 everything 是一個字，不可寫成 every thing。

I believe **everything** Tom says.
湯姆說的**每件事**我都相信。

everywhere [ˋɛvrɪˏwɛr]

副 到處

用法 也可以說 everyplace [ˋɛvrɪˏples]。

You can use your credit card **everywhere** in that country. 那個國家**到處**都可使用信用卡。

evil [ˋivḷ]

形 邪惡的；令人不舒服的

用法 ⓐ evil 也可當名詞，為「邪惡」的意思。

ⓑ an evil smell 難聞的味道

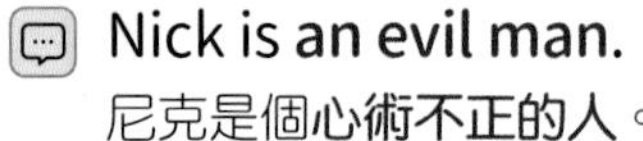

Nick is an **evil** man.

尼克是個**心術不正**的人。

exam [ɪgˋzæm]

名 考試

用法 exam 是 examination

[ɪgˏzæməˋneʃən] 的簡寫。

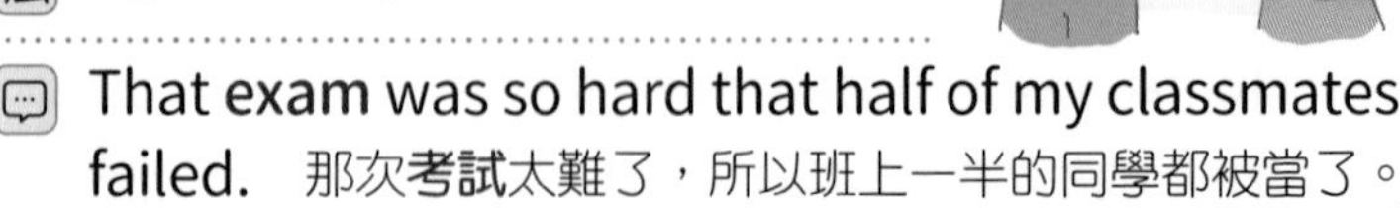

That **exam** was so hard that half of my classmates failed. 那次**考試**太難了，所以班上一半的同學都被當了。

Ee

example [ɪgˋzæmpl̩]

名 例子；模範

用法 For example, ...　譬如，⋯⋯
For example 通常放在句首，
之後要有逗點，再接句子。

Bonnie has many hobbies. For example, she enjoys singing.　邦妮有很多嗜好。**譬如說**，她喜歡唱歌。

excellent [ˋɛksələnt]

形 優異的

用法 good 相當於「不錯的」，
excellent 則相當於「極棒的」。

Dale's English is excellent. How did he learn it?
戴爾的英文**棒透了**。他是怎麼學的？

except [ɪkˋsɛpt]

介 除了⋯⋯之外

用法 except 常和 all、every、any、no 並用。
No one can sing except Peter.
（除了彼得外，誰都不會唱歌。）

All the students passed the test except David.
這次考試**除了**大衛外，所有學生都及格了。

excite [ɪkˋsaɪt]

動 使激動；使興奮

用法 excitement [ɪkˋsaɪtmənt] 名 興奮（不可數）；令人興奮的事（可數）

This good news excited all of us.

這則好消息**振奮**了我們所有人。

excited [ɪkˋsaɪtɪd]

形 感到興奮的

用法 be excited about...

對……感到興奮

Henry was excited about the good news.

亨利對這個好消息**感到興奮**。

exciting [ɪkˋsaɪtɪŋ]

形 令人興奮的

用法 -ing 作形容詞的字，均可譯成「令人……的」；而 -ed 作形容詞的字則可譯成「感到……的」。

The good news is really exciting.

這個好消息真**令人興奮**。

excuse

[ɪk\`skjuz ] 動 原諒　[ ɪk\`skjus] 名 藉口

用法
ⓐ Excuse me, but...　不好意思，……
ⓑ a good / bad excuse
很好 / 很差的藉口

Excuse me, but when is the next train?
不好意思，下一班火車什麼時候到？

exercise [\`ɛksɚ͵saɪz]

名 動 運動

用法
exercise 也可表示「練習作業」。
do an exercise　做練習作業

Exercise is good for your health.
運動有益你的健康。

exist [ɪg\`zɪst]

動 存在

用法
existence [ɪg\`zɪstəns] 名 存在

The custom still exists in that country.
那個國家仍存有這個習俗。

exit [ˋɛgzɪt / ˋɛgsɪt]

名 出口

用法 an emergency exit　緊急逃生出口

Excuse me. Where is the exit?
不好意思，**出口**在哪裡？

expect [ɪkˋspɛkt]

動 期待

用法 expect sb to V
預期某人會……；要求某人做……

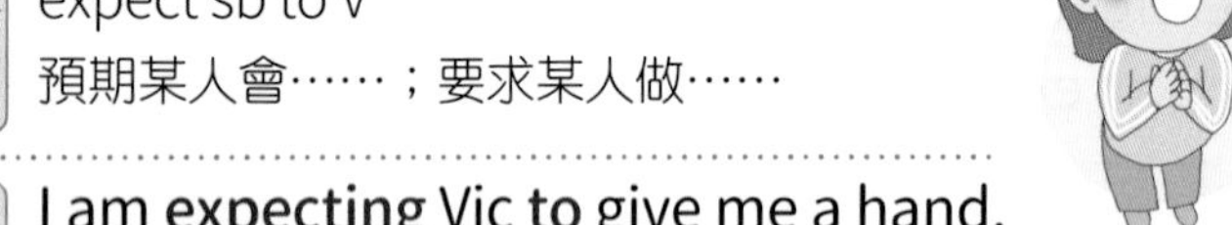

I am expecting Vic to give me a hand.
我**期待**維克幫我一個忙。

expensive [ɪkˋspɛnsɪv]

形 昂貴的

用法 expensive 指東西的「貴」，若表示價格「貴」，需要用 high 一字。
The price is too high.（這價格太貴了。）

This watch is too expensive. Do you have a cheaper one?　這只錶太**貴**了。你有便宜一點的嗎？

experience [ɪkˋspɪrɪəns]

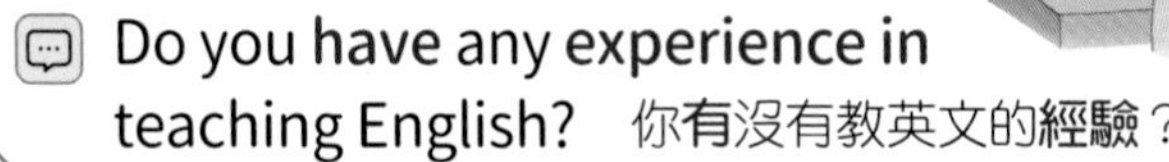

名 經驗

用法 have experience in...
在……方面有經驗

Do you have any experience in teaching English? 你有沒有教英文的經驗？

explain [ɪkˋsplen]

動 解釋

用法 ⓐ explain why / how / what...
解釋為何 / 如何 / 什麼……
ⓑ explain that... 解釋……

Can you explain to me why you were late?
你可否向我解釋你為什麼遲到了？

express [ɪkˋsprɛs]

動 表達

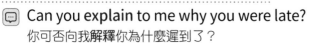

用法 express oneself
表達自己的想法 / 感受

I'd like to express my thanks to Nina.
我想要表達我對妮娜的謝意。

extra [ˋɛkstrə]

形 額外的

用法 an extra + 數字　額外若干……

Please give me an extra ten minutes.
請再多給我十分鐘。

eye [aɪ]

名 眼睛

用法 keep an eye on + sb　好好看著某人
Please keep an eye on the baby for me.
（請替我看著小寶寶。）

My little sister has beautiful eyes.
我小妹有一雙美麗的眼睛。

Notes

F f

face [fes]

名 臉蛋，面孔　動 面對

用法
- wash one's face　洗臉
- lose face　丟臉，沒面子
- face the problem　面對問題

Mary has a round face.
瑪麗有一張圓臉。

fact [fækt]

名 事實

用法
- in fact, ...　事實上，……

John isn't a good boy. In fact, he is pretty bad.　約翰不是個好孩子。事實上，他很壞。

factory [ˋfæktərɪ]

名 工廠

用法
- a car factory　汽車工廠
- a toy factory　玩具工廠

There is a shoe factory near our school.　我們學校附近有一家製鞋工廠。

F

fail [fel]

動 **失敗；沒考及格；辜負（某人期望）**

用法 fail sb　辜負某人（的期望）
Don't fail me. Study hard.
（別辜負我的期望。用功讀書。）

If George doesn't study, he'll fail the test.　喬治若不讀書，考試就會**不及格**。

fair [fɛr]

形 **公平的**

用法 fair 當名詞用有「市集」的意思。
a book fair　書展

Be fair to everyone.
對待每個人都要**公平**。

fall [fɔl]

動 **落下**　名 **秋天**

用法
ⓐ fall 當動詞使用時，三態為：
fall、fell [fɛl]、fallen [ˋfɔlən]。
ⓑ fall 當「秋天」時，等於 autumn [ˋɔtəm]。

In autumn, leaves begin to fall.
秋天時，樹葉開始**掉落**。

false [fɔls]

形 錯誤的；假的

用法 false teeth　假牙

The answer to the question is true, not false.
這題的答案是對的，不是錯的。

family [ˋfæməlɪ]

名 家庭

用法 There are five members in my family.（我家裡有五口人。）

Isaac has a big family.
艾薩克有一個大家庭。

famous [ˋfeməs]

形 出名的，有名的

用法 be famous for...　因……而出名
The factory is famous for its good cars.（這間工廠因生產好車而出名。）

My sister is a famous actress.
我姊姊是個很有名的女演員。

fan [fæn]

名 歌迷；影迷；球迷；扇子

用法
a baseball fan　棒球迷
a movie fan　影迷

Heather is a big fan of that movie star.　海瑟是那位電影明星的超級粉絲。

fancy [ˋfænsɪ]

形 華麗的，奢華的

用法
a fancy restaurant　豪華餐廳

My family stayed in a fancy hotel for three days.　我們一家人在一間奢華的飯店住了三天。

fantastic [fænˋtæstɪk]

形 很棒的

用法
fantastic 等於 wonderful [ˋwʌndɚfəl]。

That meal was fantastic. Everyone enjoyed it.　那頓飯很棒，大家吃得很開心。

far [fɑr]

形 遙遠的　副 遙遠

用法 far away from + 地方　離某地很遠

Ned lives far away from the school.　奈德住的地方離學校很遠。

farm [fɑrm]

名 農場

用法 farm 要與 on 並用。
on the farm　在農場上

John grew up on a farm.
約翰是在農場長大的。

farmer [ˋfɑrmɚ]

名 農夫

用法 a fruit farmer　果農
a pig farmer　豬農

Abby's father is a farmer.
艾比的爸爸是農夫。

fashionable

[ˋfæʃənəbl̩]

形 流行的，時髦的

用法 fashionable clothes　時髦的衣服

Mary likes to wear fashionable clothes to school.　瑪麗喜歡穿**時髦的**衣服上學。

fast [fæst]

形 快速的　副 快速地

用法 Joe's watch is five minutes fast / slow.
（喬的錶快 / 慢五分鐘。）

Jim runs faster than David.
吉姆跑得比大衛快。

fat [fæt]

形 肥胖的　名 脂肪

用法 get fat　變胖
You'll get fat if you eat junk food.
（你若吃垃圾食物就會發胖。）

The thin girl used to be very fat.
這位苗條的女孩以前很胖。

father [ˋfɑðɚ]

名 父親；(天主教) 神父

用法 father 之前有 my、your、his、her、a 等字時，father 要小寫；若無時，father 則大寫。

Ivan's **father** is an English teacher.
艾凡的**爸爸**是英文老師。

faucet [ˋfɔsɪt]

名 水龍頭

用法 「打開」水龍頭的動詞用 turn on。
「關掉」水龍頭的動詞用 turn off。

Turn on the **faucet**.
把**水龍頭**打開。

fault [fɔlt]

名 錯誤

用法 find fault with + sb
挑剔某人，找某人毛病

I don't like John because he likes to **find fault with** others. 我不喜歡約翰，因為他喜歡**挑**別人的**毛病**。

favorite [ˋfevərɪt]

形 最喜愛的

用法 ⓐ favorite 之前接所有格。如 my、your 等字。
ⓑ favorite 也可當名詞，為「最喜愛的人 / 物」的意思。

Blue is Melvin's favorite color.
藍色是馬文**最喜歡的**顏色。

fear [fɪr]

名 動 害怕

用法 等於 be afraid of。

Ellen fears dogs.
艾倫怕狗。

February [ˋfɛbrʊˏɛrɪ]

名 二月

用法 in February　在二月
on February eighth　在二月八號

My brother is going to get married in February.　我哥哥二月就要結婚了。

fee [fi]

名 費用

用法 a monthly membership fee
會員月費

What's the entrance fee?
入場費是多少？

feed [fid]

動 餵食

用法 ⓐ 三態：feed、fed [fɛd]、fed
ⓑ feed the baby　餵寶寶
feed the dog　餵狗

Peter forgot to feed his dog this morning.　今天早上彼得忘了要餵狗。

feel [fil]

動 感覺

用法 ⓐ 三態：feel、felt [fɛlt]、felt
ⓑ feel + Adj　感覺……
feel happy　感覺很快樂

Are you feeling better now?
你現在覺得好些了嗎？

feeling [ˋfilɪŋ]

名 感覺（單數）

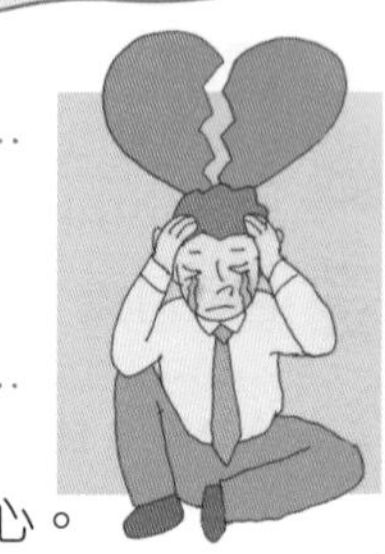

用法 feelings [ˋfilɪŋz] 名 感情（恆用複數）
Don't hurt my feelings.
不要傷了我的感情。

I have a feeling that Amy will hurt Ted's heart. 我覺得艾咪會傷了泰德的心。

female [ˋfimel]

名 女性；雌性 形 女性的；雌性的

用法 male [mel] 名 男性；雄性
形 男性的；雄性的

Our English teacher is a female.
我們的英文老師是位女性。

fence [fɛns]

名 籬笆，圍牆

用法 fence 也可以當動詞，fence sth in 就是「用籬笆圍住」的意思。

Tom painted the fence red.
湯姆把籬笆漆成紅色。

festival [ˋfɛstəvḷ]

名 節日

用法
the Mid-Autumn Festival 中秋節
Dragon Boat Festival 端午節

We have a boat race on Dragon Boat Festival. 我們在**端午節**會舉行龍舟賽。

fever [ˋfivɚ]

名 發燒

用法
have a fever 發燒
have a high fever 發高燒

Josephine doesn't feel well. She has a fever. 約瑟芬覺得不舒服。她**發燒**了。

few [fju]

形 很少的，沒幾個的

用法
few + 複數名詞 沒幾個……
a few + 複數名詞 一些……

The bad boy has few friends.
這個壞小子**沒幾個**朋友。

fifteen [fɪfˋtin]

名 十五　形 十五個的

用法 fifteen 之後要接複數名詞。

There are ten boys and fifteen girls in our class.　我們班上有十個男生及十五個女生。

fifty [ˋfɪftɪ]

名 五十　形 五十個的

用法 fifty 之後應接複數名詞。
fifty books / boys　五十本書 / 個男孩

Our English teacher is fifty years old.　我們的英文老師五十歲了。

fight [faɪt]

名 動 打架；吵架；戰鬥

用法
ⓐ 三態：fight、fought [fɔt]、fought
ⓑ have a fight with + sb
與某人吵架 / 打架

A good boy never fights with others.
好男孩從不會與人爭執。

fill [fɪl]

動 充滿

用法 be filled with...
= be full of... 充滿……

The bottle is filled with water.
瓶子灌滿了水。

film [fɪlm]

名 電影（可數）；底片，膠卷（不可數）

用法 a film / movie、two films / movies...
一部電影、兩部電影……

What do you think of the film?
這部電影你覺得怎麼樣？

final [ˋfaɪnḷ]

形 最後的；期末的 名 期末考

用法 the final exams = the finals
期末考（因有好幾項考試科目，故常用複數）

Andrea is studying for the final exams. 安德莉亞正用功準備期末考。

finally [ˋfaɪnḷɪ]

副 **終於，最後**

用法 finally 可置於句首，之後通常要有逗點；finally 也可置於句中。

Lily finally found her dog.
莉莉終於找到她的狗了。

find [faɪnd]

動 **找出，發現**

用法 三態：find、found [faʊnd]、found

Where's my pen? I can't find it.
我的筆放在哪裡了？我找不到。

fine [faɪn]

形 **美好的；不錯的；(身體) 無恙的**

用法 fine 也可作動詞用，表示「罰款」。
Victor was fined NT$ 3,000 for speeding.
(維克多因為超速被罰了新臺幣三千元。)

Don't worry. I'm fine.
別擔心。我沒事。

finger [ˋfɪŋgɚ]

名 手指

用法
thumb 拇指　index finger 食指
middle finger 中指　little finger 小指
ring finger 無名指（戴戒指用的手指）

My finger hurts!
我的手指好痛喲！

finish [ˋfɪnɪʃ]

動 完成

用法
finish 之後可接名詞或結尾為 -ing 的動名詞。
finish the homework　把家庭作業做完
finish writing the letter　寫完這封信

You have to finish your homework before you go to bed.　你必須把功課做完才能睡覺。

fire [faɪr]

名 火；火災　動 開除

用法
sb be fired　某人被開除
The lazy man was fired.
（這個懶鬼被開除了。）

A fire broke out this morning.
今天早上發生了火災。

first [fɝst]

名 第一　形 第一的

用法 It's one's first time to...
這是某人第一次……

It's Dale's first time to go abroad.
這是戴爾第一次出國。

fish [fɪʃ]

名 魚　動 釣魚

用法
ⓐ fish 單複數同形。
ⓑ go fishing　去釣魚

Cathy sees some fish in the river.
凱西看到河裡有一些魚。

fisherman [ˋfɪʃɚmən]

名 漁夫，捕魚人

用法
a fisherman　一位漁夫
two fishermen　兩位漁夫
（非 two fishermans）

John's uncle is a fisherman.
約翰的叔叔是漁夫。

fit [fɪt]

動 適合　形 適合的；強健的

用法
ⓐ fit 三態同形。
ⓑ To keep fit, you must exercise every day.（要保持健康，你每天都須運動。）

The shirt doesn't fit Toby; it's too large. 這件襯衫不合托比的身形，太大了。

five [faɪv]

名 五　形 五個的

用法
five 之後接複數名詞。
five years　五年
five boys　五個男孩

Mr. Wang has five children.
王先生有五個孩子。

fix [fɪks]

動 修理；準備（食物）

用法
fix / cook breakfast / lunch / dinner
弄早餐 / 午餐 / 晚餐
fix / make tea / coffee　泡茶 / 咖啡

Can Eric fix this machine?
艾瑞克會修理這臺機器嗎？

A B C D E F G H I J K L M N O P Q R S T U V W X Y Z

flag [flæg]

名 旗子

用法 a national flag 國旗

The national **flag** is flying.
國**旗**在飄揚。

flashlight [ˋflæʃˏlaɪt]

名 手電筒

用法 shine the flashlight 用手電筒照

The **flashlight** is very useful if you plan to go on a night trip. 如果你計劃要夜遊，**手電筒**會很管用。

flat tire [ˏflæt ˋtaɪr]

名 洩了氣的輪胎

用法 have a flat tire 汽車爆胎

Tim had a **flat tire** on his way home.
提姆在回家的路上汽車**爆胎**了。

flight [flaɪt]

名 飛行；班機

用法 Our flight was canceled because of the typhoon. （因為颱風的關係，我們的班機被取消了。）

It's a long flight from Taipei to New York. 從臺北到紐約要飛好久的時間。

floor [flɔr]

名 地板；樓層

用法 live on the ground (或 first) / second / third floor 住在一樓 / 二樓 / 三樓

Evan lives on the fifth floor. 伊凡住在五樓。

flour [flaʊr]

名 麵粉

用法
- ⓐ flour 為不可數。
- ⓑ flour 當動詞用時有「在……上灑上麵粉」的意思。

To make a cake, you need flour and eggs. 做蛋糕需要麵粉和雞蛋。

flower [ˋflaʊɚ]

名 花

用法 Don't pick flowers.
（不要摘花。）

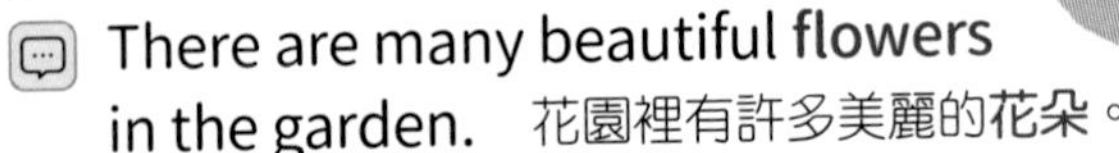

There are many beautiful flowers in the garden. 花園裡有許多美麗的花朵。

flu [flu]

名 流行性感冒（始終與 the 並用）

用法 「得到一般感冒」則用 catch (a) cold。
Candy caught a cold yesterday.
（坎蒂昨天感冒了。）

Eliot had the flu last week.
上星期艾略特得了流感。

flute [flut]

名 橫笛；笛子

用法 表示「演奏」樂器，均使用動詞 play，並與 the 並用。
play the flute　吹笛子

Mary plays the flute very well.
瑪麗笛子吹得很好。

fly [flaɪ]

名 蒼蠅　動 飛；駕駛（飛機）

用法
ⓐ 三態：fly、flew [flu]、flown [flon]
ⓑ fly an airplane　開飛機

Jacob sees a few birds flying high in the sky.　雅各看見有幾隻鳥在高空飛翔。

focus [ˋfokəs]

動 集中注意力（與 on 並用）　名 焦點，重點

用法
focus on...
將注意力集中在……之上

Hank should focus on his work.
漢克應專心工作。

fog [fɔg]

名 霧

用法
heavy fog　濃霧

The fog is so heavy that Jay can't see anything.　霧太大，因此傑什麼都看不見。

F

foggy [ˋfɔgɪ]

形 多霧的

用法 a foggy day　起霧的日子

It's dangerous to drive on foggy days.　在霧天開車很危險。

follow [ˋfalo]

動 跟隨；遵守

用法 follow the rules　遵守規定

Follow me. This way, please.
跟著我。請往這個方向走。

food [fud]

名 食物

用法 junk food　垃圾食物
（指漢堡、炸薯條等高熱量低營養的速食）

Justin is hungry. He needs some food to eat.　賈斯汀餓了，需要吃點食物。

fool [ful]

名 傻瓜

用法 April Fool's Day　愚人節

Whenever Jamie is with Eva, he feels like a **fool**.
每一次傑米跟伊娃在一起時，就覺得自己像個**傻瓜**似的。

foolish [ˋfulɪʃ]

形 愚笨的

用法 It was foolish of sb to V
某人做……很傻

Leo has made a **foolish** mistake.
李歐犯了個**愚笨的**錯誤。

foot [fʊt]

名 腳（單數）

用法 ⓐ feet [fit] 為複數。
ⓑ on foot　步行
go to school on foot　走路上學

A man has two **feet**.
人有兩隻**腳**。

football [ˋfut͵bɔl]

名 足球

用法 a football player　足球員

The football game attracted a lot of fans.　足球賽吸引了許多球迷。

for [fɔr]

介 為了；對；給

用法 Herman bought a watch for Elaine.
（赫曼買了一只錶給伊蓮。）

Smoking is bad for you, Dad.
爸爸，抽菸對您不好。

foreign [ˋfɔrɪn]

形 外國的

用法 a foreign language　外語，外國語
English is a foreign language to us.
（對我們來說，英語是外語。）

Jason collects foreign stamps.
傑森蒐集外國郵票。

foreigner [ˋfɔrɪnɚ]

名 外國人

用法 local [ˋlokḷ] 名 本地人
John is a foreigner, and I'm a local.
（約翰是外國人，而我是本地人。）

Ivan's neighbor is a foreigner.
艾凡的鄰居是個外國人。

forest [ˋfɔrɪst]

名 森林

用法 a rain forest = a rainforest
雨林

There are many kinds of animals in the forest. 森林裡有許多種動物。

forget [fɚˋgɛt]

動 忘記

用法
ⓐ 三態：forget、forgot [fɚˋgɑt]、forgotten [fɚˋgɑtn̩]
ⓑ forget to... 忘了要……

Eunice forgot that boy's name again.
尤妮絲又忘了那個男孩的名字。

forgive [fɚˋgɪv]

動 原諒

用法 三態：forgive、forgave [fɚˋgev]、forgiven [fɚˋgɪvən]。

Please forgive me for lying to you.
請**原諒**我對你說謊。

fork [fɔrk]

名 叉子

用法 eat with a knife and fork
用刀叉吃東西
eat with chopsticks　用筷子吃東西

Peter eats with a knife and fork.
彼得**用刀叉**吃飯。

form [fɔrm]

名 表格；形式

用法 an application form
申請表

Fill out the forms, please.
請填寫這些**表格**。

formal [ˋfɔrml̩]

形 正式的

用法 on a formal occasion
在正式場合中

This is a formal meeting.
這是正式的會議。

former [ˋfɔrmɚ]

形 之前的　名 前者（與 the 並用）

用法
ⓐ the former president　前任總統
ⓑ the former..., and the latter
前者……，後者……

John and Peter are good friends. The former is a teacher, and the latter is a policeman.
約翰和彼得是好朋友。前者是老師，後者則是警察。

forty [ˋfɔrtɪ]

名 四十　形 四十個的

用法 forty 之後要接複數名詞。
如 forty books / toys
四十本書 / 個玩具

Helen can type forty words a minute.　海倫一分鐘可以打四十個字。

forward [ˋfɔrwəd]

副 向前（= forwards）

用法 look forward to + V-ing / N
期待……

We're **looking forward to** seeing you again soon.　我們**期待**很快能與你再次會面。

four [fɔr]

名 四　形 四個的

用法 four 之後要接複數名詞。
如 four books / toys（四本書 / 玩具）。

There are **four** seasons in a year.
一年有**四**季。

fourteen [ˏfɔrˋtin]

名 十四　形 十四個的

用法 fourteen 之後要接複數名詞。
如 fourteen books / toys
（十四本書 / 個玩具）。

Matthew will be **fourteen** years old next month.　馬修下個月就滿**十四**歲了。

Ff

fox [fɑks]

名 狐狸

用法 fox 也可指「狡猾的人」。
That guy is an old fox. Stay away from him.（那傢伙是個老狐狸。離他遠一點。）

A fox looks like a dog.
狐狸樣子很像狗。

frank [fræŋk]

形 坦白的

用法 To be frank with you, ...
= To tell you the truth, ...
坦白跟你說，……

To be frank with you, Oliver is a bad guy. 老實跟你說，奧利佛是壞蛋。

free [fri]

形 自由的；有空的；免費的

用法 a free ticket　一張免費的票

Will you be free this afternoon?
今天下午你有空嗎？

freedom [ˋfridəm]

名 自由

用法 free [fri] 形 自由的；有空的
Are you free this afternoon?
（你今天下午有空嗎？）

Without freedom, I would rather die.
不自由毋寧死。

freezer [ˋfrizɚ]

名（冰箱內的）冷凍室；冰凍櫃

用法 refrigerator [rɪˋfrɪdʒəˏretɚ] 名 冰箱

Put the beef in the freezer.
把牛肉存放在冰凍櫃裡。

freezing [ˋfrizɪŋ]

形 極冷的，冷得快要結冰的　副 極冷地

用法 Angel's hands are freezing cold.
安琪的手凍僵了。

It's freezing outside.
外面超級冷。

French fries

[ˌfrɛntʃ ˋfraɪz]

名 薯條

用法 fries 源自動詞 fry [fraɪ]（油炸）。

Children like to eat French fries.
小朋友都喜歡吃薯條。

fresh [frɛʃ]

形 新鮮的

用法 fresh air　清新的空氣

The fruit is not fresh. Don't eat it.　這水果不新鮮，不要吃了。

Friday [ˋfraɪde]

名 星期五

用法 日子均與 on 並用。
on Friday　星期五那天
on Friday morning　星期五早上

We'll have a party on Friday night.
Will you come?　星期五晚上我們會舉辦派對。你會來嗎？

Ff

friend [frɛnd]

名 朋友

用法 make friends with...
與……交朋友（friends 要用複數）

Peter is my best friend.
彼得是我最好的朋友。

friendly [ˋfrɛndlɪ]

形 友善的

用法 be friendly to + sb　對某人友善

I like David because he is friendly to everyone.　我喜歡大衛，因為他對每個人都很友善。

friendship [ˋfrɛndʃɪp]

名 友誼

用法 treasure / cherish / value one's friendship　珍惜某人的友誼

Eric really treasures our friendship.
艾瑞克真的很珍惜我們的友誼。

frighten [ˋfraɪtn̩]

動 使害怕

用法 be frightened to death
受到極度驚嚇

Darren frightened me to death when he called my name from behind. 達倫從背後叫我名字時，把我嚇死了。

Frisbee [ˋfrɪzbi]

名 飛盤

用法 play Frisbee 玩飛盤

A boy is playing Frisbee with his dog in the park. 有個男孩子正在公園跟他的狗狗玩飛盤。

frog [frɑg]

名 青蛙

用法 tadpole [ˋtæd͵pol] 名 蝌蚪
toad [tod] 名 蟾蜍

I see a frog in the pond.
我看到池塘裡有隻青蛙。

A B C D E F G H I J K L M N O P Q R S T U V W X Y Z

from [frɑm]

介 由，從

用法 from now on　從現在起
From now on, I'll study harder.
（從現在起，我要更加用功。）

F

Where are you from?
你從哪裡來？

front [frʌnt]

名 前面

用法 in front of...　在……的前面

There is a garden in front of Jenna's house.　珍娜家前面有一座花園。

fruit [frut]

名 水果

用法
ⓐ 若強調水果為食物，fruit 不加 s。
ⓑ 若強調水果的種類，則 fruit 可加 s。

You should eat a lot of fruit and vegetables.　你應吃大量的水果和蔬菜。

fry [fraɪ]

動 煎；炸

用法 三態：fry、fried [fraɪd]、fried

Mom is frying fish in the kitchen.
媽媽正在廚房裡煎魚。

full [fʊl]

形 充滿的

用法 be full of... 充滿……
= be filled with...

This paper is full of mistakes.
這份報告到處都是錯誤。

fun [fʌn]

名 樂趣（不可數） 形 樂趣的

用法 ⓐ have fun = have a good time
玩得很愉快
ⓑ a fun movie 一部很有趣的電影

George and his friends had lots of fun at the party last night. 喬治和他的朋友昨晚在派對上玩得很開心。

F

funny [ˋfʌnɪ]

形 滑稽的，好笑的

用法
a funny man　很滑稽的人
a fun man　很有趣的人

This story isn't funny. My daughter doesn't like it.　這個故事不好笑。我女兒不喜歡。

furniture [ˋfɝnɪtʃɚ]

名 傢俱（集合名詞，不可數）

用法
a furniture (×)
→ a piece of furniture (○) 一件傢俱
some furniture (○) 一些傢俱

Winnie needs to buy several pieces of furniture.
溫妮需要買幾件傢俱。

future [ˋfjutʃɚ]

名 未來；前途　形 未來的

用法
ⓐ in the future　未來
ⓑ If you work hard, you'll have a bright future.（你若努力，就會有光明的前途。）

What do you want to be in the future?　你將來想當什麼？

gain [gen]

動 獲得

用法 gain weight 變胖
lose weight 瘦下來

Gary will gain weight if he does not control what he eats. 蓋瑞若不控制飲食就會發胖。

game [gem]

名 遊戲

用法 play games 玩遊戲

Peter is good at playing computer games. 彼得很會打電動。

garage [gəˋrɑʒ]

名 車庫

用法 garage 也有「汽車修理廠」的意思。

Donald's car is in the garage now. 唐納德的車現在停在車庫裡。

gather [ˋgæðɚ]

動 **聚集，集合**

用法 gather together
= get together 聚會

Our family **gathered together** to celebrate Grandma's birthday. 我們一家人**聚在一起**慶祝奶奶的生日。

garbage [ˋgɑrbɪdʒ]

名 **垃圾（不可數）**

用法
a piece of garbage 一件垃圾
two pieces of garbage 兩件垃圾
some garbage 一些垃圾

Please pick up the **garbage** and throw it into the **garbage can** there. 請把**垃圾**撿起來扔進那邊的**垃圾桶**。

garden [ˋgɑrdn̩]

名 **花園；菜園**

用法 grow flowers / vegetables in the garden
在花 / 菜園裡種花 / 菜

What does Greg grow in the **garden**? 葛瑞格在**花園**裡種了些什麼？

gas [gæs]

名 瓦斯，天然氣；汽油

用法
ⓐ gas 表示「汽油」時，是 gasoline [ˋgæsəlin] 的簡稱。
ⓑ gas station　加油站

Mother uses gas to cook food.
媽媽用瓦斯煮菜。

gate [get]

名 大門

用法
gate 指住家、學校、機關的圍牆大門，door 則指房間的門。

Wait for me at the school gate.
在校門口等我。

general [ˋdʒɛnərəl]

形 一般的　名 將軍

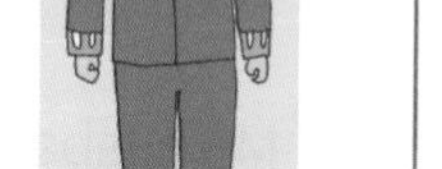

用法
In general, ... = Generally speaking, ...
一般而言，……

Francis's father is a general.
法蘭西斯的父親是一位將軍。

generous [ˋdʒɛnərəs]

形 慷慨的

用法 be generous to sb
對某人很慷慨

John's father is very generous to him. 約翰的父親對他很慷慨。

genius [ˋdʒinɪəs]

名 天才

用法 a music / mathematical genius
音樂 / 數學天才

Mozart was a music genius.
莫札特是音樂天才。

gentle [ˋdʒɛntḷ]

形 溫柔的；溫和的

用法 be gentle with...
對……很溫柔

My husband is very gentle with children and women. 我先生對小朋友及女士都十分溫柔。

gentleman

[ˋdʒɛntl̩mən]

名 紳士，君子

用法 複數為 gentlemen。

A gentleman never forgets his table manners. 紳士決不會忘記他的餐桌禮儀。

geography

[dʒiˋɑgrəfɪ]

名 地理

用法 geography 為不可數名詞。

Our geography teacher taught us to read a map. 我們地理老師教我們如何看地圖。

gesture [ˋdʒɛstʃɚ]

名 手勢

用法 make a... gesture
做……的手勢

Elva made a strange gesture to me.
艾娃向我比了一個奇怪的手勢。

get [gɛt]

動 獲得；變成

用法
ⓐ 三態：get、got [gɑt]、gotten [ˋgɑtn̩] / got
ⓑ get 表示「變成」時，之後須接形容詞。
如 get angry　變得生氣起來

Where did you **get** this toy, Johnny?
強尼，你這玩具是在哪兒得到的？

ghost [gost]

名 鬼

用法
believe in ghosts
相信有鬼（存在）

Are you afraid of **ghosts**?
你怕鬼嗎？

giant [ˋdʒaɪənt]

名 巨人　形 巨大的

用法
a giant　巨人
a giant tree = a very big tree
巨大的樹

In the story, the prince killed the **giant**.　故事中，王子把巨人殺死了。

gift [gɪft]

名 禮物；天分

用法 have a gift for music
有音樂的天分

Thank you for the gift.
謝謝你送的禮物。

girl [gɝl]

名 女孩，女生

用法 boy [bɔɪ] 名 男孩，男生
We have more girls than boys in our class. （我們班上女生比男生多。）

Who is that beautiful girl?
那位美麗的女孩是誰？

give [gɪv]

動 給予

用法 ⓐ 三態：give、gave [gev]、given [ˋgɪvən]
ⓑ give + sb + sth = give + sth + to + sb

Eric gave Jane a watch for her birthday.
艾瑞克送給珍一只錶當作她的生日禮物。

glad [glæd]

形 高興的

用法 be glad to... 很高興……
I'm glad to meet you.
(幸會 / 很高興與你見面。)

I'm glad to see you again.
我很高興再次與你見面。

glass [glæs]

名 玻璃；玻璃杯

用法 ⓐ 表示「玻璃」時為不可數名詞。
It is made of glass.（這是玻璃做的。）
ⓑ 表示「玻璃杯」時為可數名詞。

Arthur needs a glass of water.
亞瑟需要一杯水。

glasses [ˋglæsɪz]

名 眼鏡

用法 因眼鏡有兩個鏡片，故 glasses 始終都是複數。
a pair of glasses 一副眼鏡

Mary just bought a new pair of glasses. 瑪麗剛買了一副新眼鏡。

glove [glʌv]

名 手套

用法 put on the gloves 戴上手套
take off the gloves 脫下手套

It's very cold outside, so you'd better **put on** your coat and **gloves**. 外面很冷，你最好穿上外套並**戴上手套**。

glue [glu]

名 黏膠，漿水 動 黏住

用法 ⓐ a bottle of glue 一瓶膠水
ⓑ Glue this paper to the wall.
（把這張紙黏在牆上。）

Brad used **glue** to **glue** the paper.
布萊德用**膠水黏**紙。

go [go]

動 走，去；從事

用法 ⓐ 三態：go、went [wɛnt]、gone [gɑn]
ⓑ 表示「從事」時，之後的字結尾要加 -ing。
go swimming 去游泳

Elva will **go to** junior high school next year. 艾娃明年就要**上**國中了。

goal [gol]

名 目標

用法 achieve one's goal
達成某人的目標

The team has achieved their goal at last. 這個團隊最後終於達成目標。

goat [got]

名 山羊

用法 sheep [ʃip] 名 綿羊（單複數同形）
one sheep、two sheep（非 sheeps）

A goat looks different from a sheep.
山羊與綿羊外型不同。

gold [gold]

名 金 形 金的，金製的

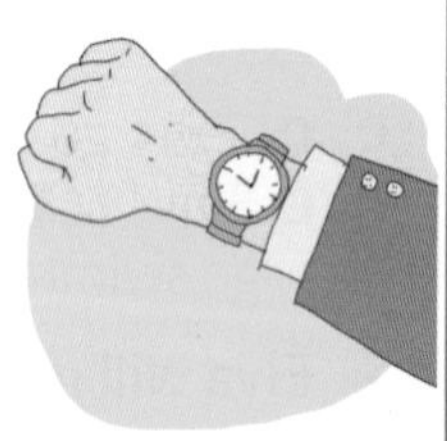

用法 The watch is made of gold.
（這只錶是黃金打造的。）

Ivy wears a gold watch.
艾薇戴著一只金錶。

golden [ˋgoldən]

形 金色的，金黃色的

用法 golden 也可表示「非常有利的；成功的」。
a golden opportunity　大好機會

Jenna's golden hair is shining in the sun.　珍娜的金髮在陽光下閃耀。

golf [galf]

名 高爾夫球　動 打高爾夫球

用法
ⓐ golf 為不可數。
ⓑ go golfing　打高爾夫球

Laura goes golfing every Saturday.
蘿拉每個星期六會去打高爾夫球。

good [gʊd]

形 好的，不錯的

用法
be good at...　擅於 / 精通⋯⋯
be bad at...　不擅於⋯⋯

Ken is good at English, but he is bad at math.　肯英文不錯，但數學就差了。

G

goodness [ˋgʊdnɪs]

感歎 God 的代用語，表示驚訝

用法 (My) goodness!　天哪！

My goodness, you have bought so many things!　我的天，你買了這麼多的東西！

good-bye [gʊdˋbaɪ]

感歎 名 再見

用法 say good-bye to + sb　向某人道別
We say good-bye to our teacher before we go home.（我們回家前都會跟老師再見。）

Good-bye, everybody.
再見了，各位。

goose [gus]

名 鵝

用法 goose 的複數為 geese [gis]。
one goose　一隻鵝
two geese　兩隻鵝

Hannah sees two ducks and three geese in the pond.　漢娜看到池塘裡有兩隻鴨子及三隻鵝。

government

名 政府 [ˋgʌvɚnmənt]

用法 central / local government
中央 / 地方政府（皆不可數）

Randy works for the government.
藍迪任職政府單位。

grade [gred]

名 年級；成績

用法 ⓐ be in the first / second / third...grade
念一年級 / 二年級 / 三年級……
ⓑ 表示「成績」時，應使用複數 grades。

Grace is in the fifth grade now.
葛瑞絲現在念五年級了。

gram [græm]

名 公克

用法 one gram 一公克
two grams 兩公克

A kilogram is 1,000 grams.
一公斤等於一千公克。

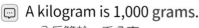

granddaughter

[ˋgræn(d)ˏdɔtɚ]

名 孫女

用法 great-granddaughter 名 曾孫女

Mabel has two **granddaughters**.
梅寶有兩個孫女。

grandfather

[ˋgræn(d)ˏfɑðɚ]

名（外）祖父；**爺爺**

用法 口語中常用 grandpa [ˋgrɑn(d)pɑ] 取代。

My **grandfather** loves my grandmother very much. 我**爺爺**很愛我奶奶。

grandmother

[ˋgræn(d)ˏmʌðɚ]

名（外）祖母；奶奶

用法 口語中常用 grandma [ˋgrɑn(d)mɑ] 取代。

My **grandmother** is going to see us today.
我**奶奶**今天會來看我們。

grandson

名 孫子 [ˋgræn(d)ˏsʌn]

用法 grandparent [ˋgræn(d)ˏpɛrənt]
名 祖父，祖母

Miranda's grandson is serving in the army. 米蘭達的孫子正在軍中服役。

grape [grep]

名 葡萄

用法 a grape 一粒葡萄
a bunch of grapes 一串葡萄

These grapes taste sweet.
這些葡萄味道很甜。

grass [græs]

名 草

用法 下列例子是公園草地上常見的英文標示用語。其中 keep off 表示「遠離⋯⋯」或「勿走在⋯⋯之上」的意思。

Keep off the grass.
請勿踐踏草地。

gray [gre]

名 灰色　形 灰色的

用法 gray 也可指頭髮的「銀白色」。
gray hair　白髮
turn gray　變成灰白色

Grandpa's hair is turning gray.
爺爺的頭髮漸漸灰白了。

great [gret]

形 很棒的；偉大的

用法
a great idea　很棒的點子
a great man　偉人

It's great to see you again.
與你再次見面真棒。

greedy [ˋgridɪ]

形 貪心的

用法
be greedy for...　對……貪心

Nobody likes greedy people.
誰都不喜歡貪心的人。

green [grin]

名 綠色　形 綠色的

用法
green tea　綠茶
black tea　紅茶（非 red tea）

Max doesn't drink **green tea**. He drinks black tea.　麥克斯不喝**綠茶**。他喝紅茶。

greet [grit]

動 打招呼

用法
greet sb with sth
以……來迎接某人

Wesley **greeted** everyone with smile.
衛斯理微笑地和每一個人**打招呼**。

ground [graʊnd]

名 地面

用法
play（玩耍）與 ground 結合在一起就成了 playground（學校的操場；公園內小朋友玩耍的地方）。

What is it on the **ground**?
地上那個是什麼東西？

group [grup]

名 群；團體

用法
a group of people　一群人
a group of students　一群學生

A group of foreign students are visiting us today.　一群外籍學生今天會來拜訪我們。

grow [gro]

動 生長；種植

用法
ⓐ 三態：grow、grew [gru]、grown [gron]
ⓑ grow up　長大

Roy wants to be a doctor when he grows up.　羅伊長大後要當醫生。

guard [gɑrd]

名 守衛者，警衛　動 守衛

用法
be on guard　守衛
stand guard　站衛兵，守衛

The guard stopped us from going inside.　警衛不讓我們進去。

guava [ˋgwavə]

名 芭樂，番石榴

用法 guava juice　芭樂汁

Does your son like guavas?
你兒子喜歡芭樂嗎？

guess [gɛs]

名 動 猜

用法
ⓐ I guess that...　我猜想……
ⓑ Make a guess!　猜猜看嘛！

Teddy guesses that it will rain this afternoon.　泰迪猜想今天下午會下雨。

guest [gɛst]

名 客人

用法 a special guest　特別來賓

Many guests were invited to the party.　這場派對邀請了很多客人。

guide [gaɪd]

動 引導，引領　名 嚮導

用法 The man guided us to the hall.
（那名男子帶領我們到大廳去。）

My brother is a tour guide.
我哥哥是個導遊。

guitar [gɪˋtɑr]

名 吉他

用法 表示「彈奏」樂器，一律使用動詞 play。
play the guitar / piano / flute
彈吉他 / 彈鋼琴 / 吹笛子

Can Will play the guitar?
威爾會彈吉他嗎？

gun [gʌn]

名 槍

用法 carry a gun　配帶槍枝

It's against the law to buy guns in Taiwan.　在臺灣買槍械是犯法的。

Gg

guy [gaɪ]

名 傢伙，男子

用法
a good guy　好人
a bad guy　壞蛋，壞傢伙

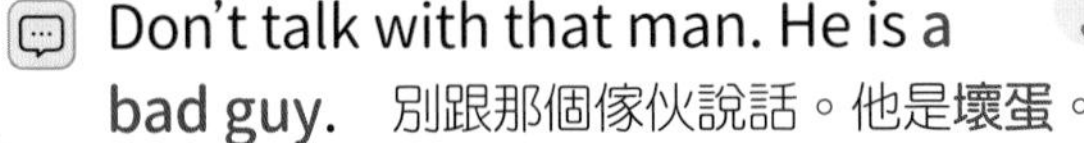

Don't talk with that man. He is a bad guy.　別跟那個傢伙說話。他是壞蛋。

gym [dʒɪm]

名 體育館；健身房

用法
ⓐ gym 是 gymnasium [dʒɪmˋnezɪəm] 的簡寫。
ⓑ work out in the gym　在健身房健身

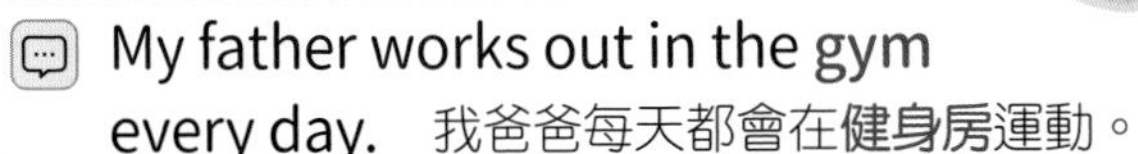

My father works out in the gym every day.　我爸爸每天都會在健身房運動。

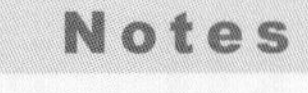

Notes

H h

habit [ˋhæbɪt]

名 習慣

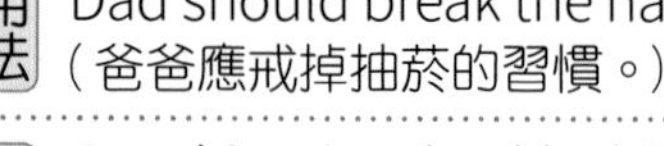

用法 break the habit of... 戒掉……的習慣
Dad should break the habit of smoking.
（爸爸應戒掉抽菸的習慣。）

Smoking is a bad habit.
抽菸是惡習。

hair [hɛr]

名 頭髮；毛

用法 gray hair 白頭髮

Amy has beautiful long hair.
艾咪有一頭漂亮的長髮。

haircut [ˋhɛrˏkʌt]

名 理髮

用法 have / get a haircut 剪頭髮

Derek's hair is too long. He needs a haircut. 德瑞克的頭髮太長了，需要理髮了。

Hh

hairdresser

[ˋhɛrˏdrɛsɚ]

名 美髮師，理髮師

用法 hairstyle [ˋhɛrˏstaɪl] 名 髮型

Mary used to be a hairdresser.
瑪麗曾經當過美髮師。

hall [hɔl]

名 大廳

用法
a lecture hall 演講廳
a city hall 市政府大樓

We'll meet in the hall tomorrow morning. 我們明早將在大廳見面。

Halloween [ˏhæloˋin]

名 萬聖節前夕

用法 萬聖節前夕指十月三十一日夜晚。小朋友會向住處附近的鄰居討糖果吃，是西方小朋友最愛的節慶之一。

Children enjoy Halloween.
孩子們都喜歡萬聖節。

half [hæf]

名 一半 形 一半的

用法 half of the... 一半的……
Johnny ate half of the cake.
(強尼把一半的蛋糕吃掉了。)

Half of the students failed the test. 有半數的學生考試不及格。

ham [hæm]

名 火腿

用法 a ham sandwich
一份火腿三明治

Harry often has ham and eggs for breakfast. 哈利早餐常吃火腿及雞蛋。

hamburger [ˋhæmbɝgɚ]

名 漢堡

用法 在賣漢堡的速食餐廳常說：I'd like three hamburgers to go, please.
(我想要三份漢堡外帶，麻煩您。)

I'd like two hamburgers, please.
我想要兩個漢堡，麻煩您。

hammer [ˋhæmɚ]

名 鎚子，鐵鎚

用法 hammer 當動詞用時，為「用槌子敲擊」的意思。

You need a hammer for the work.
這工作需要用到鐵鎚。

hand [hænd]

名 手

用法 Give me a hand, please.
（請幫我一個忙。）

You should wash your hands before eating. 吃東西前你應該先洗手。

handkerchief [ˋhæŋkɚtʃɪf]

名 手帕

用法 複數形為 handkerchiefs。

Ted used a handkerchief to blow his nose. 泰德用手帕擤鼻涕。

handle [ˋhændḷ]

動 處理　名（門、刀等）把柄

用法
ⓐ handle a problem　處理問題
ⓑ a door handle　門把

Handle it with care.
請小心處理。

handsome [ˋhænsəm]

形 英俊的，瀟灑的

用法
handsome 通常用以修飾男孩，beautiful 或 pretty [ˋprɪtɪ] 則通常用以修飾女孩。

Who is that handsome boy over there?　那邊那個帥哥是誰呀？

hang [hæŋ]

動 懸掛

用法
三態：hang、hung [hʌŋ]、hung

Please hang the picture on the wall.　請把畫掛在牆上。

hanger [ˋhæŋɚ]

名 衣架

用法 也可以說 clothes hanger。

Hang your coat on a hanger.
把你的外套用**衣架**掛起來。

happen [ˋhæpən]

動 發生

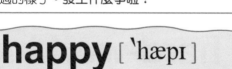

用法 What happened to you?
= What's the matter with you?
= What's wrong with you? （怎麼了？）

You look sad. What happened to you?
你一副難過的樣子。**發生**什麼事啦？

happy [ˋhæpɪ]

形 快樂的；幸福的

用法 be happy for sb　為某人感到開心
I feel happy for you.
（我為妳感到高興。）

Ian felt happy when he heard the good news. 伊恩聽到這個好消息時感到很**高興**。

hard [hɑrd]

形 堅硬的；困難的　副 努力地

用法
ⓐ The test yesterday was very hard.
（昨天的測驗很難。）
ⓑ work / study hard　努力工作；努力用功

Harold should work hard if he wants to pass the test.　哈洛德若想通過考試就應用功。

hardly [ˋhɑrdlɪ]

副 幾乎不

用法
與 hardly 相似的字有：
barely [ˋbɛrlɪ] 副 幾乎沒有
scarcely [ˋskɛrslɪ] 副 幾乎不

The old woman can hardly walk now.　那位老太太現在幾乎走不動了。

hard-working

形 努力的　[ˏhɑrdˋwɝkɪŋ]

用法
Hank is hard-working.
（漢克很努力。）

All teachers like hard-working students.　所有的老師都喜歡用功的學生。

hat [hæt]

名 帽子

用法 Put on your hat. （戴上帽子。）
Take off your hat. （脫下帽子。）

Peter is wearing a yellow hat today.
彼得今天戴了一頂黃色的帽子。

hate [het]

動 憎恨，討厭

用法 Hugo hates to talk to Ella.
= Hugo hates talking to Ella.
（雨果討厭跟艾拉說話。）

Why does Duke hate me so much? 杜克為何如此討厭我？

have [hæv]

動 有 助 已經；曾經

用法 ⓐ 第三人稱單數現在式用 has，過去式用 had。
ⓑ have 表示「已經」或「曾經」時，之後接過去分詞。I have seen him before.（我曾見過他。）

Gordon doesn't have much money, but he is happy. 戈登沒有什麼錢，但他很快樂。

he [hi]

代 他

用法 he 是作主詞的代名詞，him [hɪm]
也表示「他」，要放在動詞的後面。

Amber likes John because he is friendly. 安柏喜歡約翰，因為他待人和善。

head [hɛd]

名 頭

用法 Keep your head. （你要保持冷靜。）
Don't lose your head.
（不要失去理智。）

Keep your head. Don't get angry.
你要冷靜。別生氣。

headache [ˋhɛd͵ek]

名 頭痛

用法 have a headache 頭痛

Denise had a headache this morning, but she's feeling better now. 丹妮絲今天早上頭痛，不過她現在好多了。

health [hɛlθ]

名 健康（不可數）

用法
be in good health　身體很健康
be in bad health　身體不健康

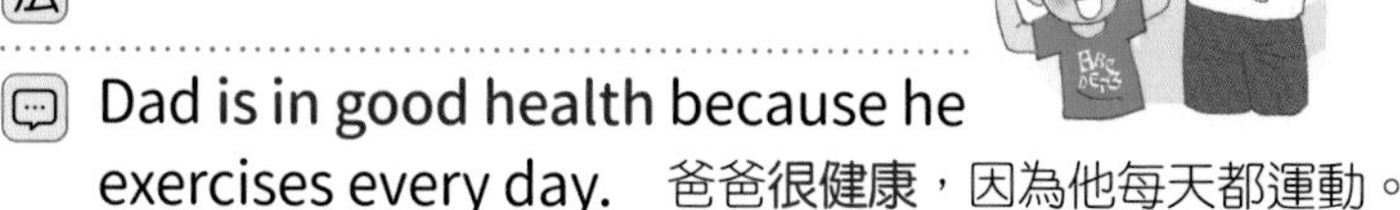

Dad is in good health because he exercises every day.　爸爸很健康，因為他每天都運動。

healthy [ˋhɛlθɪ]

形 健康的

用法
stay healthy　保持健康
To stay healthy, you must exercise.
（要保持健康，你就必須運動。）

Mr. and Mrs. Li have two healthy children.　李氏夫婦有兩個健康的孩子。

hear [hɪr]

動 聽到，聽見

用法
ⓐ 三態：hear、heard [hɝd]、heard
ⓑ hear 指「無意間聽到」，listen to 則指「注意聽」、「聆聽」。

Did you hear that noise?
你聽到那個雜音了嗎？

heart [hɑrt]

名 心；心臟

用法 have a heart of gold　有一顆善心
a heart of gold　用黃金打造的心
（喻「善心」）

Mary has a heart of gold.
瑪麗有顆善心。

heat [hit]

名 熱　動 加熱

用法 heat 作動詞時，有下列用法：
heat the food　把食物加熱
heat the milk　把牛奶加熱

Danny can't stand the heat.
丹尼受不了這麼酷熱。

heater [ˋhitɚ]

名 暖氣機；加熱器

用法 air-conditioner [ˋɛrkənˏdɪʃənɚ]
名 冷氣機

We need a heater to keep us warm in winter.　我們冬天需要暖氣機保暖。

heavy [ˋhɛvɪ]

形 重的

用法 heavy 表示「重的」，light [laɪt] 表示「輕的」。

a heavy / light box　很重／輕的箱子

This box is too heavy.

這個箱子太重了。

height [haɪt]

名 高度；身高

用法 Jay is 180 centimeters in height.

= Jay is 180 centimeters tall.

（傑身高一百八十公分。）

What's Abe's height?

亞伯的身高有多高？

hello [həˋlo]

感歎 名 哈囉，喂

用法 say hello to + sb　向某人打招呼／問候

say goodbye to + sb　向某人道別

Hello? Who is it, please?

哈囉？請問哪位？（電話用語）

helicopter

[ˋhɛlə͵kɑptɚ]

名 直升機

用法 a helicopter pilot　直升機駕駛員

Can Barry fly a helicopter?
貝瑞會駕駛直升機嗎？

help [hɛlp]

名 動 幫助

用法 help + sb + (to) + V　幫某人
Can you help me wash the car, son?
（兒子，能否請你幫我洗車？）

May I help you?
我可以幫您什麼忙嗎？

helpful [ˋhɛlpfəl]

形 有幫助的；樂於助人的

用法
ⓐ a helpful idea　有幫助的點子
ⓑ a helpful child　樂於助人的孩子

Yvonne likes David because he is very helpful.　伊芳喜歡大衛，因為他很樂意幫助人。

hen [hɛn]

名 母雞

用法 ⓐ「公雞」則為 rooster [ˋrustɚ]。
ⓑ lay an egg　生蛋

The hen lays an egg a day.
這隻**母雞**每天生一顆蛋。

here [hɪr]

副 這裡

用法 在速食店點餐後，店員把食物拿給我們時，都會說：Here you go.（東西請拿去 / 食物給您。）

Come, Billy. I have some candy for you here.
來，比利。我**這裡**有一些糖果要給你。

hero [ˋhɪro]

名 英雄

用法 heroine [ˋhɛroɪn] 名 女英雄

The hero killed the bad guy and married the princess.　那個**英雄**把壞蛋殺死，娶了公主。

hey [he]

感歎 嘿

用法 hey 是用以喚醒對方注意力或表示驚訝、憤怒的感歎詞。
Hey, don't touch me! （嘿，不要碰我！）

Hey, wait for me!
嘿，等我一下！

hi [haɪ]

感歎 嗨

用法 hi 是用以向對方打招呼的感歎詞，相當於 hello（哈囉），有「你好」的意思。美國人見面時，常會說：Hi, there!（嗨！你好！）

Hi, Peter, how're you doing?
嗨，彼得，你好嗎？

hide [haɪd]

動 躲藏；將…… 藏起來

用法
ⓐ 三態：hide、hid [hɪd]、hidden [ˋhɪdn̩]
ⓑ hide the ball under the bed
把球藏在床下

The little boy is hiding behind the door. 小男孩正躲在門後。

high [haɪ]

形 高的　副 高高地

用法 high 指東西的高，tall 則指人或樹等會繼續成長的高。

The mountain is very high.
這座山很高。

highway [ˋhaɪˏwe]

名 公路（通常指高速公路）

用法 on a highway　在公路上

Chuck’s car broke down on the highway.　查克的車在公路上拋錨了。

hike [haɪk]

名 動（在山中或鄉間）遠足；健行

用法 go hiking　去健行

Evan likes to go hiking on Sundays.　星期天伊凡喜歡去健行。

hill [hɪl]

名 丘陵，小山丘

用法 hill 指高度在兩、三百公尺以下的「小山丘」，而 mountain [ˋmaʊntn̩] 則指「高山」、「大山」。

There is a big tree on top of the hill. 山丘頂上有一棵大樹。

hip [hɪp]

名 臀部；屁股

用法 臀部因有兩片，故常用複數。

Bonnie put her hands on her hips.
邦妮把兩手放在臀部上。

hippo [ˋhɪpo]

名 河馬

用法 hippo 是 hippopotamus [ˌhɪpəˋpɑtəməs] 的簡稱。

Hippos enjoy staying in the water.
河馬喜歡待在水裡。

history [ˋhɪst(ə)rɪ]

名 歷史

用法 in history　在歷史中
Yue Fei was a great man in Chinese history. （岳飛在中國歷史中是個偉人。）

John is studying Chinese history.
約翰正在研讀中國史。

hire [haɪr]

動 名 僱用；租用

用法 for hire　可供租用
The cabins over there are for hire.
（那邊的小木屋可供租用。）

We need to hire two more people for the job. 這工作我們需要再僱兩個人手。

hit [hɪt]

動 名 打；碰撞

用法
ⓐ 三態同形
ⓑ Ted was hit by a car.
（泰德被車子撞到了。）

The ball almost hit me.
這顆球差一點打到我。

hobby [ˋhɑbɪ]

名 嗜好

用法 Daisy's hobby is singing / dancing / swimming.
（黛西的嗜好是唱歌 / 跳舞 / 游泳。）

Hank's hobby is listening to music.
漢克的**嗜好**是聽音樂。

hold [hold]

動 握住，抱住；舉行

用法
ⓐ 三態：hold、held [hɛld]、held
ⓑ hold the key　拿著鑰匙
hold the meeting　舉行會議

Eric will hold a meeting today.
艾瑞克今天將會**舉行**會議。

hole [hol]

名 洞

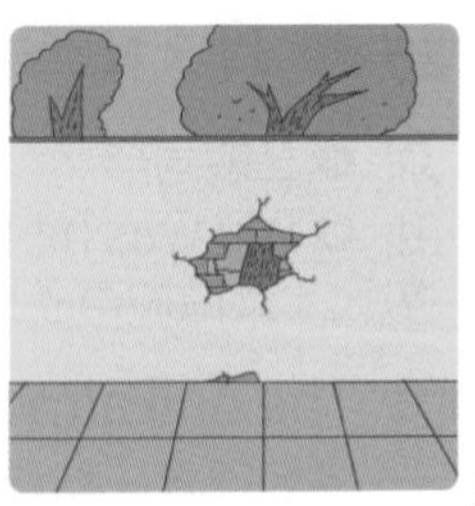

用法 dig a hole　挖洞

There is a hole in the wall.
牆上有個**洞**。

holiday [ˋhɑlə,de]

名 假日，假期

用法 be on holiday　在度假 / 休假
Mom and Dad are on holiday in New York.（爸媽正在紐約度假。）

What are you going to do during the holiday?　你在**假期**期間會做什麼？

home [hom]

名 家　副 在家；回家

用法
ⓐ be at home　在家裡
ⓑ go home　回家（非 go to home）

It's getting dark. Let's **go home** now.　天色漸漸暗了。咱們現在就**回家**吧。

homesick [ˋhom,sɪk]

形 思鄉的

用法 類似字有：nostalgic [nɑsˋtældʒɪk] 形 鄉愁的

Some people get **homesick** when they are abroad.　有些人在海外時會**思念家鄉**。

homework [ˋhom͵wɜk]

名 家庭作業，功課

用法 homework 為不可數。
some homework 一些功課
a lot of homework 許多功課

George has a lot of homework to do tonight. 喬治今晚有許多**功課**要做。

honest [ˋɑnɪst]

形 誠實的

用法 be honest with + sb
對某人很誠實

I like John because he is honest with people. 我喜歡約翰，因為他對人很誠實。

honesty [ˋɑnəstɪ]

名 誠實

用法 honesty 為不可數。

Honesty is the best policy.
誠實為上策。—— 諺語

honey [ˋhʌnɪ]

名 蜂蜜（不可數）

用法 honey 有甜美的味道，英美人士常以 honey（親愛的、甜心）稱呼心愛的人。

Honey tastes sweet.
蜂蜜的味道很甜。

hop [hɑp]

動 跳躍

用法
ⓐ 三態：hop、hopped [hɑpt]、hopped
ⓑ hop 多指昆蟲、小鳥的跳躍。

The little bird hopped onto my finger.
這隻小鳥跳到我的手指上。

hope [hop]

名 動 希望

用法
ⓐ hope to + V　希望……
ⓑ Don't give up hope.（別放棄希望。）

Jacob hopes to take a trip to Tainan next week.　雅各希望下星期到臺南走一趟。

horrible [ˋhɔrəbḷ]

形 可怕的，糟糕的

用法 相似的字有：terrible [ˋtɛrəbḷ]
形 可怕的；很糟的

I had a horrible day yesterday.
我昨天很慘。

horse [hɔrs]

名 馬

用法 ride a horse　騎馬

Harriet is learning to ride a horse.
哈莉特正在學習騎馬。

hospital [ˋhɑspɪtḷ]

名 醫院

用法 be in the hospital　住院

The sick man has been in the hospital for two months.　這位男病患住院已兩個月了。

host [host]

名（男）主人

🔍用法 hostess [ˋhostɪs] 名 女主人

Mr. Chen is the host of the party.
陳先生是派對的主人。

hot [hat]

形 熱的

🔍用法 hot 也可表示「辣的」。
The food tastes hot.
（這道食物味道很辣。）

It's very hot today.
今天天氣很熱。

hot dog [ˋhat ˏdɔg]

名 熱狗

🔍用法 在美國的電影院大多設有販賣部，販賣的東西有 hot dog（熱狗）、soda [ˋsodə]（汽水）及 popcorn [ˋpapˏkɔrn]（爆米花）。

Peter likes to eat hot dogs.
彼得很喜歡吃熱狗。

hotel [ho`tɛl]

名 旅館，飯店

用法 hostel [`hɑstl̩]
名 便宜的小旅舍，青年旅館

Dennis is going to stay in this hotel for three nights. 丹尼斯打算在這家飯店住三個晚上。

hour [aʊr]

名 小時

用法 half an hour 半個小時
an hour 一個小時
an hour and a half 一個半小時

Doris will be back in an hour.
朵瑞絲一個小時後就會回來。

house [haʊs]

名 房子；家

用法 Come to my house for dinner this weekend, OK?
（這個週末到我家來吃晚飯，好嗎？）

Peter's father has just bought a big house in the country. 彼得的父親剛在鄉下買了一棟大房子。

housewife [ˋhaʊsˏwaɪf]

名 家庭主婦

用法 ⓐ 複數為 housewives [ˋhaʊsˏwaɪvz]。
ⓑ 如果是丈夫待在家洗衣、煮飯、帶孩子，就稱作 house husband（家庭「煮夫」）。

My mother is a housewife.
我媽媽是家庭主婦。

housework

[ˋhaʊsˏwɝk]

名 家事（不可數）

用法 do the housework 做家事

Betty often helps her mom do the housework. 貝蒂常幫她媽媽做家事。

how [haʊ]

副 怎麼，如何；多麼，好

用法 ⓐ how 表示「怎麼」或「如何」時，是疑問詞。
ⓑ how 後加形容詞表示「多麼」時，是感歎詞。

How cute the little girl is!
這個小女孩好可愛哦！

however [haʊˋɛvɚ]

副 然而，不過

用法 使用時，however 之後要加逗點。

The man is poor. **However**, he is happy. 這個男子很窮，**不過**他卻很快樂。

hug [hʌg]

名 動 擁抱

用法
ⓐ 三態：hug、hugged [hʌgd]、hugged

ⓑ give sb a hug 給某人一個擁抱

Debbie **hugged** her grandpa tight when she saw him. 黛比看到爺爺時，緊緊地**擁抱**著他。

human [ˋhjumən]

形 人類的 名 人類，人

用法
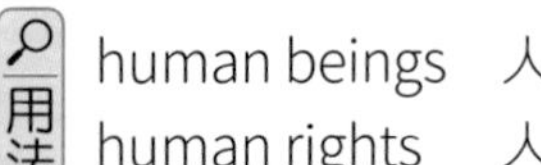
human beings 人類
human rights 人權

All **human** beings make mistakes.
凡人都會犯錯。

humble [ˋhʌmbl̩]

形 謙遜的

用法 a humble opinion　淺見

We all like humble people.
我們都喜歡謙遜的人。

humid [ˋhjumɪd]

形 溼度高的

用法 humidity [hjuˋmɪdətɪ]
名 溼氣，溼度（不可數）

It's very hot and humid in summer here.　這裡夏天又熱又潮溼。

humor [ˋhjumɚ]

名 幽默

用法
ⓐ humor 為不可數。
ⓑ a sense of humor　幽默感

It's important to have a sense of humor in life.　生活中帶點**幽默感**是挺重要的。

humorous [ˋhjumərəs]

形 **幽默的**

🔍用法 a humorous personality
個性幽默

💬 **Elaine likes to make friends with humorous people.** 伊蓮喜歡跟**幽默的**人做朋友。

hundred [ˋhʌndrəd]

名 **一百** 形 **一百個的**

🔍用法 hundred 前有數字（如 a / one、two...）時，不可加 -s。若無數字時，則要寫成 hundreds of...（數百個……）。

💬 **Can I borrow one hundred dollars from you?** 我可以向你借一百元嗎？

hunger [ˋhʌŋgɚ]

名 **飢餓（不可數）**

🔍用法 hunger 當動詞用時有「渴望」的意思。
After years of war, we all hunger for peace.
（經過多年戰爭，我們都渴望和平。）

💬 **Many people die of hunger in that poor country every year.** 那個窮國每年都有好多人餓死。

hungry [ˋhʌŋgrɪ]

形 飢餓的

用法 get hungry　肚子餓
Jerry gets hungry before noon.
（傑瑞中午以前肚子就會餓。）

Lance is hungry. He needs something to eat.　蘭斯餓了，需要吃點東西。

hunt [hʌnt]

名 動 打獵

用法 go hunting　去打獵

John's uncle goes hunting every weekend.　約翰的叔叔每個週末都會去打獵。

hunter [ˋhʌntɚ]

名 獵人

用法 a job-hunter　求職者

The soldier used to be a hunter.
這個軍人以前曾是個獵人。

hurry [ˋhɝɪ]

名 匆忙　動 趕快

用法
ⓐ 三態：hurry、hurried [ˋhɝɪd]、hurried
ⓑ hurry up　趕快
ⓒ in a hurry　匆促地

Hurry up! We're late.
快點！我們就要遲到了。

hurt [hɝt]

動 名 傷害；疼痛

用法
ⓐ 三態同形
ⓑ hurt 之後有受詞時，hurt 譯成「傷害」。
ⓒ hurt 之後無受詞時，hurt 譯成「疼痛」。

Don't hurt Larry.
別傷害賴瑞。

husband [ˋhʌzbənd]

名 丈夫，老公

用法
wife [waɪf] 名 妻子，老婆

Mary's husband is very nice to her.
瑪麗的老公對她很好。

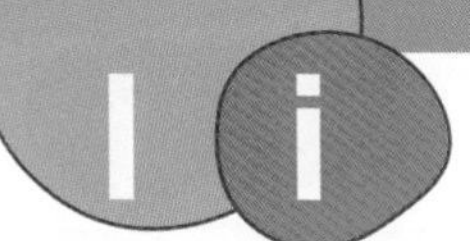

I [aɪ]

代 我

用法 I 及 me [mi] 都表示「我」，
I 要作主詞，me 要作受詞。

I need your help right now.
我現在需要你的幫助。

ice [aɪs]

名 冰

用法 ice cube [ˋais ˏkjub] 名 冰塊

Would you like some ice cubes in your drink? 你的飲料要不要加點冰塊？

ice cream [ˋaɪs ˏkrim]

名 冰淇淋

用法 vanilla ice cream 香草冰淇淋
（vanilla [vəˋnɪlə] 名 香草）

Children love ice cream.
小朋友都喜歡冰淇淋。

A B C D E F G H I J K L M N O P Q R S T U V W X Y Z

idea [aɪˋdɪə]

名 點子，主意，想法

用法 (It) Sounds like a good idea.
（聽起來像是個好點子。）
上列句子的 It 通常不說出來。

That's really **a good idea.**
那真是個好點子。

if [ɪf]

連 如果

用法 even 與 if 並用時，表示「即使」。
Even if I have money, I won't lend Tim any.（即使我有錢，也不會借給提姆。）

I'll call Olivia **if** I have time.
我若有時間就會打電話給奧莉薇雅。

ignore [ɪgˋnɔr]

動 忽視

用法 ignorance [ˋɪgnɔrəns] 名 無知
ignorant [ˋɪgnɔrənt] 形 無知的；不知道的

Eddy will be sorry if he **ignores** my advice. 艾迪要是忽視我的忠告，有天會後悔的。

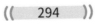

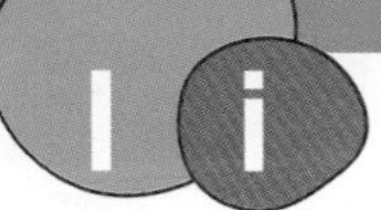

ill [ɪl]

形 生病的

用法 fall ill　生病

Gary **fell ill** and had to lie in bed for a week.
蓋瑞生病了，得在床上躺了一個星期。

imagine [ɪˋmædʒən]

動 想像

用法 You can't imagine...
你無法想像……（表示強調）

Isaac **can't imagine** what life would be like without his girlfriend.　艾薩克不敢想像如果沒有他女友，人生會怎樣。

impolite [ˌɪmpəˋlaɪt]

形 不禮貌的

用法 polite [pəˋlaɪt] 形 禮貌的

It's very **impolite** to point your finger at others.　用手指指著他人很不禮貌。

A B C D E F G H I J K L M N O P Q R S T U V W X Y Z

importance

[ɪm`pɔrtəns]

名 重要，重要性

用法 important [ɪm`pɔrtn̩t] 形 重要的

Our teacher's words are of great **importance** to us. 我們老師的話對我們很重要。

important [ɪm`pɔrtn̩t]

形 重要的

用法 It's important for + sb + to...
……對某人而言是很重要的

It's important for us **to** learn English.
學英文對我們來說是很重要的。

impossible [ɪm`pasəbl̩]

形 不可能的

用法 possible [`pasəbl̩] 形 可能的

Nothing is **impossible** in this world.
在這個世界上，沒有不可能的事。

improve [ɪmˋpruv]

動 改善，改進

用法 improved [ɪmˋpruvd] 形 已改善的，有改進的

Reading newspapers is a good way to improve your writing. 看報紙是使寫作進步的一個好方法。

in [ɪn]

介 在……裡 面

用法 in the box 在盒子裡
on the box 在盒子上
by the box 在盒子旁邊

What's in the bag?
袋子裡有什麼東西？

inch [ɪntʃ]

名 英寸

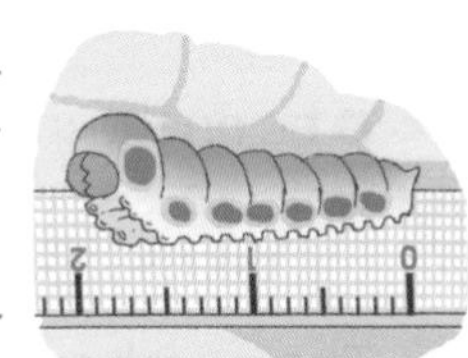

用法 Give him an inch, and he'll take a yard.（給他一英寸，他就會要一碼。——他這個人會得寸進尺。）

This worm is two inches long.
這隻蟲長兩英寸。

include [ɪnˋklud]

動 包括

用法 including [ɪnˋkludɪŋ] 介 包括

Does the price **include** tax?
這個價錢有沒有含稅？

income [ˋɪnkʌm]

名 收入

用法 have a high / low income
收入高 / 低

Doctors in Taiwan **have a high income.**
臺灣的醫生收入很高。

increase

[ɪnˋkris] 動 增加　[ˋɪnkris] 名 增加

用法
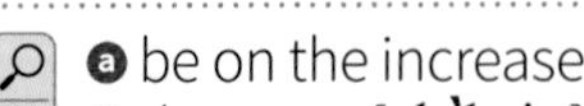
ⓐ be on the increase　增加中
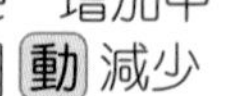
ⓑ decrease [dɪˋkris] 動 減少
[ˋdikris] 名 減少

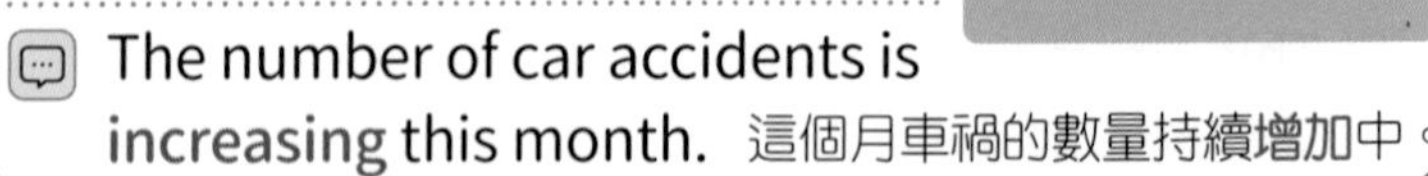
The number of car accidents is **increasing** this month.　這個月車禍的數量持續增加中。

I i

independent

[ˌɪndɪˋpɛndənt]

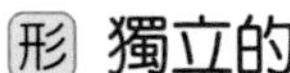

形 獨立的

用法 be independent of... 脫離……而獨立

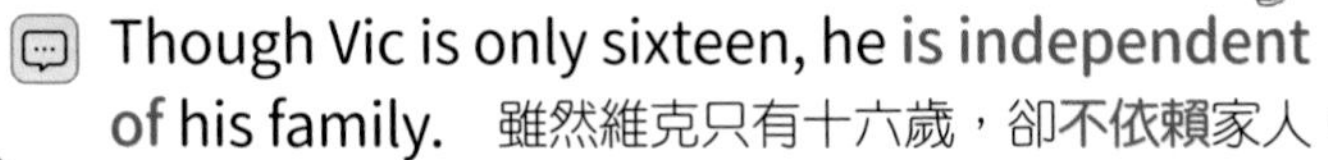

Though Vic is only sixteen, he **is independent of** his family. 雖然維克只有十六歲，卻不依賴家人。

indicate [ˋɪndɪˌket]

動 顯示

用法 indicate 也可等於 show。

The report **indicates** that there are more boys than girls in that country today. 該報告顯示該國的男孩比女孩多。

influence [ˋɪnflʊəns]

名 動 影響

用法 have a / an... influence on...
對……有影響

Don't be **influenced** by Jared's words.
不要被傑瑞德的話所影響。

information

[ˌɪnfɚˋmeʃən]

名 消息，資料

用法 information 為不可數名詞。

Eve got some **information** from the internet. 伊芙從網路上找了一些資料。

ink [ɪŋk]

名 墨水

用法 in blue ink 用藍墨水
（非 with blue ink）

Write your name **in blue ink.**
用藍墨水寫下你的名字。

insect [ˋɪnsɛkt]

名 昆蟲

用法 美國人在口語中常用 bug [bʌg]
取代 insect，均表示「小昆蟲」之意。

Spiders catch small **insects** and eat them. 蜘蛛會捕食小昆蟲。

inside [ɪnˋsaɪd / ˋɪnˏsaɪd]

副 在裡面　介 在……裡 面（= in）

用法 What's inside the box?
= What's in the box?
（盒子裡面有什麼東西？）

It's cold outside. Let's stay **inside**.
外面很冷。咱們待在**裡面**吧。

insist [ɪnˋsɪst]

動 堅持

用法 insist on...　堅持要……

Erin **insisted on** staying at home.
艾琳**堅持要**留在家裡。

inspire [ɪnˋspaɪr]

動 啟發，激勵

用法 inspire sb to + V
激發某人做……

I hope my words can **inspire** Jay **to** work even harder.　希望我的話能**激勵**傑更加用功。

instant [ˋɪnstənt]

名 一剎那 形 立即的；立即可用的

用法 ⓐ in an instant 剎那間
（= in a moment = in a minute）
ⓑ instant noodles 速食麵

Dinner will be ready **in an instant.**
晚飯馬上就好了。

instrument

[ˋɪnstrəmənt]

名 樂器；儀器

用法 a musical instrument 樂器

How many **instruments** does Olivia play? 奧莉薇亞會玩幾種樂器？

intelligent

[ɪnˋtɛlədʒənt]

形 有智力的，聰明的

用法 intelligence [ɪnˋtɛlədʒəns] 名 聰明才智

Renee is the most **intelligent** student in her class. 芮妮是她班上最聰明的學生。

interest [ˋɪnt(ə)rɪst]

名 興趣

用法
ⓐ have / take an interest in...
對……有興趣
ⓑ interest 也可當動詞，為「使……感興趣」的意思。

My brother **has no interest in** music.
我哥哥對音樂沒**興趣**。

interested [ˋɪnt(ə)rɪstɪd]

形 感興趣的

用法
be interested in + N/V-ing
對……感興趣

This book is interesting. Pamela is

interested in it. 這本書很有趣，潘蜜拉對它變**感興趣的**。

interesting [ˋɪnt(ə)rɪstɪŋ]

形 有趣的

用法
interesting 表示「令人有趣的」，修飾事物；
interested 則表示「感到有趣的」，修飾人。

This lesson is **interesting**.
這一課很**有趣**。

international

形 國際的，國際性的 [ˌɪntɚˋnæʃənḷ]

用法
ⓐ international trade 國際貿易
ⓑ the International Date Line
國際換日線

English is an **international** language. 英語是國際語言。

internet [ˋɪntɚˌnɛt]

名 網際網路

用法
internet 之前要置 the。
surf the internet 上網

Timothy **surfs the internet** when he has time. 提摩西有空時都會上網。

interrupt [ˌɪntəˋrʌpt]

動 打斷

用法
interrupt sb = cut in on sb
打斷某人的話

It's impolite to **interrupt** others when they are talking. 別人在講話時打斷他們的話是不禮貌的。

interview [ˋɪntɚ͵vju]

名 動 會見；訪問

用法
interview + sb
與某人會談；訪問某人
have a job interview　去求職面試

My sister will **have a job interview** this afternoon.　我姊姊今天下午會去求職面試。

into [ˋɪntʊ]

介 進入

用法
walk into...　走入……
run into...　跑入……
jump into...　跳入……

Walter saw nobody when he **walked into** the classroom.　華特走進教室時沒看到任何人。

introduce [͵ɪntrəˋdjus]

動 介紹

用法
ⓐ introduction [͵ɪntrəˋdʌkʃən]
名 介紹
ⓑ introduce A to B　將 A 介紹給 B

Let me **introduce** this man **to** you, Miss Wang.　王小姐，讓我向妳介紹這位先生。

invent [ɪnˋvɛnt]

動 發明

用法 invention [ɪnˋvɛnʃən]
名 發明（不可數）；發明物（可數）

Bell invented the telephone in 1876. 貝爾於一八七六年發明電話。

invitation [ˏɪnvəˋteʃən]

名 邀請，請帖

用法 accept one's invitation
接受某人的邀請

Walter went to Mary's party at her invitation. 在瑪麗的邀請下，華特參加了她的派對。

invite [ɪnˋvaɪt]

動 邀請

用法 invite + sb + to...
邀請某人參加……

Mary invited me to her birthday party. 瑪麗邀請我參加她的生日派對。

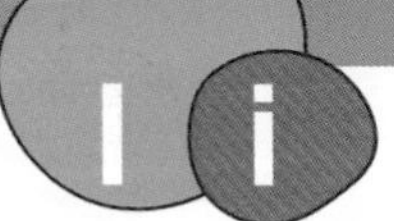

iron [ˋaɪɚn]

名 鐵；熨斗　動（用熨斗）燙（衣服）

用法 iron 為「鐵」的意思時，為不可數。
iron 為「熨斗」的意思時，為可數。

Could you **iron** this shirt for me?
您可否替我燙這件襯衫？

island [ˋaɪlənd]

名 島

用法 live on the island　住在島上

No one lives on this **island**.
這座島上沒人住。

it [ɪt]

代 它；牠

用法 it 可代替除人之外任何單數的生物，
也可代替單數無生物，更可代替抽象
的東西（如 時間、美麗、誠實）。

The dog is strange. **It** has very
small eyes.　這隻狗很怪，牠的眼睛好小喲。

item [ˋaɪtəm]

名 物品；項目

用法 item by item　逐項

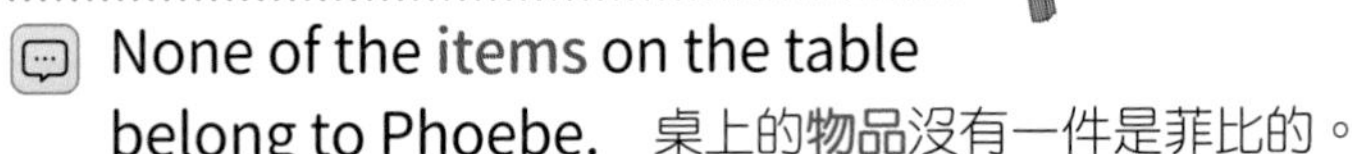

None of the **items** on the table belong to Phoebe.　桌上的物品沒有一件是菲比的。

Notes

jacket [ˋdʒækɪt]

名 夾克

用法
put on the jacket 穿上夾克
take off the jacket 脫下夾克

Put on your **jacket** before you go out. 你把夾克穿上再外出。

jam [dʒæm]

名 果醬；阻塞

用法
traffic jam [ˋtræfɪk ˏdʒæm] 名 交通阻塞
Vince was late because of a traffic jam.
（因為塞車所以文斯遲到了。）

Wesley always eats bread with **jam**.
衛斯理吃麵包時一向塗抹果醬。

January [ˋdʒænjʊˏɛrɪ]

名 一月

用法
in January 在一月（月份用 in）
on January fifth
在一月五日那一天（日期用 on）

Melinda will go to Hong Kong in **January**. 梅琳達會在一月的時候到香港去。

jazz [dʒæz]

名 爵士樂

用法
ⓐ jazz 為不可數。
ⓑ jazz = jazz music

My father is crazy about jazz.
我父親很迷爵士樂。

jealous [ˋdʒɛləs]

形 忌妒的

用法
be jealous of... 忌妒……

Mary is jealous of Jane's beauty.
瑪麗很忌妒珍的美。

jeans [dʒinz]

名 牛仔褲

用法
牛仔褲因為有兩條褲管，故 jeans 始終是複數。a jean (×)
→ a pair of jeans (○) 一條牛仔褲

Young people like to wear jeans.
年輕人喜歡穿牛仔褲。

jeep [dʒip]

名 吉普車

用法 drive a jeep 開吉普車

Stan enjoys **driving a jeep** on weekends. 史坦喜歡在週末**開吉普車**兜風。

job [dʒab]

名 工作；職業

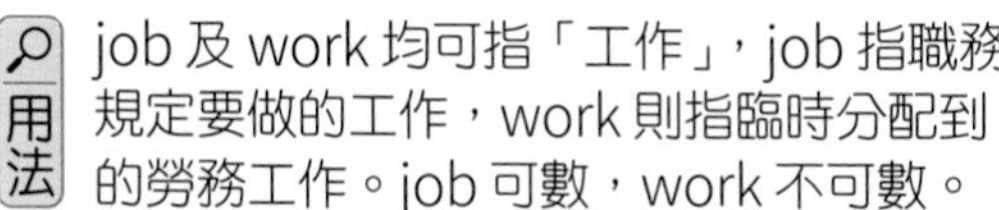

用法 job 及 work 均可指「工作」，job 指職務規定要做的工作，work 則指臨時分配到的勞務工作。job 可數，work 不可數。

My brother found a **job** as a waiter. 我哥哥找了一份當服務生的工作。

jog [dʒag]

名 動 **慢跑**

用法
ⓐ 三態：jog、jogged [dʒagd]、jogged
ⓑ go for a jog 去慢跑

My parents **jog** in the park every morning. 我爸媽每天早上都會在公園內**慢跑**。

J j

join [dʒɔɪn]

動 參加

用法
- ⓐ join the chess club　參加西洋棋社
- ⓑ join + sb + in...　加入某人一起……

My friend and I are going fishing tomorrow. Would you like to **join** us?　我和我朋友明天會去釣魚。你要加入嗎？

J

joke [dʒok]

名 玩笑

用法
play a joke / jokes on + sb
對某人開玩笑

Tim likes to **play jokes on** me.
提姆喜歡跟我開玩笑。

journalist [ˋdʒɝnḷɪst]

名 新聞從業人員（包括記者、編輯）

用法
純粹指「記者」則使用 reporter [rɪˋpɔrtɚ] 一字。

My teacher used to be a **journalist**.
我的老師曾經當過新聞工作者。

joy [dʒɔɪ]

名 歡樂，喜悅

用法 jump for joy　高興得跳起來

Stuart **jumped for joy** when he heard the good news.　史都華聽到這個好消息時，高興得跳起來。

judge [dʒʌdʒ]

名 法官　動 判斷

用法 Do not judge a man by his looks.
（勿以貌取人。）

All **judges** should be fair.
所有的法官都應公正。

juice [dʒus]

名 果汁（不可數）

用法 a glass of orange / tomato juice
一杯柳橙 / 番茄汁

Jenny likes **orange juice**. How about you?　珍妮喜歡柳橙汁。你呢？

July [dʒuˋlaɪ]

名 七月

用法 in July　在七月（月份用 in）
on July third　在七月三日那天
（日期用 on）

Summer vacation starts in July.
暑假自七月開始。

jump [dʒʌmp]

動 跳

用法 jump up　跳起來
jump down　跳下來
jump into...　跳入……

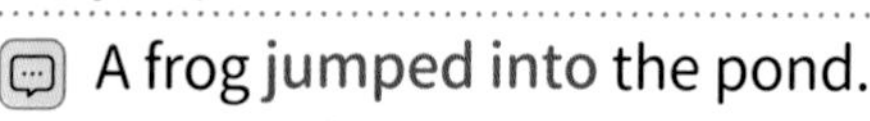

A frog **jumped into** the pond.
一隻青蛙跳到池塘裡。

June [dʒun]

名 六月

用法 in June　在六月（月份用 in）
on June sixth　在六月六日那天
（日期用 on）

Mary and Peter are getting married in June.　瑪麗和彼得將在六月結婚。

junior high school

[ˌdʒunjɚ ˋhaɪ ˌskul]

名 國中

用法 go to junior high school　念國中

David is an elementary school student, and his sister is a junior high school student.
大衛是小學生，他姊姊則是國中生。

just [dʒʌst]

副 剛剛；僅僅（= only）

用法 My little brother is just five years old.
= My little brother is only five years old.
（我小弟只有五歲大。）

I just saw David in the library.
我剛剛在圖書館看到大衛。

Notes

kangaroo [ˌkæŋgəˋru]

名 袋鼠

用法
one kangaroo　一隻袋鼠
two kangaroo**s**　兩隻袋鼠
(非 kangarooes)

We can see **kangaroos** in the zoo.
我們可以在動物園裡看到**袋鼠**。

keep [kip]

動 保留；保持

用法
ⓐ 三態：keep、kept [kɛpt]、kept
ⓑ 保留：keep + N
ⓒ 保持：keep + Adj

Please **keep quiet**. I'm studying.
請**保持安靜**。我正在念書。

ketchup [ˋkɛtʃəp]

名 番茄醬

用法
ketchup 為不可數。

Can you pass me the **ketchup**, please?　麻煩你把**番茄醬**遞給我好嗎？

key [ki]

名 鑰匙；關鍵　形 重要的　動 用鍵盤輸入

用法 key 當動詞用時，
三態為 key, keyed [kid], keyed。

Where is my **key**?
我**鑰匙**在哪裡？

kick [kɪk]

動 踢

用法 kick 也可表示「戒除」之意。
kick the bad habit of smoking
戒掉抽菸的惡習

Don't **kick** the dog, Johnny.
強尼，別**踢**狗。

kid [kɪd]

名 小孩　動 開玩笑，說著玩的

用法
ⓐ 三態：kid、kidded [ˋkɪdɪd]、kidded
ⓑ Jane will marry you? You are kidding!
（珍要嫁給你？你在開玩笑吧！）

Mr. Johnson has three **kids**.
強森先生有三個**孩子**。

kill [kɪl]

動 殺，殺死

用法 kill time　殺時間，消磨時間
Chloe kills time by listening to music.
（克洛伊聽音樂消磨時間。）

Don't hurt or kill animals.
別傷害或宰殺動物。

kilogram [ˋkɪləˏgram]

名 公斤

用法 kilogram 常簡稱 kilo [ˋkɪlo]
Mary weights forty kilos.
（瑪麗體重四十公斤。）

Cathy weighs about thirty kilograms.　凱西體重約三十公斤。

kilometer

[kəˋlamətɚ / ˋkɪləˏmitɚ]

名 公里

用法 本字亦可寫成 km。

This highway is 250 kilometers long.
這條公路有兩百五十公里長。

kind [kaɪnd]

名 種類　形 親切的，仁慈的

用法 kind 表示「種類」時，有下列用法：
a kind of bird　某種鳥
this kind of bird　這種鳥

The old man is **kind** to children.
這位老伯伯對小朋友很**和藹**。

kindergarten

[ˋkɪndɚˏgartn̩]

名 幼稚園

用法 nursery [ˋnɝsərɪ] 名 托兒所，托嬰中心

There are several public **kindergartens** nearby.
這附近有幾所公立的**幼稚園**。

king [kɪŋ]

名 國王

用法 國王的妻子或女王稱作 queen [kwin]。

The **king** and queen live in a beautiful castle.　**國王**和王后住在一座美麗的城堡裡。

kingdom [ˋkɪŋdəm]

名 王國

用法 the United Kingdom
大英聯合王國

The **kingdom** is ruled by a young king. 這個**王國**由一個年輕的國王所統治。

kiss [kɪs]

名 動 吻

用法 kiss + sb + on the + 被親吻的部位
Amy kissed me on the mouth.
（艾咪吻我的嘴。）

The young boy almost passed out when the beautiful girl **kissed** him. 美少女**吻**了這位少男時，他差點昏倒。

kitchen [ˋkɪtʃɪn]

名 廚房

用法 cook in the kitchen
在廚房裡做菜

Mom is cooking in the **kitchen**.
媽媽正在**廚房**做菜。

kite [kaɪt]

名 風箏

用法 fly a kite　放風箏

Some kids are flying kites by the river.　一些孩子在河邊**放風箏**。

kitten [ˋkɪtn̩]

名 小貓

用法 cat [kæt] 名 貓

My mom won't allow me to keep a **kitten** at home.　我媽媽不讓我在家裡養**小貓**。

knee [ni]

名 膝蓋

用法 fall to one's knees　跪下

Donald fell down and hurt his **knees**.　唐納德跌倒，把**膝蓋**弄傷了。

knife [naɪf]

名 刀子

用法 knife 是單數，knives [naɪvz] 是複數。
如 a knife、two knives
（一把刀、兩把刀）。

The cook uses a **knife** to cut meat.
這名廚師用**刀子**切肉。

knock [nɑk]

動 敲

用法 knock the door. (×)
→ knock on the door. (○)

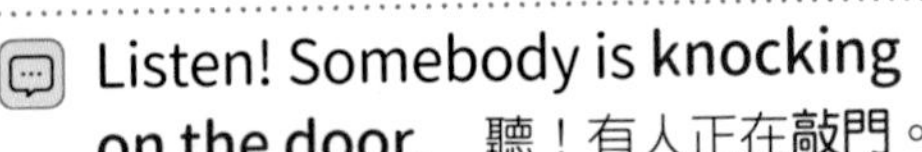

Listen! Somebody is **knocking on the door**. 聽！有人正在**敲門**。

know [no]

動 知道，認識

用法
ⓐ 三態：know、knew [n(j)u]、known [non]
ⓑ Do you know...? 你知道……嗎？

Do you **know** this guy?
你**認識**這個傢伙嗎？

knowledge [ˋnalɪdʒ]

名 知識（不可數）

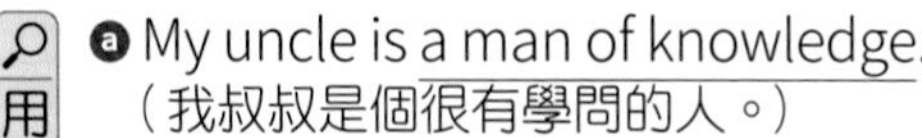

用法
ⓐ My uncle is a man of knowledge.
（我叔叔是個很有學問的人。）

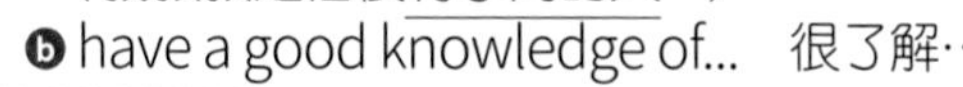

ⓑ have a good knowledge of... 很了解……

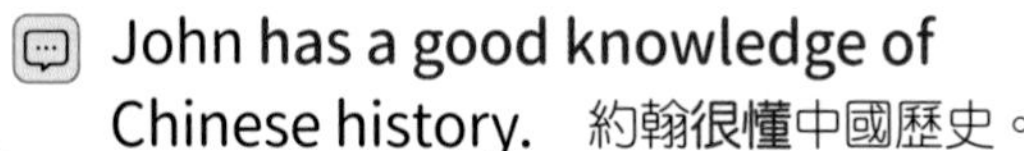

John has a good knowledge of Chinese history. 約翰很懂中國歷史。

koala [koˋalə]

名 無尾熊

用法
koala 也稱作 koala bear [koˋalə ˏbɛr]。
（bear [bɛr] 名 熊）

Koalas are cute animals.
無尾熊是可愛的動物。

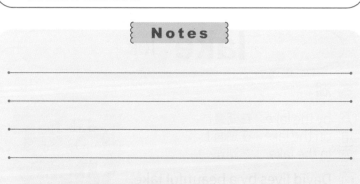

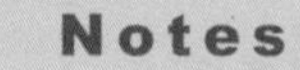

lack [læk]

名 動 缺乏

用法 for lack of... 由於缺乏……
Dennis looks tired for lack of sleep.
(丹尼斯因為缺乏睡眠，看起來很疲憊。)

Duke lacks the skills for the job.
杜克**缺乏**做這件工作的技能。

lady [ˋledɪ]

名 女士；淑女

用法
ⓐ 複數為 ladies [ˋledɪz]。
ⓑ a ladies' room 女用洗手間

Mary was taught to be a lady at an early age. 瑪麗在年輕時就被教導要當**淑女**。

lake [lek]

名 湖

用法 by the lake 在湖邊
on the lake 在湖面上
in the lake 在湖裡

David lives by a beautiful lake.
大衛住在美麗的**湖畔**。

lamb [læm]

名 小綿羊，羔羊

用法 請注意 lamb 的 b 不發音喲！

The little girl stayed close to her mother like a **lamb**. 小女孩就像隻**小綿羊**般地依偎在她母親身旁。

lamp [læmp]

名 檯燈

用法
beside lamp 床頭燈
desk lamp 書桌燈

There is a **lamp** on the desk.
書桌上有一盞**檯燈**。

land [lænd]

名 陸地 動 降落，著地

用法
ⓐ a piece of land 一塊土地（非 a land）
ⓑ The airplane landed at 10 a.m.
（飛機在上午十點降落。）

Dad bought **a piece of land** in the country. 爸爸在鄉下買了**一塊地**。

language [ˋlæŋgwɪdʒ]

名 語言

用法 foreign language　外語
Cathy wants to learn another foreign language.（凱西想再學一種外語。）

I speak English, Spanish, and Russian.

How many languages does Eric speak?　艾瑞克能說多少種語言？

lantern [ˋlæntɚn]

名 燈籠

用法 carry a lantern around
提著燈籠到處走

Tomorrow is the Lantern Festival.　明天就是元宵節。

large [lɑrdʒ]

形 大的

用法 large 與 big 是同義字，均表示「大的」。
a large car = a big car　大車

This car is large, but that one is small.　這輛車很大，那一輛卻很小。

last [læst]

形 最後的　動 持續

用法
ⓐ last 表示「最後的」時，之前要加 the。
ⓑ The rain lasted two days.
（這場雨持續下了兩天。）

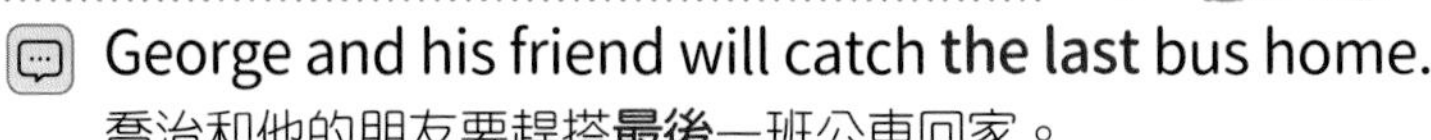

George and his friend will catch the last bus home.
喬治和他的朋友要趕搭**最後**一班公車回家。

late [let]

形 遲的，晚的　副 遲到地

用法
ⓐ be + 一段時間 + late　遲到一段時間
be two hours late　遲到兩小時
ⓑ be late for school / work　上學 / 上班遲到

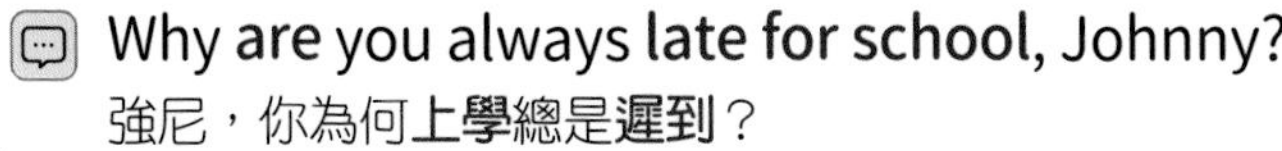

Why are you always late for school, Johnny?
強尼，你為何**上學**總是**遲到**？

later [ˋletɚ]

副 後來，稍後

用法
ⓐ See you later.（待會兒見 / 再見。）
ⓑ 一段時間 + later　一段時間之後
five minutes later　五分鐘後

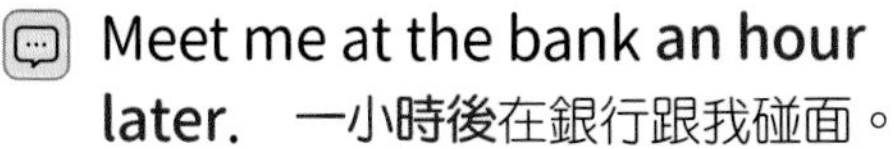

Meet me at the bank an hour later.　**一小時後**在銀行跟我碰面。

A B C D E F G H I J K L M N O P Q R S T U V W X Y Z

latest [ˋletɪst]

形 最新的，最近的

用法 the latest news　最新消息

Have you read the **latest** novel of *Harry Potter*?　你讀過了**最新的**《哈利波特》小說嗎？

latter [ˋlætɚ]

名 後者（與 the 並用）

用法 the latter　後者
the former [ˋfɔrmɚ]　前者

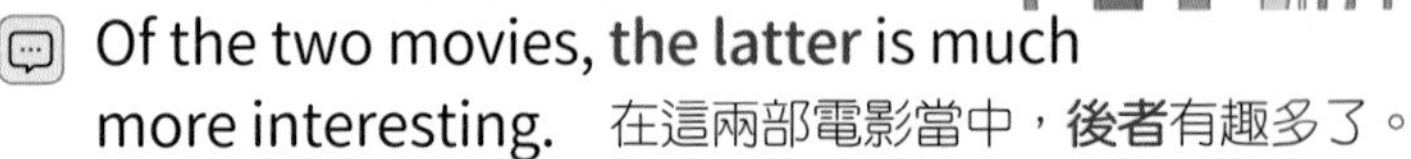

Of the two movies, **the latter** is much more interesting.　在這兩部電影當中，**後者**有趣多了。

laugh [læf]

動 笑

用法 laugh at...　取笑……

Peter got angry when John **laughed at** him.　約翰**取笑**彼得時，彼得生氣了。

law [lɔ]

名 法律

用法 against the law 違法

Drunk driving is against the law.
酒醉駕車是**違法**的。

lawyer [ˋlɔjɚ]

名 律師

用法 lawyer 源自 law。

Jane wants to be a lawyer when she grows up. 珍長大想當**律師**。

lay [le]

動 放置；生（蛋）

用法 三態：lay、laid [led]、laid
George laid the book on the desk.
（喬治把書放在桌上。）

The hen lays an egg every day.
這隻母雞每天**下**一顆蛋。

lazy [ˋlezɪ]

形 **懶惰的**

用法 lazy 與 bones [bonz]（骨頭）結合在一起就成 lazybones [lezɪˏbonz]，指「懶人」，單複數同形。

No teacher likes **lazy** students.

沒有老師喜歡**懶惰的**學生。

lead

[lid] 動 **引導，帶領**　[lɛd] 名 **鉛（金屬）**

用法
ⓐ 三態：lead、led [lɛd]、led
ⓑ lead + sb　帶領某人

We need a good teacher to **lead** us.

我們需要一位好老師來**帶領**我們。

leader [ˋlidɚ]

名 **領袖，領導者**

用法 class leader　班長

John is our **class leader**.

約翰是本班的**班長**。

leaf [lif]

名 葉子

用法 複數為 leaves [livz]。

The dead **leaves** were falling down from the trees. 枯葉正從樹上飄落下來。

learn [lɝn]

動 學習

用法 learn English / Chinese 學英文 / 中文
learn to swim / sing / dance
學習游泳 / 唱歌 / 跳舞

Learning English is very important.
學英文很重要。

least [list]

副 最少地 名 最少

Call me at least once a week.

用法 at least + 數字 至少……
at least once a week 至少一星期一次

Eric should call me **at least once a week.** 艾瑞克應**每個星期至少**打**一次**電話給我。

leave [liv]

動 離開；遺留

用法 ⓐ 三態：leave、left [lɛft]、left
ⓑ leave for + 地方　前往某地

Hurry up! The train will be **leaving** soon.　快點！火車就快**開**了。

left [lɛft]

形 左方的　名 左方　副 在左邊

用法 turn left　向左轉
= turn to the left

Turn left, and you'll see the bank.
向左轉，你就可以看到銀行了。

leg [lɛg]

名 腿

用法 break a leg
弄斷一條腿；祝演出成功

Mary has long **legs**.
瑪麗的**腿**很修長。

lemon [ˋlɛmən]

名 檸檬

用法 lemonade [ˏlɛməˋned] 名 檸檬水
a glass of lemonade　一杯檸檬水

Elmer doesn't like **lemon juice**.
艾爾不喜歡**檸檬汁**。

lend [lɛnd]

動 借給

用法 ⓐ 三態：lend、lent [lɛnt]、lent
ⓑ lend + sb + sth　把某物借給某人
= lend + sth + to + sb

Can you **lend** me some money?
你可否**借**我一點錢？

less [lɛs]

形 較少的　副 較少地

用法 less 由 little（很少的、沒多少的）變化而成。
less... than...　比……更少的

Derek has **less** money **than** you.
德瑞克的錢**比**你的**少**。

lesson [ˋlɛsn̩]

名 課；教訓

用法
take piano lessons　上鋼琴課
take driving lessons　上駕駛課
learn a lesson　學到一個教訓

This **lesson** is boring. Evan doesn't like it.　這堂**課**很無聊。伊凡不喜歡。

let [lɛt]

動 讓，允許

用法
ⓐ 三態同形
ⓑ let + sb + V　讓某人做某事
Let me go.（讓我走。）

My mom won't **let** me go out after dark.　我媽媽不**讓**我在天黑後外出。

letter [ˋlɛtɚ]

名 信；字母

用法
ⓐ send a letter to + sb　寄信給某人
ⓑ The word "book" has four letters.
（book 這個字有四個字母。）

Write me a **letter** when you have time.　你有空時寫封**信**給我。

lettuce [ˋlɛtəs]

名 萵苣

用法 lettuce 多半當作生菜供生食用。「生菜」的英文稱做 salad [ˋsæləd]，有人譯成「沙拉」。

Adam doesn't eat lettuce.
亞當不喜歡吃**萵苣**。

level [ˋlɛvəl]

名 **程度；水平面**

用法 above sea level 海拔
The church is 445 meters above sea level.
(教會的海拔高度為四百四十五公尺。)

The **level** of this book is too high for children. 這本書的**程度**對小朋友來說太高了。

library [ˋlaɪˏbrɛrɪ]

名 **圖書館**

用法 study in the library
在圖書館念書

Alicia likes to **study in the library** because it's quiet there. 艾莉西亞喜歡**在圖書館念書**，因為那裡很安靜。

lick [lɪk]

動 名 舔

用法 lick one's lips
舔嘴唇；垂涎欲滴地期待

Denise hates it when her dog **licks** her. 丹妮絲最討厭她的狗狗**舔**她了。

lid [lɪd]

名 蓋子

用法 put the lid on...
把蓋子蓋在……之上

Please **put the lid on** the garbage can.
請**把**垃圾桶的**蓋子蓋上**。

lie [laɪ]

動 撒謊；躺 名 謊言

用法 ⓐ 表示「撒謊」，三態：lie、lied、lied。
ⓑ 表示「躺」，三態：lie、lay [le]、lain [len]。

Don't **lie** to me.
別對我**說謊**。

life [laɪf]

名 生命；生活

用法
ⓐ life 的複數形為 lives [laɪvz]。
ⓑ live a... life　過著……的生活

John lives a happy life.
約翰**過著**快樂**的生活**。

lift [lɪft]

動 舉起　名 搭便車

用法
give + sb + a lift　讓某人搭便車
= give + sb + a ride

The box is so heavy that Greg can't **lift** it.　箱子太重了，葛瑞格**搬**不動。

lightning [ˋlaɪtnɪŋ]

名 閃電

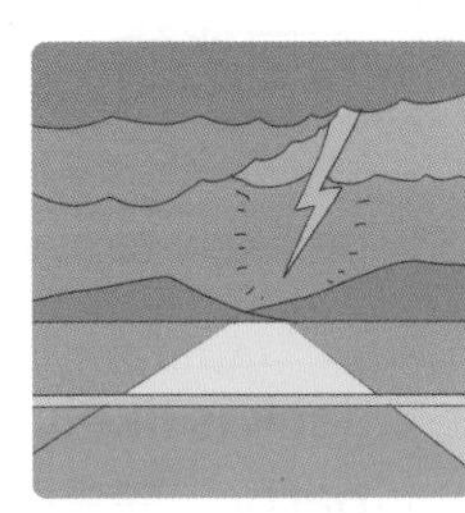

用法
ⓐ lightning 為不可數。
ⓑ a bolt of lightning　一道閃電

Lightning comes before thunder.　雷聲伴隨著**閃電**而來。

light [laɪt]

名 光線；電燈　形 輕的

用法
ⓐ The box is light / heavy.
（這箱子很輕 / 很重。）
ⓑ turn on / off the light　打開 / 關掉電燈

Turn on the light, please. I can't see anything in here.　請把**電燈打開**。這裡面我什麼也看不見。

like [laɪk]

動 喜歡　介 像

用法
look like...　看起來像……
Tom looks like his father.
（湯姆看起來像他爸爸。）

I like John because he never lies.
我**喜歡**約翰，因為他從不說謊。

likely [ˋlaɪklɪ]

形 有可能的

用法
be likely to...　有可能……

Jack is likely to come to my birthday party.　傑克**可能**會前來參加我的生日派對。

limit [ˋlɪmɪt]

名 動 限制

用法 limit 一字多與介詞 to 並用。
There is a limit to everything.
（每件事都有限制。）

My mother **limits** my daily expenses to NT$100. 我媽**限制**我每天的開銷最多新臺幣一百元。

line [laɪn]

名 線；電話線 動 排隊

用法
ⓐ The line is busy. （忙線 / 占線中。）
ⓑ Line up! Don't cut in line.
（排隊！不要插隊。）

The **line** is busy. Please call later.
現在**占線中**。請稍後再打。

link [lɪŋk]

名 關聯 動 連接，使有關聯

用法
ⓐ be linked to... 與……有關
ⓑ link A to / with B 將 A 與 B 連結

Doctors say that there is a **link** between smoking and lung cancer. 醫生說抽菸和肺癌有**關聯**。

lion [ˋlaɪən]

名 獅子

用法 pride [praɪd] 是名詞，原指「驕傲」，但也可指「獅群」。
a pride of lions　一群獅群

There is a **lion** in the cage.
籠子裡有一頭**獅子**。

lip [lɪp]

名 嘴唇

用法 因為嘴唇有兩片，所以常用複數 lips。

Mary has beautiful **lips**.
瑪麗的**嘴唇**很漂亮。

liquid [ˋlɪkwɪd]

名 液體　形 液體的

用法
ⓐ solid [ˋsɑlɪd] 名 固體　形 固體的
ⓑ Water is a liquid.（水是液體。）

Small children take medicine in **liquid** form.　小孩子服用藥**水**。

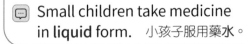

list [lɪst]

名 名單；表

用法 make a list of... 列下……
Make a list of the things you want to buy.
（列下你要買的東西。）

I can't see your name **on the list**, Peter.
彼得，**在名單上**我看不到你的名字。

listen [ˋlɪsn̩]

動 聆聽，注意聽

用法 listen 要與 to 並用。
不要說：listen music
而要說：listen to music 聽音樂

You'll be sorry if you don't **listen to** your teacher. 你若不**聽**老師的話會後悔的。

liter [ˋlitɚ]

名 公升

用法 縮寫為 l。

Could you buy me a **liter** bottle of wine? 你可以幫我買瓶一**公升**的葡萄酒嗎？

little [ˋlɪtḷ]

形 小的；少到幾乎沒有的

用法
- ⓐ a little boy　小男孩
- ⓑ little 表示「少到幾乎沒有的」時，之後接不可數名詞。

My **little** sister is three years old now.　我**妹妹**現在已經三歲了。

live

[lɪv] 動 住　[laɪv] 形 現場的

用法
- ⓐ live in + 地方
- ⓑ a live [laɪv] show
  現場節目（非事先錄影的節目）

Where do you **live**, John?
約翰，你**住**在哪兒呢？

living room

名 客廳　[ˋlɪvɪŋ ˏrum]

用法
dinning room [ˋdaɪnɪŋ ˏrum]
名（家中的）餐廳

Mom and Dad are watching TV in the **living room**.　爸媽正在**客廳**看電視。

loaf [lof]

名 一條（麵包）

用法 loaves [lovz] 名 數條（麵包）
a loaf of bread　一條麵包
two loaves of bread　兩條麵包

Dora ate a whole loaf of bread.
朵拉吃了**一整條**的**麵包**。

local [ˋlokḷ]

形 地方的；當地的　名 當地人

用法 a local newspaper / custom
當地的報紙 / 地方風俗

My brother can take a computer class at a local school. 我弟弟可以在**本地的**學校上電腦課。

lock [lɑk]

動 上鎖　名 鎖

用法 Remember to lock the door before going out.
（出門前記得把門鎖上。）

Erica turned the key in the lock.
艾瑞卡轉動鎖裡面的鑰匙。

locker [ˋlakɚ]

名 置物櫃

用法 a locker room
（健身房內有置物櫃的）更衣間

Put your bag in the locker.
把你的袋子放進**置物櫃**裡。

lonely [ˋlonlɪ]

形 **孤單的，寂寞的**

用法 feel lonely　感到寂寞的

When Eve **feels lonely**, she listens to music.　伊芙**感到寂寞**時會聽音樂。

long [lɔŋ]

形 **長的；長久的**

用法 for a long time　好一陣子，好一段時間
Nora has lived here for a long time.
（諾拉在這裡已住了好一段時間。）

The dog has a **long** tail.
這隻狗的尾巴很**長**。

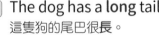

look [lʊk]

動 看；看起來

用法
ⓐ 看（與 at 並用）
ⓑ 看起來（之後接形容詞）

James **looks** angry. What's wrong with him? 詹姆士**看起來**很生氣的樣子。他怎麼啦？

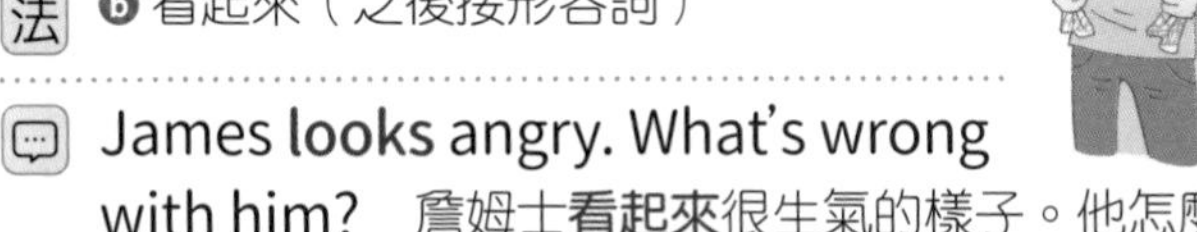

lose [luz]

動 失去；丟掉；輸

用法
ⓐ 三態：lose、lost [lɔst]、lost
ⓑ lose the game 輸掉比賽
ⓒ lose the chance 失去機會

Jessica **lost** her watch on her way home. 潔西卡回家途中把手錶**弄丟**了。

loser [ˋluzɚ]

名 失敗者

用法
winner [ˋwɪnɚ] 名 勝者；得獎者

Losers always find an excuse for their failure. **失敗者**永遠會為他們的失敗找藉口。

loud [laʊd]

動 大聲的　副 大聲地

🔍用法 speak louder　說話大聲點
Speak louder. I can't hear you.
（說大聲點。我聽不見。）

💬 **Vic's voice is too loud. I can't stand it.**
維克說話的聲音太大了。我受不了。

love [lʌv]

名 動 愛

🔍用法 fall in love with + sb　愛上某人
I think I'm falling in love with Mary.
（我想我愛上瑪麗了。）

💬 **I love my parents, and they love me, too.**　我愛我爸媽，他們也愛我。

lovely [ˋlʌvlɪ]

形 漂亮的，動人的

🔍用法 lovely 也可表示「美好的」、「愉快的」。
Nancy had a lovely morning.
（南西早上過得很愉快。）

💬 **Mary is a lovely girl.**
瑪麗是個很甜美的女孩。

low [lo]

形 低的　副 低地　名 低點

用法
- ⓐ in low voices　小聲地
- ⓑ be in a low mood　心情低落
- ⓒ reach a new low　創新低

Keep your voices low, boys.
小子們，小聲點。

lucky [ˋlʌkɪ]

形 幸運的

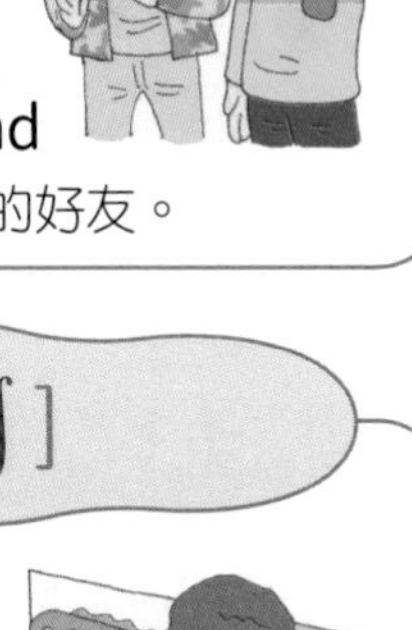

用法
lucky 源自名詞 luck [lʌk]（幸運）。
Good luck to you!
（祝你好運！）

David is lucky to have a good friend like you.　大衛很幸運有一個像你這樣的好友。

lunch [lʌntʃ]

名 午餐

用法
- ⓐ a lunch break　午休
- ⓑ prepare lunch　準備午餐
- ⓒ eat / have... for lunch　午餐吃……

It's time for lunch now.
現在該是吃午餐的時候了。

Mm

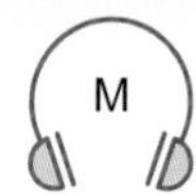

ma'am [mæm]

名 夫人；小姐

用法 ma'am 是 madam [ˋmædəm] 的簡寫。

May I take your order now, ma'am?
小姐，我可以幫妳點餐了嗎？

machine [məˋʃin]

名 機器

用法
- ⓐ by machine　用機器做的
- ⓑ by hand　用手工做的

This machine doesn't work. Can you fix it?　這臺機器壞掉了。你能修理嗎？

mad [mæd]

形 生氣的；熱衷的

用法
- ⓐ be mad at + sb　生某人的氣
- ⓑ be mad about + sb / sth　瘋狂喜愛某人 / 某東西

Why is Charlie so mad at me?
查理為何那麼生我的氣？

magazine [ˌmægəˋzin]

名 雜誌

用法 a fashion / computer / travel magazine　時尚 / 電腦 / 旅遊雜誌

Cassie likes to read fashion magazines.　凱西喜歡閱讀時尚雜誌。

magician [məˋdʒɪʃən]

名 魔術師

用法 magical [ˋmædʒɪkḷ] 形 魔術的，神奇的
magically [ˋmædʒɪkḷɪ] 副 魔術般地，神奇地

David is a famous magician.
大衛是個有名的魔術師。

magic [ˋmædʒɪk]

名 魔術　形 魔術的

用法
ⓐ magic 當名詞時為不可數。
ⓑ a magic trick　魔術把戲

Does your sister believe in magic?　你妹妹相信魔術嗎？

mail [mel]

名 郵件　動 寄（信、包裹等）

用法 mail a letter to + sb　寄信給某人
= send a letter to + sb

Could you mail the letter for me?
你能否幫我寄這封信？

mailman [ˋmel͵mæn]

名 郵差

用法 a mailman　一位郵差
= a postman [ˋpostmən]（英式用法）
two mailmen [ˋmel͵mɛn]　兩位郵差

John's father is a mailman.
約翰的爸爸是郵差。

main [men]

形 主要的

用法 a main point　重點

What's Duke's main reason for going alone?　杜克要單獨前往的主要理由是什麼？

major [ˋmedʒɚ]

形 主要的　名 主修課程　動 主修

用法 English is my major.
= I major in English.
（我的主修是英文。）

Parking is a major problem in many cities.　在許多城市裡，停車是個大問題。

make [mek]

動 製作；使；叫

用法
ⓐ 三態：make、made [med]、made
ⓑ 使；叫：make + sb + V
Dad made me wash the car.（爸爸叫我洗車。）

Mom is making a birthday cake for me.
媽媽正在為我做生日蛋糕。

male [mel]

名 男性；雄性　形 男性的；雄性的

用法 female [ˋfimel]
名 女性；雌性 形 女性的；雌性的

I have two dogs. One is a male, and the other is a female.　我有兩隻狗，一隻是公的，另一隻是母的。

mall [mɔl]

名 大賣場；購物中心

用法 a shopping mall　購物中心

There is a big **mall** near where Clara lives.　克萊拉家附近有一家大賣場。

man [mæn]

名 男人；人類

用法
ⓐ man 的複數為 men [mɛn]。
ⓑ man 表示「人類」時，之前不可加 a、the、this、that 等字。

Who is that **man** over there?
那邊那個男子是誰？

manager [ˋmænədʒɚ]

名 經理

用法 a general manager　總經理

My father is the **general manager** of this company.　我爸爸是這家公司的總經理。

many [ˋmɛnɪ]

形 許多的

用法 many 之後的名詞一定是複數。
many students / books / people
許多學生 / 書 / 人

My little sister has many toys.
我妹妹有許多玩具。

mango [ˋmæŋgo]

名 芒果

用法 複數為 mangoes。

Mangoes are in season now.
現在是盛產芒果的季節。

manner [ˋmænɚ]

名 態度；禮貌（恆用複數）；方法

用法
ⓐ table manners　餐桌禮儀
ⓑ in a(n) + Adj + manner
以……的方式

We should treat people in a friendly manner.　我們應採友善的態度待人。

map [mæp]

名 地圖

用法 read the map 看地圖
(非 see the map)

Follow the map, and you'll get to the bank. 照著地圖走，你就會找到銀行。

March [mɑrtʃ]

名 三月

用法 in March 在三月（月份用 in）
on March fifth 在三月五號
（日期用 on）

It is still cold here in March.
這裡三月仍然很冷。

mark [mɑrk]

名 記號 動 做記號

用法 mark 也可表示考試的「分數」。
get full marks on the English test
英文考試得了滿分

Do not make any marks in this book.
不要在這本書裡做任何記號。

marker [ˋmarkɚ]

名 奇異筆

用法 write / draw with a marker
用奇異筆寫字 / 畫畫

The boy is drawing a picture with a marker. 這個男孩正用奇異筆畫畫。

market [ˋmarkɪt]

名 市場

用法 go to the market to buy...
到市場買……

Mom will go to the market to buy some vegetables. 媽媽要到市場買些蔬菜。

married [ˋmærɪd]

形 **結婚的，已婚的**

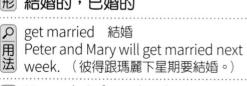

用法 get married 結婚
Peter and Mary will get married next week. （彼得跟瑪麗下星期要結婚。）

My uncle is forty, but he is not married yet. 我叔叔四十歲了，但是他尚未結婚。

marry [ˋmærɪ]

動 與……結婚；娶，嫁

用法
ⓐ 三態：marry、married [ˋmærɪd]、married
ⓑ marry sb　嫁 / 娶某人
Will you marry me?（妳願意嫁給我嗎？）

John asked Judy to marry him.
約翰要茱蒂嫁給他。

marvelous

形 好極的；不可思議的；了不起的 [ˋmɑrvələs]

用法
marvel [ˋmɑrvḷ] 名 令人驚歎的事物
動 感到讚歎

John's English is marvelous.
約翰的英語棒透了。

mask [mæsk]

名 面具；口罩

用法
wear a mask　戴面具；戴口罩

You have to wear a mask when you are in the hospital.　你在醫院時必須戴口罩。

mass [mæs]

名 團；塊；多數（大量） 形 大眾的

用法 a mass of... 一塊／團⋯⋯；大量的⋯⋯
Cindy has a mass of packages to send.
（辛蒂有一大堆的包裹要寄。）

Edwin can't move such a mass of rock. 愛德溫搬不動這麼大塊的岩石。

master [ˋmæstɚ]

名 大師；主人 動 精通

用法 Without hard work, you can't master English.
（不努力你就無法把英文學通。）

Who is the master of the dog?
這隻狗的主人是誰？

match [mætʃ]

名 對手；火柴 動 與⋯⋯匹配；與⋯⋯相配

用法 He has never met his match at chess.
（他從未在西洋棋上遇到過對手。）

The tie doesn't match your suit.
這條領帶和你的西裝不搭配。

mat [mæt]

名 墊子

用法 Wipe your feet on the mat.
（在墊子上把你的腳抹乾淨。）

My pet dog likes to sleep on the mat. 我的寵物狗喜歡睡在墊子上。

math [mæθ]

名 數學（不可數）

用法 math 是 mathematics [ˌmæθəˋmætɪks] 的簡寫。

Mary is good at math.
瑪麗數學很行。

matter [ˋmætɚ]

名 事情；麻煩

用法 matter 也可當動詞，為「重要，有關係」的意思。It doesn't matter when he'll come. （他何時來並不重要。）

The girl is crying. What's the matter with her? 這個女孩在哭泣。她怎麼了？

maximum

[ˋmæksəməm]

名 最大值；最大量

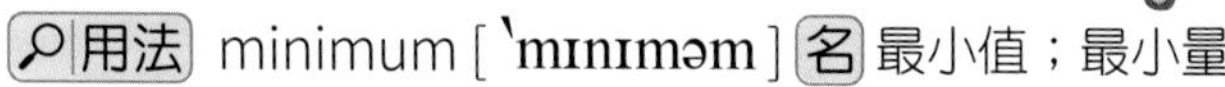

用法 minimum [ˋmɪnɪməm] 名 最小值；最小量

Twenty kilograms of baggage is the maximum allowed. 你最多可攜帶二十公斤的行李。

May [me]

名 五月

用法
in May 在五月（月份用 in）
on May first 在五月一日
（日期用 on）

David's baby sister was born in May last year. 大衛的小妹妹是去年五月出生的。

may [me]

助 可以；可能

用法
ⓐ 可以：You may leave now. （你現在可以離開了。）
ⓑ 可能：It may rain this afternoon.
（今天下午可能會下雨。）

May I help you, sir?
先生，我可以為您效勞嗎？

Mm

maybe [ˋmebɪ]

副 也許

用法 maybe 要放在句首。
Maybe we should take a rest now.
（也許我們現在應該休息一下。）

Maybe Robert is right.
也許羅伯特是對的。

M

meal [mil]

名 一餐

用法 Don't eat between meals.
（不要吃零食——不要在兩餐之間吃東西。）

Ross has three meals a day.
羅斯一天吃三餐。

mean [min]

動 意指，意思就是　形 卑鄙的

用法 三態：mean、meant [mɛnt]、meant

What does this word mean?
這個字是什麼意思？

Mm

meaning [ˋminɪŋ]

名 意思，意義

用法 meaning behind...
……背後的含義

Not many people understand the **meaning behind** his words. 不是很多人了解隱藏在他話**背後的含意**。

measure [ˋmɛʒɚ]

動 度量（長、寬、高等） 名 措施，方法

用法 take measures 採取措施
We should take measures to deal with pollution.（我們應採取措施來處理汙染的問題。）

The nurse **measured** my son's height.
護士**量**了我兒子的身高。

meat [mit]

名 肉

用法 各種食用的肉均稱 meat，為不可數名詞。

Lucy doesn't eat **meat**. She only eats vegetables. 露西不吃**肉**。她只吃青菜。

mechanic [məˋkænɪk]

名 技工

用法 technician [tɛkˋnɪʃən]
名 技術人員，技師

My father worked as a mechanic three years ago. 我父親三年前是名技工。

medicine [ˋmɛdəsn̩]

名 藥

用法 take medicine 吃藥 / 服藥
不可說：eat medicine

Remember to take the medicine after the meal. 記得飯後要吃藥。

media [ˋmidɪə]

名 媒體；媒介物

用法 ⓐ media 為 medium [ˋmidɪəm] 的複數。
ⓑ the mass media 大眾傳播媒體

TV and newspapers are both important media. 電視和報紙都是重要的媒體。

medium [ˋmidɪəm]

形 **中等的，中號的**

用法 表示衣服、鞋子的「大」、「中」、「小」號，分別是 large、medium、small。

I want a medium-size shirt.
我要一件中號的襯衫。

meet [mit]

動 **遇見；與……見面**

用法
ⓐ 三態：meet、met [mɛt]、met
ⓑ Meet me at the train station.
（在火車站跟我碰面。）

Let's meet at the coffee shop.
咱們咖啡廳見。

meeting [ˋmitɪŋ]

名 **會議**

用法 hold a meeting　舉行會議，開會
= have a meeting

We'll have a meeting this afternoon.　我們今天下午會開會。

member [ˋmɛmbɚ]

名 成員；會員

用法 How many members are there in your family?
（你家裡有幾位成員？）

John is a member of the club.
約翰是該俱樂部的**會員**。

memory [ˋmɛm(ə)rɪ]

名 記憶力，記憶；記念

用法 in memory of... 以記念……
They built a park in memory of the hero.
（他們蓋了一座公園以記念這位英雄。）

Mary has a good memory.
瑪麗的**記憶力**很好。

men's room

[ˋmɛnz ˌrum]

名 男廁

用法 ladies' room [ˋledɪz ˌrum] 名 女廁

Excuse me, where is the men's room? 不好意思，請問**男廁**在哪裡？

menu [ˋmɛnju]

名 菜單

用法 What's on the menu?
（菜單上有什麼吃的？）

Can I have a look at the **menu**, please? 請問我可以看一下**菜單**嗎？

message [ˋmɛsɪdʒ]

名 信息

用法 leave a message 留話

I'd like to **leave a message**.
我想要**留話**。

metal [ˋmɛtḷ]

名 金屬

用法 metal 當形容詞用時，也可以解釋為「堅強的」。

Iron is a useful **metal**.
鐵是用途很多的**金屬**。

meter [ˋmitɚ]

名 公尺

用法 可縮寫成 m。

The bed is two meters long.
這張床有兩公尺長。

method [ˋmɛθəd]

名 方法

用法 way [we] 名 方法

Andy's method doesn't work.
安迪的方法行不通。

metro [ˋmɛtro]

名 地鐵

用法 a metro station　地鐵站

Excuse me, where is the metro station?　請問一下，地鐵站在哪兒？

microwave

[ˋmaɪkrə͵wev]

名 微波；微波爐　動 微波

用法 a microwave oven　微波爐

A microwave oven is easy to use.　微波爐操作很簡單。

middle [ˋmɪdl̩]

名 中間，中央　形 中間的

用法
- ⓐ in the middle of...　在……中間
- ⓑ middle height　中等身高

John fell asleep in the middle of the movie.　約翰在電影放映到一半時睡著了。

midnight [ˋmɪd͵naɪt]

名 午夜（不可數）

用法 at midnight　在午夜時分
Annie received a strange call at midnight.（安妮在半夜接到一通怪電話。）

It was already midnight when we got home.　我們到家時已經是午夜了。

mile [maɪl]

名 英里

用法 kilometer [kɪˋlɑmətɚ] 是「公里」。
1 英里約 1.6 公里。

My brother jogs five miles a day.
我哥哥一天慢跑五英里。

milk [mɪlk]

名 牛奶

用法 在英美國家，牛奶均為冷飲，所以用玻璃杯裝，因此表示「一杯牛奶」要說：a glass of milk（非 a cup of milk）。

You should drink more milk. It's good for your health. 你應該多喝牛奶，這有益你的健康。

million [ˋmɪljən]

名 百萬 形 百萬的

NT$2,000,000

用法
ⓐ one million books 一百萬本書
two million books 兩百萬本書
ⓑ millions of books 好幾百萬本書

This car cost my father two million NT dollars. 這輛車花了我爸爸新臺幣兩百萬。

Mm

mind [maɪnd]

動 介意　名 心；心意

用法
ⓐ make up one's mind　下定決心
ⓑ Would you mind + V-ing ?
你介意……嗎？

Would you mind opening the window?　你介意把窗戶打開嗎？

minor [ˋmaɪnɚ]

形 較小的；次要的；未成年的　名 未成年者

用法
It's just a minor change.
（這只是個小小的改變。）

We won't sell cigarettes to minors.
我們不會把香菸賣給未成年的人。

minus [ˋmaɪnəs]

介 減

用法
plus [plʌs] 介 加
Two plus two is four.
（二加二等於四。）

Ten minus two is eight.
十減二等於八。

A B C D E F G H I J K L M N O P Q R S T U V W X Y Z

minute [ˋmɪnɪt]

名 分鐘

用法 second [ˋsɛkənd] 名 秒鐘
in a minute　片刻後，稍後
= in a second / moment

Chloe will be back in a minute.
克洛伊稍後就會回來。

mirror [ˋmɪrɚ]

名 鏡子

用法 look in / into a mirror　照鏡子

Betty looked at herself in the mirror.　貝蒂看著鏡子裡的自己。

Miss [mɪs]

名 小姐

用法 Miss 是稱呼語，要放在姓氏前面。
Miss Wang　王小姐

Miss Chen is our English teacher.　陳小姐是我們英文老師。

miss [mɪs]

動 錯過；想念

用法 ⓐ 錯過：miss the chance　錯過這個機會
miss the train　錯過火車
ⓑ 想念：I miss you.（我想念你。）

Ben got up late, so he missed the bus.　班起床晚了，因此錯過了公車。

mistake [məˋstek]

名 錯誤

用法 make a mistake　犯錯

Don't be afraid to make mistakes when you speak English.　說英語時別怕犯錯。

mix [mɪks]

名 動 混合

用法 mix A with B
將 A 與 B 混合在一起

You can't mix water with oil.
油和水是無法混合的。

modern [ˋmadɚn]

形 現代的；現代化的

用法
the modern world　現代的世界
a modern city　現代化的都市

This is a modern city.
這是座**現代化的城市**。

model [ˋmadḷ]

名 模型；模特兒

用法
ⓐ a role model　楷模，模範
ⓑ a fashion model　時尚模特兒

The architect will show us a model of the building.　這名建築師會把建築物的**模型**給我們看。

moment [ˋmomənt]

名 片刻

I will call you back in a moment.

用法
ⓐ in a moment / minute / second　片刻後
ⓑ at this moment　目前
I'm busy at this moment.（我目前很忙。）

I will call you back in a moment.
我**稍後**會回你電話。

Mm

Monday [ˋmʌnde]

名 星期一

用法
on Monday　星期一
next Monday　下星期一
last Monday　上星期一

Next Monday is a holiday.
下星期一是假日。

money [ˋmʌnɪ]

名 錢（不可數）

用法
make money　賺錢
spend money　花錢
save money　省錢

Brad needs some **money** to buy a camera.　布萊德需要一些**錢**買相機。

monkey [ˋmʌŋkɪ]

名 猴子

用法
monkey 也可以作動詞，有下列用語：
monkey around　胡鬧，搗蛋
Stop monkeying around!（別再胡鬧了！）

Monkeys like to eat bananas.
猴子喜歡吃香蕉。

M m

monster [ˋmɑnstɚ]

名 怪物

用法 a sea monster　海怪

Shrek is a monster with green skin.
史瑞克是個綠皮膚的怪物。

month [mʌnθ]

名 月

It's the first month.
January
1

用法 this month　這個月
last month　上個月
next month　下個月

January is the first month of the year.　一月是一年的第一個月。

moon [mun]

名 月

用法 a full moon　滿月
a new moon　上弦月，新月

The moon is bright tonight.
今晚的月亮很明亮。

mop [mɑp]

名 拖把　動 用拖把拖地

用法 ⓐ 三態：mop、mopped [mɑpt]、mopped
ⓑ mop the floor　拖地板

My mother uses a **mop** to **mop** the floor.　我媽媽用**拖把拖**地板。

more [mɔr]

形 更多的（many, much 的比較級）　副 更加

用法 more... than...　比……更多 / 更加……
more handsome / beautiful than...
比……更帥 / 美

Mary is much **more** beautiful **than** her younger sister.　瑪麗要**比**她妹妹漂亮多了。

morning [ˋmɔrnɪŋ]

名 早上

用法 ⓐ Good morning.　早安。
ⓑ in the morning　在早上

Benjamin usually gets up at six **in the morning**.　班傑明早上通常在六點起床。

mosquito [mə`skito]

名 蚊子

用法 複數為 mosquitoes。

Some **mosquitoes** can spread diseases. 某些**蚊子**會傳播疾病。

most [most]

形 大多數的 代 大部分 副 最

用法
ⓐ the most + Adj 最……的
ⓑ most of the/my...
大部分的 / 我大部分的……

Jane is the **most** beautiful girl in our class. 珍是我們班上**最**漂亮的女生。

motion [`moʃən]

名 運動；移動

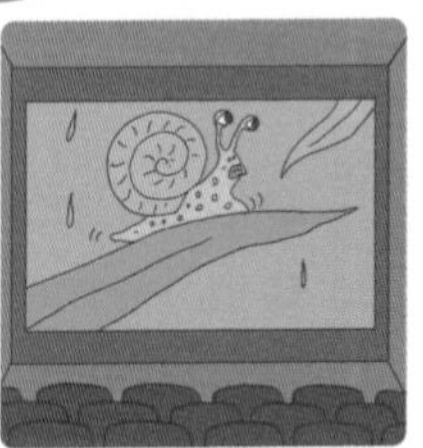

用法 in motion 移動中
Do not get off when the bus is in motion. （公車在行駛中不要下車。）

Parts of the film were shown in slow **motion**. 電影中有若干部份是以慢**動作**放映。

mother [ˋmʌðɚ]

名 媽媽

用法 口語中，常將 mother 簡稱 mom [mɑm]。mommy [ˋmɑmɪ]（媽咪）則是小朋友的用語。

Paul's mother cooks very well.
保羅的**媽媽**很會做菜。

motorcycle

名 摩托車，機車 [ˋmotɚˏsaɪkḷ]

用法 motorcycle 也常簡稱為 motorbike [ˋmotɚˏbaɪk]。

My father rides a motorcycle to and from work every day. 我爸爸每天騎**機車**上下班。

mountain [ˋmaʊntṇ]

名 高山，大山

用法 ⓐ hill [hɪl] 指「小山」，通常指高度在兩、三百公尺以下的小丘陵。
ⓑ live in the mountains　住在群山之中

Mr. and Mrs. Wang live in the mountains.
王先生和王太太住在**山**中。

mouse [maʊs]

名 老鼠

用法 mouse 的複數為 mice [maɪs]。
two mice　兩隻老鼠

Cats are good at catching mice.
貓擅長捉老鼠。

mouth [maʊθ]

名 嘴，口

用法 我們若用英文說髒話時，外國人聽到了就會不悅地說：Watch your mouth.（注意你的嘴巴 / 別說髒話。）

The dentist asked me to open my mouth.　牙醫要我張開嘴巴。

move [muv]

動 移動；搬家

用法 move 也可作名詞，意為「動作，行動」。
the next move　下一步

Aaron moved to Taipei two years ago.　亞倫兩年前搬到臺北。

movie [ˋmuvɪ]

名 電影

用法 go to the movies　看電影

My wife and I go to the movies every weekend.　我和我太太每個週末都會去看電影。

movement [ˋmuvmənt]

名 （社會或政治的）運動；移動

用法 the women's movement
婦女運動

The dancer's movement is graceful.
舞者的動作很優美。

Mr. [ˋmɪstɚ]

名 先生

用法 Mr. 是稱呼語，要放在姓氏的前面。
Mr. Wang　王先生

Mr. Li is my neighbor.
李先生是我的鄰居。

Mrs. [ˋmɪsɪz]

名 太太

用法 Mrs. 是稱呼語，要放在姓氏前面。
Mrs. Chang　張太太

Mrs. Wu keeps a cat as a pet.
吳太太養了一隻貓當寵物。

MRT [ˋɛmˏɑrˋti]

名 捷運

用法 MRT 是 mass rapid transit（大眾捷運系統）的縮寫。

Barry takes the MRT to school every day.　貝瑞每天搭捷運上學。

Ms. [mɪz]

名 小姐；女士

用法 我們已知王小姐未婚時，就可說：Miss Wang；我們若不知王小姐是否已婚，則應說：Ms. Wang。

Glad to see you, Ms. Wilson.
很高興見到您，威爾遜女士。

much [mʌtʃ]

形 許多的　副 更加

用法 much 與 many 均表示「許多的」，但 much 之後接不可數名詞，many 則接可數名詞。

I feel much better now. Thank you very much.　我現在感到好多了。非常謝謝妳。

mud [mʌd]

名 泥巴（不可數）

用法 be covered in mud　被泥巴覆蓋
= be covered with mud

The dog is covered in mud.
這隻狗滿身都是泥巴。

museum [mjuˋzɪəm]

名 博物館

用法 visit the museum
參觀博物館

The students visited a museum this morning.　今天早上這群學生參觀了一間博物館。

music [ˋmjuzɪk]

名 音樂（不可數）

用法 listen to music　聽音樂
Belle enjoys listening to music.
（貝兒喜歡聽音樂。）

What kind of music does Charlie like?　查理喜歡哪一類音樂？

musician [mjuˋzɪʃən]

名 音樂家

用法 musical [ˋmjuzɪkl̩] 形 音樂的　名 音樂劇
Ashley has a musical talent.
（艾希莉有音樂天賦。）

Mr. Wang is a great musician.
王先生是偉大的音樂家。

must [mʌst]

助 必須；一定（猜測）

用法 ⓐ 必須：You must work hard.（你必須努力。）
ⓑ 一定：That man must be fifty years old.
（那名男子一定有五十歲了。）

You must finish your homework right now.　你現在就必須把你的作業做完。

Nn

N

nail [nel]

名 釘子；指甲

用法 hit the nail into the wall
把釘子釘入牆面

Don't bite your nail.
別咬你的指甲。

name [nem]

名 名字　動 命名

用法 name + sb + 名字　把某人命名為……
Mr. Wang named his son John.
（王先生把他的兒子取名為約翰。）

May I have your name, please?

May I have your name, please?
請問貴姓大名？

napkin [ˋnæpkɪn]

名 餐巾

用法 towel [ˋtaʊəl] 名 毛巾

Can I have some napkins, please?　請給我一些餐巾紙好嗎？

A B C D E F G H I J K L M N O P Q R S T U V W X Y Z

narrow [ˋnæro]

形 狹窄的

用法 wide [waɪd] 形 寬廣的

Drive carefully. The road is **narrow.** 小心駕駛，這條路很窄。

nation [ˋneʃən]

名 國家

用法 the United Nations 聯合國

People of this nation are **friendly.** 此國的人民很友善。

national [ˋnæʃənl̩]

形 國家的；國立的；全國的

用法
a national flag 國旗
a national meeting 全國會議

There are many different animals **in this national park.** 這座**國家公園**有許多不同的動物。

Nn

natural [ˋnætʃərəl]

形 自然的

用法 natural resources　天然資源

We should eat more natural food.
我們應多吃**天然食物**。

nature [ˋnetʃɚ]

名 大自然（不可數）；性質

用法 nature 表示「大自然」時，之前不可放 the。
I love the nature. (×)
→ I love nature. (○)（我喜歡大自然。）

Elva loves nature.
艾娃喜歡**大自然**。

naughty [ˋnɔtɪ]

形 頑皮的

用法 a naughty boy　調皮的小男孩

Cassie's brother is very naughty.
凱西的弟弟非常**頑皮**。

Nn

near [nɪr]

介 在……附近，接近

用法 live near... 住在……的附近

Grace lives near the post office.
葛瑞絲住在郵局附近。

nearly [ˋnɪrlɪ]

副 幾乎

N

用法 almost [ˋɔlˏmost] 副 幾乎

Duke's mother is nearly fifty now.
杜克的母親現在年近五十。

necessary [ˋnɛsəˏsɛrɪ]

形 必需的（常與 for 並用）

用法 It is necessary (for sb) to V
（某人）做……是必要的

Water is necessary for life.
水是生命所必需的。

neck [nɛk]

名 頸，脖子

用法 neck and neck　並駕齊驅
The two parties are still neck and neck.（這兩黨仍不分上下。）

That man has a long neck.
那個男子的**脖子**好長。

necklace [ˋnɛkləs]

名 項鍊

用法 a gold / pearl necklace
金 / 珍珠項鍊

Jane is wearing a pearl necklace today.　珍今天戴了一條珍珠項鍊。

need [nid]

名 動 需要

用法
ⓐ a basic need　基本需求
ⓑ need to + V

I need your help, John.
約翰，我**需要**你的**幫助**。

needle [ˋnidḷ]

名 針

用法 a needle and thread　針線

There's a hole in my pants. Give me a **needle and thread.**　我褲子破了一個洞，請給我**針線**。

negative [ˋnɛgətɪv]

形 否定的；負面的

用法 positive [ˋpɑzətɪv] 形 肯定的；正面的

Derek gave me a **negative** answer.
德瑞克給了我一個**否定的**答案。

neighbor [ˋnebɚ]

名 鄰居

用法 neighborhood [ˋnebɚˏhʊd] 名 鄰近地區
There is a market in Amy's neighborhood.
（艾咪的住處附近有一個菜市場。）

Hannah's **neighbors** are helpful.
漢娜的**鄰居**們很樂於助人。

Nn

neither [ˋniðɚ]

代 兩者皆不　副 既不……也不……

用法 neither... nor... 連接主詞時，動詞按最近的主詞變化。Neither he nor I am wrong.（他沒錯，我也沒錯。）

Neither of my parents loves music.
我爸媽都不喜歡音樂。

nephew [ˋnɛf ju]

名 姪兒；外甥

用法 niece [nis] 名 姪女；外甥女

My nephew's girlfriend just came back from Canada. 我姪子的女友剛從加拿大回來。

nervous [ˋnɝvəs]

形 緊張的；神經的

用法 a nervous system　神經系統

Chloe gets nervous among strangers. 在陌生人之中克洛伊會緊張。

Nn

nest [nɛst]

名 巢，窩

用法 a bird's nest　鳥巢

There's a bird's nest in the tree.
樹上有個鳥巢。

net [nɛt]

名 網

用法
ⓐ slip through the net　漏網脫逃
ⓑ the Net / internet　網路

John used a net to catch fish.
約翰用網子捕魚。

never [ˋnɛvɚ]

副 從不，絕不

用法 have never...　從來沒有……

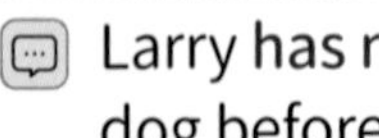

Larry has never seen such a big dog before.　賴瑞以前從未見過這麼大隻的狗。

Nn

new [n(j)u]

形 新的

用法 new 的反義詞為 used [juzd]（舊的）。
a new car　新車
a used car　舊車

Irene's watch is broken. She needs to buy a new one.　艾琳的錶壞了。她需要買一只新的。

news [n(j)uz]

名 新聞，消息（不可數）

用法 a good piece of news　一則好消息
some good news　一些好消息

Did you watch the news on TV yesterday?　你昨天看到電視播的新聞了嗎？

newspaper

名 報紙　[ˋn(j)uzˏpepɚ]

用法 read a newspaper　看報紙
a daily newspaper　日報

Dad is reading a newspaper in the living room.　爸爸正在客廳看報紙。

next [nɛkst]

形 下一個的

用法 next 也可表示「相鄰的」，與 to 並用。
Heidi lives next to her school.
（海蒂就住在她學校的隔壁。）

Leo and his friend will go fishing next week. 李歐和他朋友**下星期**要去釣魚。

nice [naɪs]

形 好的

用法
ⓐ We had a nice day yesterday.
（我們這邊昨天天氣很好。）
ⓑ a nice boy / girl　好男孩 / 好女孩

John is a **nice** boy, so we all like him. 約翰是個**好孩子**，因此我們都喜歡他。

nice-looking

[ˌnaɪsˈlʊkɪŋ]

形 漂亮的；俊美的

用法 等於 good-looking。

Who's that **nice-looking** young man? 那位年輕的**帥哥**是誰呀？

N n

niece [nis]

名 姪女；外甥女

用法 aunt [ænt] 名 阿姨；姑姑
uncle [ˋʌŋkl̩] 名 叔叔；伯父；舅舅

My **niece** is a junior high school student.
我**姪女**是個國中生。

night [naɪt]

名 晚上

用法 at night　在晚上
during the day　在白天

The city looks beautiful **at night**.
這座城市**在夜間**看起來很美。

nine [naɪn]

名 九　形 九個的

用法 work nine to five
從早上九點上班到下午五點

Dad gets to work **at nine in the morning**.　爸爸都是在**早上九點**上班。

Nn

nineteen [ˌnaɪnˋtin]

名 十九　形 十九個的

用法 nineteen books / toys
十九本書 / 十九個玩具

John's brother is nineteen years old.　約翰的哥哥十九歲了。

ninety [ˋnaɪntɪ]

名 九十　形 九十個的

用法 get ninety-five points on a test
某項測驗得九十五分

Mark got ninety-five points on the English test.　馬克這次的英文測驗考了九十五分。

no [no]

限 沒有　副 不

用法 no 常大寫，形成下列常用語：
No Smoking　禁止吸菸
No Parking　禁止停車

Matt has no money. Could you lend him some?　麥特沒錢。你能否借他一些？

nobody [ˋno,badɪ]

代 沒有人

用法 nobody 也可作「無名小卒」，之前要加 a。
Lee is a nobody. （李是個無名小卒。）

John lies all the time, so nobody believes his words. 約翰一直在說謊，因此沒人相信他的話。

nod [nad]

動 點頭

用法
ⓐ 三態：nod、nodded [ˋnadɪd]、nodded
ⓑ nod at + sb 向某人點頭打招呼

When I asked Mary whether she would go swimming with us, she nodded quickly. 我問瑪麗是否要跟我們去游泳時，她很快就點頭了。

noise [nɔɪz]

名 噪音

用法 make noise(s) 發出噪音；吵鬧

Stop making noises. Be quiet.
別再吵鬧了。安靜下來。

noisy [ˋnɔɪzɪ]

形 吵鬧的

用法 noisy 也有「（電子設備）干擾的」之意。
a noisy signal　干擾信號

Debbie doesn't like noisy neighbors.　黛比不喜歡**喧鬧的**鄰居。

none [nʌn]

代 一點（個）也沒有

用法 None of your business!
（不關你的事！/ 少管閒事！）

None of Gary's friends love music.　蓋瑞的朋友**沒有一個**喜歡音樂。

noodle [ˋnudḷ]

名 麵條

用法 吃麵條時通常有很多條，因此常用複數 noodles。

My mom loves to eat rice, but my dad loves to eat **noodles**.　我媽媽喜歡吃飯，不過我爸爸則喜歡吃**麵**。

noon [nun]

名 中午

用法
at noon 中午
in the morning 早上
in the afternoon 中午

Let's go out for lunch at noon.
我們**中午**到外面吃午餐吧。

nor [nɔr]

連 也不

用法
nor 作連接詞連接兩個主要子句時，第一個主要子句必須是否定句，第二個主要子句一定採倒裝句型。

Frank doesn't like Gerald, nor do I.
法蘭克不喜歡傑拉德，我**也**是。

north [nɔrθ]

副 往北　名 北方　形 北方的

用法
go north 往北走
in the north 在北方
North America 北美

It's cold in the north.
北方天氣很冷。

Nn

nose [noz]

名 鼻子

用法 blow one's nose　擤鼻涕
John used a handkerchief to blow his nose. （約翰用一條手帕擤鼻涕。）

Tom has a big nose.
湯姆的鼻子很大。

not [nɑt]

副 不

用法 not 要放在 is、am、are 之後。
不要說：He not is a good student. (×)
而要說：He is not a good student. (○)

This is not the pen Matt wants.
這不是麥特要的筆。

note [not]

名 筆記，便條

用法 ⓐ 筆記：take notes　做筆記
ⓑ 便條：Luke left a note on the desk.
（路克在桌上留了一張便條。）

You should take notes in class.
你上課應該做筆記。

notebook [ˋnot͵bʊk]

名 筆記本

用法 notebook 也可指「筆記型電腦」。

Jane wrote many notes in the notebook. 珍在**筆記本**內寫了許多筆記。

nothing [ˋnʌθɪŋ]

名 代 沒有任何東西；沒事

用法 have nothing to do / say / eat
沒事做 / 沒話說 / 沒東西吃

Owen has nothing to do this afternoon. 歐文今天下午**沒事**做。

notice [ˋnotɪs]

名 動 注意；通知

用法
ⓐ notice (that)... 注意到
ⓑ take notice (of) 注意……

Did you notice Mary's new watch? 你**注意到**瑪麗的新手錶了嗎？

novel [ˋnɑvḷ]

名 小說　形 新奇的

用法
ⓐ novelist [ˋnɑvḷɪst] 名 小說家
ⓑ a novel idea　新穎的點子

Dolly likes to read novels when she has time.　朵莉有空時喜歡看小說。

November [noˋvɛmbɚ]

名 十一月

用法
in November　在十一月（月分用 in）
on November first　在十一月一日（日期用 on）

The weather will get cold in November.　十一月的天氣會變冷。

now [naʊ]

副 現在

用法
right now　馬上
by now　到目前
from now on　從現在開始

Jack is writing a letter now.
傑克正在寫一封信。

number [ˋnʌmbɚ]

名 數字；號碼

用法 telephone number　電話號碼
= phone number

What's Joy's **telephone number**?
喬伊的**電話號碼**是幾號？

nurse [nɝs]

名 護士

用法 由 nurse 衍生出 nursery 一字。
nursery [ˋnɝsərɪ] 名 托兒所

A **nurse** must be kind.
護士必須要有愛心。

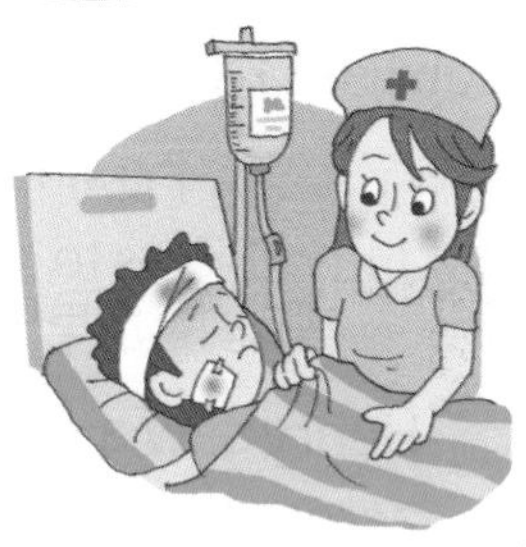

nut [nʌt]

名 堅果

用法 nuts [nʌts] 形 發瘋的
go nuts　氣瘋，大發雷霆

Many kinds of **nuts** can be eaten.
很多種**堅果**是可以吃的。

obey [oˋbe]

動 服從；遵守

用法 obey the law　守法

Everyone should **obey the law.**
人人皆應守法。

object

[ˋɑbdʒɪkt] 名 物體；目標　[əbˋdʒɛkt] 動 反對

用法 object to + N/V-ing　反對……
Judy objects to setting out so early.
（茱蒂反對這麼早出發。）

Henry saw a strange **object** flying across the sky.　亨利看見一個奇怪的物體飛過天空。

ocean [ˋoʃən]

名 海洋

用法 sea [si] 名 海（洋）

Diving **in the ocean** is exciting.
在海中潛水很刺激。

o'clock [ə'klɑk]

副 ……點鐘

用法 ⓐ o'clock 之前一定要有數字。
five o'clock　五點鐘
ⓑ clock [klɑk] 名 鐘

It's ten o'clock now.
現在是十點鐘。

October [ɑk'tobɚ]

名 十月

用法 in October　在十月（月份用 in）
on October fifth　在十月五日
（日期用 on）

October comes after September.
九月之後就是十月。

of [əv]

介 ……的

用法 the color of this car　這輛車的顏色
a cup of coffee　一杯咖啡

Candy likes the color of this car.
坎蒂喜歡這輛車的顏色。

off [ɔf]

副 介 脫離，離去

用法 take off... 脫下（穿戴在身上的衣物，如 帽子、鞋子、衣服、手錶等）
put on... 穿／戴上（上列東西）

Take off your coat.
把妳的外套**脫下**。

offer [ˋɔfɚ]

動 提供 名 提議

用法 I think Hank will accept their offer.（我想漢克會接受他們的提議。）

They will **offer** Elaine a job.
他們會**給**伊蓮這個工作。

office [ˋɔfɪs]

名 辦公室

用法 go to the office 到辦公室／公司上班
take office 就職

There is no one **in the office** now.
現在**辦公室裡**沒人。

officer [ˋɔfəsɚ]

名 警官；軍官

用法 police officer [pəˋlis ˏɔfəsɚ]
名 警官；警察

My father is a **police officer.**
我爸爸是**警察**。

often [ˋɔfən]

副 經常

用法 How often...? ……多久一次？
How often does David come here?
（大衛多久來此一次？）

My parents **often** take a walk in the park. 我爸媽**常**在公園裡散步。

oil [ɔɪl]

名 油

用法 oil 指一般的食用油或汽車的機油。
汽油則稱 gas [gæs]。
vegetable oil 植物油

When Mom cooks, she uses **vegetable oil.** 媽媽做飯的時候都使用**植物油**。

Oo

OK [ˋoˋke]

感歎 好　形 不錯的；身體好的

用法 OK 是 okay [ˋoˋke] 的縮寫。
"Let's go." "OK."
「咱們走吧。」「好。」

Don't worry. Everything is OK.
別擔心。一切都沒事。

old [old]

形 老的；…… 歲的

用法 be + 數字 + years old　是……歲
My brother is ten years old now.
（我弟弟現在十歲了。）

My grandmother is already seventy years old.　我奶奶已經七十歲了。

omit [oˋmɪt]

動 省略；遺漏

用法 三態：omit、omitted [ɔˋmɪtɪd]、omitted

Please do not omit any details.
請勿遺漏任何細節。

O

on [ɑn]

介 在⋯⋯之上

用法 on the desk 在桌上
on the wall 在牆上
on the floor 在地板上

Put the dictionary **on the desk.**
把字典放在桌上。

once [wʌns]

副 一次 連 一旦

用法 ⓐ 一旦：Once you see Carrie, let me know.（你一旦見到凱莉，就通知我。）
ⓑ at once 馬上

Chloe has been to the United States **once.** 克洛伊曾去過美國一次。

one [wʌn]

名 一個 形 一個的

用法 one day 有一天
I saw Fred on the train one day.
（有一天我在火車上看到弗瑞德。）

Gary has **one** brother and two sisters. 蓋瑞有一個哥哥、兩個妹妹。

Oo

oneself [wʌnˋsɛlf]

代 自己

用法 為 one 的反身代名詞。

One should depend on oneself.
每個人都應靠**自己**。

onion [ˋʌnjən]

名 洋蔥

用法
onion soup　洋蔥湯
onion rings　洋蔥圈

Doris doesn't like **onion soup.**
朵瑞絲不喜歡**洋蔥湯**。

O

only [ˋonlɪ]

形 唯一的　副 僅僅

用法
ⓐ an only child　獨生子（女）
ⓑ I have only five dollars with me.
（我身上只有五塊錢。）

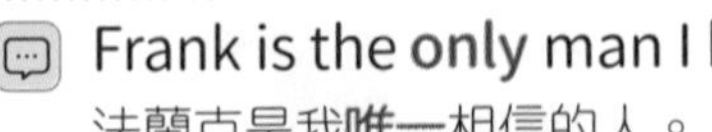

Frank is the **only** man I believe.
法蘭克是我**唯一**相信的人。

open [ˋopən]

動 打開　形 開著的

用法 ⓐ 打開：Open the door!（開門！）
ⓑ 開著的：The door is open.（門是開著的。）

Open the door. Don’t close it.
把門打開。不要關起來。

operation [ˏɑpəˋreʃən]

名 手術（與 on 並用）；操作

用法 Harry is going to have an operation on his heart tomorrow.
（明天哈利將要動心臟手術。）

The **operation** of this digital camera is easy.
這臺數位相機的**操作**很簡單。

opinion [ˋəpɪnjən]

名 意見；見解

用法 in one’s opinion
依某人之見

In my opinion, students should not be allowed to bring cellphones to school. **依我之見**，不應允許學生帶手機到學校。

or [ɔr]

連 或；要不然，否則

用法 ⓐ 或：Coffee or tea?（咖啡或茶？）
ⓑ 要不然：Put on a coat, or you'll catch (a) cold.（穿上外套，不然你會感冒。）

Study hard, **or** you will fail the test.
要用功，否則這次考試你會不及格。

orange [ˋɔrɪndʒ]

名 橘色；柳橙　形 橘色的

用法 orange 就是我們常吃的「柳丁」。
「橘子」則稱作 tangerine [ˌtændʒəˋrin]。

There are two apples and five **oranges** in the basket.　籃子裡有兩顆蘋果和五顆柳橙。

order [ˋɔrdɚ]

動 點餐；命令　名 命令；次序

用法 keep... in order　將……整理有序
Keep your books in order.
（把你的書弄整齊。）

Are you ready to **order** now, sir?
先生，您準備點餐了嗎？

Oo

ordinary [ˋɔrdṇˏɛrɪ]

形 平常的；普通的

用法 extraordinary [ɪkˋstrɔrdṇˏɛrɪ]
形 非凡的

What is Erin's **ordinary life** like?
艾琳的日常生活是什麼樣子？

other [ˋʌðɚ]

形 限 其它的（東西）；其他的（人）

用法 one... the other...　一個……另一個……

Hugo cannot go out with you. He has some **other** things to do.　雨果不能跟你出去。他有一些其它事要做。

out [aʊt]

副 到外面

用法 go out　到外面去，外出
come out　走出來

Don't **go out**. It's raining.
別出門。現在正在下著雨。

A B C D E F G H I J K L M N O P Q R S T U V W X Y Z

Oo

outside [ˌaʊtˋsaɪd]

副 在外面

🔍用法 inside [ɪnˋsaɪd] 副 在裡面
stay outside　待在外面
stay inside　待在裡面

💬 There is a dog **outside**.
外面有一隻狗。

oven [ˋʌvən]

名 烤箱，烤爐

🔍用法 be like an oven　熱得像火爐

💬 Hazel used an **oven** to bake a cake.　海柔用**烤箱**烤蛋糕。

o

over [ˋovɚ]

介 副 越過　形 結束的

🔍用法
ⓐ 越過：jump over the wall　跳過牆
ⓑ 結束的：The meeting is over.
（會議結束了。）

💬 Can you **come over**? I have something to tell you.　你能否**過來**一下？我有話要跟你說。

Oo

overpass [ˋovɚˏpæs]

名 天橋

用法 underpass [ˋʌndɚˏpæs] 名 地下道

You should use the **overpass** when you cross the street. 過馬路時，你應利用**天橋**。

overseas [ˏovɚˋsiz]

形 海外的，國外的　副 在海外，在國外

用法 an overseas student　僑生

Mary is going to work **overseas**. 瑪麗將要到**國外**工作。

overweight [ˏovɚˋwet]

形 過重的

用法 Louis is 20 kilograms overweight.（路易斯過重二十公斤。）

Many school children are **overweight**. 許多學童體重**過重**。

own [on]

動 擁有　形 屬於自己的

用法
❶ 擁有：The rich man owns five cars.
（這個有錢人擁有五部車。）
❷ 屬於自己的：his own car　他自己的車

Hank can't help you. He has his **own** problems.　漢克沒辦法幫助你。他有他自己的問題。

owner [ˋonɚ]

名 擁有者，所有人

用法
the owner of...　……的所有人

Jack is **the owner of** the car.
傑克是這臺車的所有人。

ox [ɑks]

名（閹過的）公牛，牛

用法
❶ ox 的複數為 oxen [ˋɑksn̩]。
❷ 未閹過的公牛稱作 bull [bʊl]，
母牛或乳牛則稱作 cow [kaʊ]。

Jerry sees an **ox** and a few cows on the farm.　傑瑞看到農場有一隻公牛和幾隻母牛。

P p

pack [pæk]

動 打包，裝箱　名 背包

用法
pack things　把東西打包好
pack books　把書打包好

Let me help you **pack** things.
讓我來協助你打包東西吧。

package [ˋpækɪdʒ]

名 包裹

用法
a package of...　一包……的東西
a package of books / toys...
一包書 / 玩具……

My uncle sent me **a package of** books.　我叔叔寄給我一包書。

page [pedʒ]

名 頁

用法
ⓐ on page ten　在第十頁
ⓑ Turn to page twenty, please.
（請翻到第二十頁。）

Please open your books to **page** five.　請打開你的書到第五頁。

A B C D E F G H I J K L M N O P Q R S T U V W X Y Z

pain [pen]

名 痛苦

用法 feel a pain in sth　感到某部位一陣劇痛
Thomas felt a sharp pain in his stomach.
（湯瑪斯感到胃一陣劇痛。）

Daniel **has a pain in his leg.**
丹尼爾腿痛。

painful [ˋpenfəl]

形 痛苦的

用法 a painful experience　痛苦的經驗

The accident is **a painful experience** to Evan.　這次意外對伊凡是場痛苦的經歷。

paint [pent]

名 油漆；顏料　動 漆；畫（油彩畫）

用法 paint the wall white / red / yellow...
把牆壁漆成白色 / 紅色 / 黃色……

The **paint** is still wet.
油漆未乾。

P p

painter [ˋpentɚ]

名 油漆匠；畫家

用法 Michael worked as a house painter in the US.
（麥可在美國時當過房屋的油漆工。）

My father used to be a **painter**.
我爸爸之前是位畫家。

pair [pɛr]

名 一雙；一對；一副

用法 a pair of... 一雙 / 一對 / 一副……
a pair of glasses 一副眼鏡
a pair of shoes 一雙鞋子

My mom bought me **a** new **pair of shoes**. 我媽媽買了一雙新鞋給我。

pajamas

名 睡衣褲 [pəˋdʒæməz]

用法 ⓐ pajamas 含上衣及褲子，故恆用複數。
ⓑ a pair of pajamas 一套睡衣

Denise bought **a pair of** pink **pajamas** yesterday. 丹妮絲昨天買了一套粉紅色的睡衣。

pale [pel]

形 蒼白的

用法 turn / go pale　變蒼白

Cynthia looks **pale** today. What's the matter?　辛西亞今天看起來臉色蒼白。怎麼了？

pan [pæn]

名 平底鍋

用法 a flash in the pan　曇花一現

My mother uses a **pan** to fry eggs.
我媽媽用平底鍋煎蛋。

panda [ˋpændə]

名 貓熊

用法 也叫 giant panda。

Pandas are very cute animals.
貓熊是很可愛的動物。

P p

pants [pænts]

名 褲子

用法 因為褲子有兩條褲管，所以 pants 一定是複數。表示「一條褲子」不可說：a pant，而要說：a pair of pants。

The dirty **pants** need to be washed. 這條髒褲子需要清洗了。

papaya [pəˋpɑjə]

名 木瓜

用法 papaya 的複數為 papayas。
two papayas　　兩顆木瓜
a piece of papaya　一片木瓜

Dave doesn't like to eat **papayas**.
戴夫不喜歡吃木瓜。

paper [ˋpepɚ]

名 紙（不可數）；報紙（可數）

用法
ⓐ 紙：two pieces of paper　兩張紙
ⓑ 報紙：two papers = two newspapers
　　　兩份報紙

Can I have **a piece of paper**? I need to write something. 我可以要一張紙嗎？我需要寫些東西。

Pp

pardon [ˋpardn̩]

名 動 原諒；寬恕

用法 May I beg your pardon?
= Pardon me?
= Pardon? （抱歉，請再說一次好嗎？）

May I beg your pardon?
抱歉，請再說一次好嗎？

parent [ˋpɛrənt]

名 父或母

用法 因為每個人都有爸爸及媽媽，
所以 parents 常用複數。

My **parents** love to sing.
我爸媽都喜愛唱歌。

P

park [park]

名 公園　動 停車

用法 You can't park (your car) here.
（你不可在這裡停車。）

Some children are playing in the park.　公園裡有一些小朋友在玩耍。

part [pɑrt]

名 部分

用法 ⓐ the first / second part of...
……的第一 / 第二部分
ⓑ part of...　部分的……

💬 Duke doesn't like **the first part of** this lesson.　杜克不喜歡這課的第一部分。

parking lot

[ˋpɑrkɪŋ ˏlɑt]

名 停車場

用法 a parking space　停車位

💬 There is no **parking lot** here.
這裡沒有停車場。

parrot [ˋpærət]

名 鸚鵡

用法 parrot 可當動詞用，有「機械式地模仿」的意思。

💬 Jeff keeps a **parrot** as a pet.
傑夫養了一隻鸚鵡當寵物。

Pp

partner [ˋpartnɚ]

名 夥伴；合夥人

用法
a dancing partner 舞伴
a trading partner 貿易夥伴

Nancy and I are good partners.
南西和我是好夥伴。

party [ˋpartɪ]

名 聚會，派對；政黨

用法
ⓐ throw / hold a party 舉辦派對
ⓑ invite + sb + to the party
邀請某人參加派對

Thank you for inviting me to your party. 謝謝你邀我參加你的派對。

pass [pæs]

動 通過；經過

用法
pass a test 通過考試；考及格
pass the post office / station
經過郵局 / 車站

Peter studies hard, so he passed the test. 彼得很用功，因此他考及格了。

passenger [ˋpæsṇdʒɚ]

名 乘客

用法 a passenger plane　客機

The train was crowded with passengers.　這班火車擠滿了乘客。

past [pæst]

介 副 經過　名 過去

用法 ⓐ past 表示「經過」時，之前要有動詞。
walk past the station　走路經過車站
ⓑ past 也可當形容詞用，表示「過去」的意思。

Eric has lived here for the past three years.　過去三年來艾瑞克都住在這裡。

paste [pest]

名 糨糊　動 黏

用法 paste a notice on...
把一張公告黏在……

Evan pasted a notice on the door.　伊凡在門上貼了一張公告。

path [pæθ]

名 小徑

用法 a path to success / freedom
(前往)成功 / 自由之路

My boyfriend and I took a walk along the **path** in the park. 我和男友沿著公園的小徑散步。

patient [ˋpeʃənt]

形 有耐心的(與 with 並用) 名 病人

用法 The child is a brave patient.
(這孩子是個勇敢的病人。)

The teacher **is patient with** his students. 那名老師對他的學生很有耐心。

pattern [ˋpætɚn]

名 型式

用法 a sentence pattern 句型

Just follow these **sentence patterns**. 就按照這些句型。

P p

pause [pɔz]

動 停頓　名 暫停

用法 There was a pause before the teacher continued to talk.（老師停頓了一下才又接著說。）

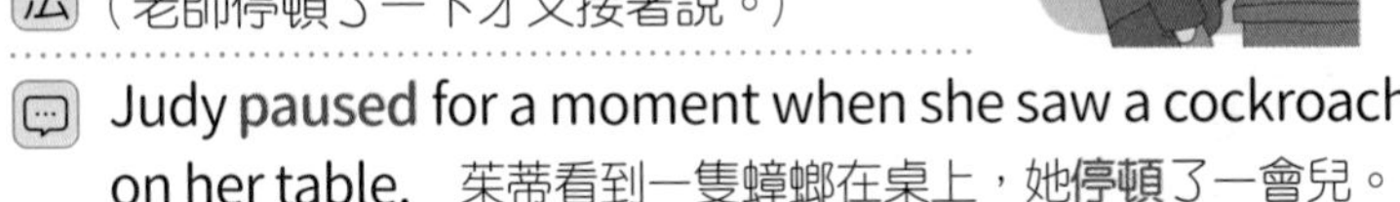

Judy **paused** for a moment when she saw a cockroach on her table.　茱蒂看到一隻蟑螂在桌上，她**停頓**了一會兒。

pay [pe]

動 付（錢）　名 薪水，待遇

用法
ⓐ 三態：pay、paid [ped]、paid
ⓑ pay + 金錢 + for + sth　付錢買某物
ⓒ The pay is good.（這個待遇不錯。）

Cindy **paid** NT$500 for this dictionary.
辛蒂**付**了新臺幣五百元買了這本字典。

PE [ˌpi`i]

名 體育課

用法
PE 是 physical education 的縮寫
physical [`fɪzɪkḷ] 形 身體的
education [ˌɛdʒəˈkeʃən] 名 教育

We have two **PE** classes every week.　我們每週有兩堂**體育課**。

Pp

peace [pis]

名 和平；平靜

用法
ⓐ peace 為不可數。
ⓑ be at peace with...
與……和平相處

The two countries are now at peace with each other. 這兩國目前和平共處。

peaceful [ˋpisfəl]

形 和平的；平靜的

用法
a peaceful afternoon / place
平靜的下午 / 地方

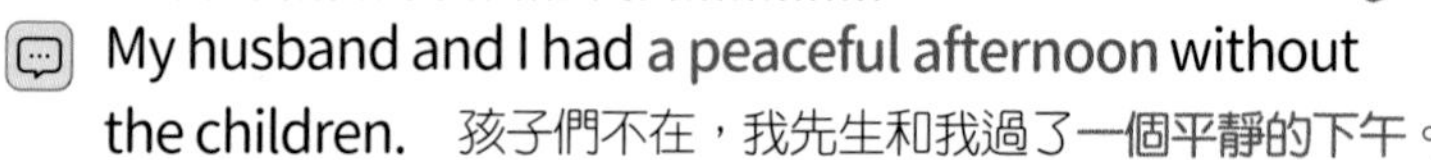
My husband and I had a peaceful afternoon without the children. 孩子們不在，我先生和我過了一個平靜的下午。

peach [pitʃ]

名 桃子

用法
peach 也可以表示「桃紅色」，此時為不可數。

The peach is sweet.
這顆桃子很甜。

pear [pɛr]

名 梨

用法 酪梨則為 avocado [ˌævəˋkɑdo]。

Pears are my son's favorite fruit.
梨子是我兒子最喜愛的水果。

pen [pɛn]

名 筆（原子筆或鋼筆）

用法 pen 也可作動詞用，為「寫」的意思。
pen a letter / poem　寫信／詩

Diana needs a pen to write a letter.
戴安娜需要一隻筆來寫信。

pencil [ˋpɛnsḷ]

名 鉛筆

用法 draw a picture with a pencil
用鉛筆畫畫

Very few people use pencils now.
現在很少人使用鉛筆了。

people [ˋpipl̩]

名 人

用法
ⓐ people 指兩個以上的人。
ⓑ 若表示「一個人」時，要說：a person（非 a people）

Why are there so many **people** there? 那邊為什麼有那麼多人？

pepper [ˋpɛpɚ]

名 胡椒粉

用法
pepper 當「胡椒粉」時為不可數名詞。另外還有「甜椒」的意思，為可數名詞。

Pass me the **pepper**, please.
請把**胡椒**遞給我。

perfect [ˋpɝfɪkt]

形 完美的

用法
Practice makes perfect.
（熟能生巧。—— 諺語）

Ella's English is almost **perfect**.
艾拉的英文幾近**完美**。

P p

period [ˋpɪrɪəd]

名 時期；期間

用法 a period of + 時間　一段……時間

Gina is going to stay there for a short period of time.　吉娜準備在那裡作短期居留。

perhaps [pɚˋhæps]

副 也許

用法 perhaps 常放在句首，等於 maybe。
Perhaps John will come.
（也許約翰會來。）

Perhaps Dave is right.
也許戴夫是對的。

person [ˋpɝsn̩]

名 人

用法 in person　親自
I will call Candy in person.
（我會親自打電話給坎蒂。）

I don't like that person. He lies.
我不喜歡那個人，他會說謊。

personal [ˋpɜsn̩l]

形 個人的，私人的

用法 personal belongings
隨身私人物品（恆用複數）

May I ask you a personal question?
我能問你一個私人問題嗎？

pet [pɛt]

名 寵物

用法 keep + 動物 + as a pet
養某動物當寵物

That boy keeps a little pig as a pet. 那個男孩子養了一條小豬當寵物。

photo [ˋfoto]

名 照片

用法 photo 是 photograph [ˋfotə͵græf] 的簡寫。
take a photo / picture of...
拍一張……的照片

Could you take a photo of me?
能否請你幫我拍張照？

physics [ˋfɪzɪks]

名 物理學

用法
ⓐ physics 為不可數。
ⓑ physicist [ˋfɪzɪsɪst] 名 物理學家

Will is not interested in physics.
威爾對物理學沒興趣。

piano [pɪˋæno]

名 鋼琴

用法
ⓐ play the piano　彈鋼琴
ⓑ pianist [pɪˋænɪst] 名 鋼琴家

Mary's sister plays the piano very well.　瑪麗的姊姊鋼琴彈得很好。

pick [pɪk]

動 摘；撿起

用法
ⓐ 撿起：pick up the garbage　撿起垃圾
ⓑ（開車）接（某人）：Pick me up at the post office.（到郵局來接我。）

Do not pick flowers in the garden.
不要在花園裡摘花。

picnic [ˋpɪknɪk]

名 野餐

用法 have a picnic　去野餐
= go on a picnic

Claire and her boyfriend will **have a picnic** tomorrow.　克萊兒和她男友明天會**去野餐**。

picture [ˋpɪktʃɚ]

名 圖畫；照片

用法 ⓐ draw a picture　畫一張畫
ⓑ take a picture of...
拍一張……的照片

Daisy's little brother can **draw a picture** of an elephant.　黛西的弟弟會**畫**大象。

pie [paɪ]

名 派，餡餅

用法 It's easy as pie. = It's very easy.
（這件事太容易了 —— 容易得就像做派一樣。）

Gary likes **apple pie** very much.
蓋瑞很喜歡**蘋果派**。

piece [pis]

名 片，塊，張

用法 a piece of paper　一張紙
a piece of cake
一塊蛋糕；比喻輕而易舉的事

Can I have a piece of that cake?
那個蛋糕我可否吃一塊？

pig [pɪg]

名 豬

用法 pig 也可指「討厭的傢伙」。
I don't like Peter. He is a pig!
（我不喜歡彼得。他是個討厭鬼！）

The little pig is very cute.
這隻小豬好可愛喲。

pigeon [ˋpɪdʒən]

名 鴿子

用法 a racing pigeon　賽鴿

My uncle raises a lot of pigeons.
我叔叔養了許多鴿子。

Pp

pile [paɪl]

名 堆

用法 a pile of... 一堆……

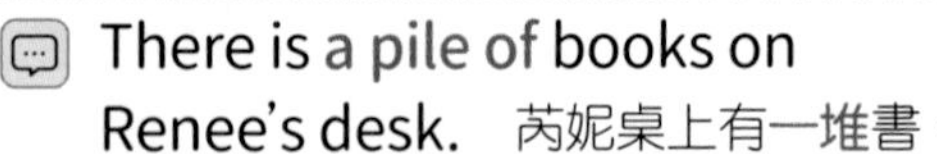

There is a pile of books on Renee's desk. 芮妮桌上有一堆書。

pillow [ˋpɪlo]

名 枕頭

用法 pillow talk （情人間的）枕邊細語

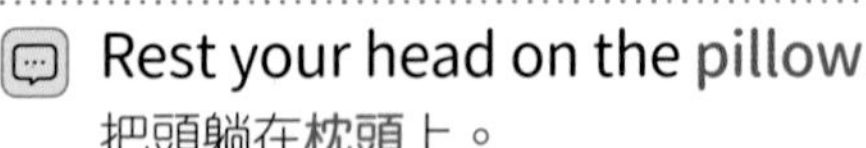

Rest your head on the pillow.
把頭躺在枕頭上。

P

pin [pɪn]

名 大頭針，別針

用法
ⓐ safety pin [ˋsefti ˏpɪn] 名 安全別針
ⓑ pin 也可當動詞，為「用別針別住」的意思。

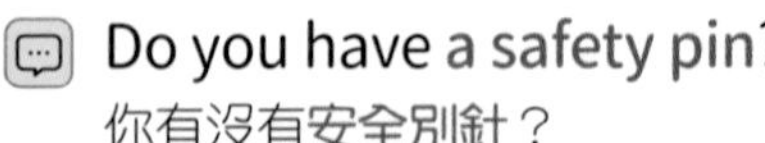

Do you have a safety pin?
你有沒有安全別針？

pineapple [ˋpaɪnˏæpl̩]

名 鳳梨

用法 pineapple juice　鳳梨汁

The pineapple is a tropical fruit.
鳳梨是一種熱帶水果。

pink [pɪŋk]

名 粉紅色　形 粉紅色的

用法 a pink flower　粉紅色的花

Pink is Jane's favorite color.
粉紅色是珍最喜愛的顏色。

pipe [paɪp]

名 管，管子

用法 a gas pipe　瓦斯管
a water pipe　水管

We should change the old water pipe.　我們應該換掉這根舊水管。

A B C D E F G H I J K L M N O P Q R S T U V W X Y Z

Pp

pizza [ˋpitsə]

名 披薩

用法
a pizza　一整個披薩
a piece of pizza　一小片披薩

Would you like one more piece of **pizza**?　你要不要再來一片**披薩**？

place [ples]

名 地方　動 放

用法
ⓐ take place　舉行；發生
ⓑ place a book on the desk
　把一本書放在桌上

Let's find a quiet **place** to study.
咱們找個安靜的**地方**讀書吧。

plan [plæn]

名 動 計劃

用法
ⓐ 三態：plan、planned [**plænd**]、planned
ⓑ make a plan　訂定計畫
ⓒ plan to...　計劃 / 打算要……

My sister is **planning** to study abroad this summer.　我姊姊**計劃**今年夏天要出國念書。

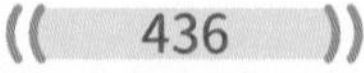

P p

planet [ˋplænɪt]

名 行星

用法 地球、月亮等會轉動的行星均稱為 planet。恆星或天上所有不會移動的星星則稱 star [stɑr]。

Is there life on other planets?
其他行星上有生物嗎？

plain [plen]

形 樸素的

用法 plain 當名詞為「草原」的意思。
Most of the city is built on the plain.
（這城市大部分建在平原上。）

Sally usually wears plain clothes.
莎莉通常穿著樸素。

plant [plænt]

名 植物（尤指盆栽）；工廠　動 種植

用法
ⓐ a power plant　發電廠
ⓑ plant a tree　種一棵樹

Don’t forget to water those plants every morning.　每天早上別忘了要對這些盆栽澆水。

plate [plet]

名 盤子

用法

ⓐ a plate of... 一盤……
ⓑ put food on the plate
把食物放在盤子上

Eliot ate **a whole plate** of French fries. 艾略特吃了一整盤的薯條。

platform [ˋplætˏfɔrm]

名 月臺

用法
platform 還有「舞臺」的意思。
Ella stepped up onto the platform and sang a song. （艾拉走上舞臺，唱了一首歌。）

There are many people waiting for the train **on the platform**. 很多人在月臺上等火車。

play [ple]

動 玩耍；吹奏（樂器）；扮演 名 戲劇

用法
play + 球類運動 打（球）
play the + 樂器 彈奏……
play a role in... 扮演……角色

Tom and his friends plan to **play** in the park after school. 湯姆和他的朋友計劃放學後到公園裡玩耍。

player [ˋpleɚ]

名 球員，選手

用法 a basketball player 籃球員
a baseball player 棒球員

Peter is a very good **basketball player.** 彼得是很優秀的籃球員。

playground

[ˋpleˏgraʊnd]

名 操場；(公園) 遊樂場

用法 a school playground 學校操場

Some children are running around the **playground.** 一些小朋友正繞著操場跑步。

pleasant [ˋplɛzənt]

形 令人愉快的

用法 unpleasant [ʌnˋplɛzn̩t] 形 令人不愉快的

It's **pleasant** to work with Peter. 和彼得共事令人愉快。

please [pliz]

感歎 **請**

用法
ⓐ please 可置於句首或句尾。置於句尾時，之前要加逗點。
ⓑ Please 也可作動詞用，有「取悅；喜歡」的意思。

Sit down, please.
請坐下。

pleased [plizd]

形 **感到滿足的；感到高興的**

用法
be pleased with...　對……很滿意
= be satisfied with...

Ruth is pleased with her job.
露絲很滿意她的工作。

pleasure [ˋplɛʒɚ]

名 **愉快，樂趣**

用法
It's a pleasure to...　……是件樂事
It's a pleasure to talk to you.
（與您談話是件樂事。）

It's a pleasure to meet you, Mr. Johnson.　強森先生，幸會。

plus [plʌs]

介 加

用法 Six plus six is / equals twelve.
六加六等於十二。

Three **plus** two is five.
三加二等於五。

p.m. [ˏpiˋɛm]

副 下午時分

用法 p.m. 也可寫成 pm、P.M. 或 PM。

The train leaves at five **p.m.**
火車將於下午五點發車。

pocket [ˋpɑkɪt]

名 口袋

用法
ⓐ pocket money　零用錢
ⓑ a pocket dictionary
口袋字典，袖珍字典

My father gives me some **pocket money** once a week.　我爸爸一星期發一次零用錢給我。

poem [ˋpoɪm]

名 詩

用法 poetry [ˋpoɪtrɪ] 名 詩
（集合名詞，不可數）
poet [ˋpoɪt] 名 詩人

John is good at **writing poems.**
約翰擅長寫詩。

point [pɔɪnt]

動 指著　名 觀點，要點

用法 ❶ point 表示「指著」時，要與 at 並用。
❷ What's your point?
（你的觀點是什麼？ / 你有什麼觀點？）

Don't **point at** others.
別指著別人。

P

poison [ˋpɔɪzn̩]

名 毒藥　動 使中毒；使汙染

用法 William used poisons to kill mice.
（威廉用毒藥殺老鼠。）

A lot of garbage **poisoned** the river.　大量的垃圾汙染了這條河。

police [pə\`lis]

名 警察們，警方

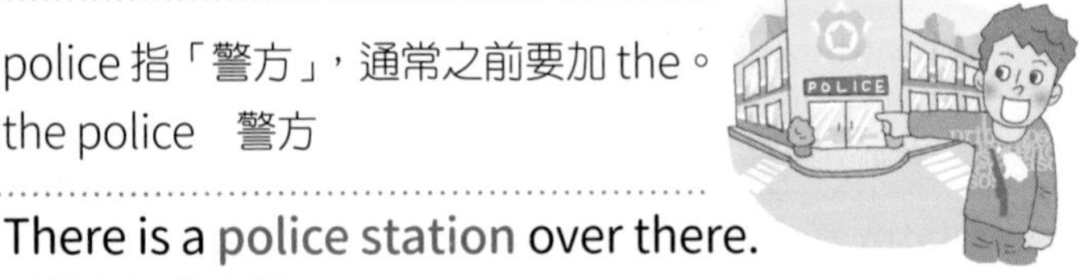

用法 police 指「警方」，通常之前要加 the。
the police　警方

There is a **police station** over there.
那裡有個警察局。

polite [pə\`laɪt]

形 禮貌的

用法 be polite to...　對……有禮貌

We should all be **polite**.
我們大家都要有禮貌。

pollute [pə\`lut]

動 汙染

用法 pollutant [pə\`lutənt] 名 汙染物

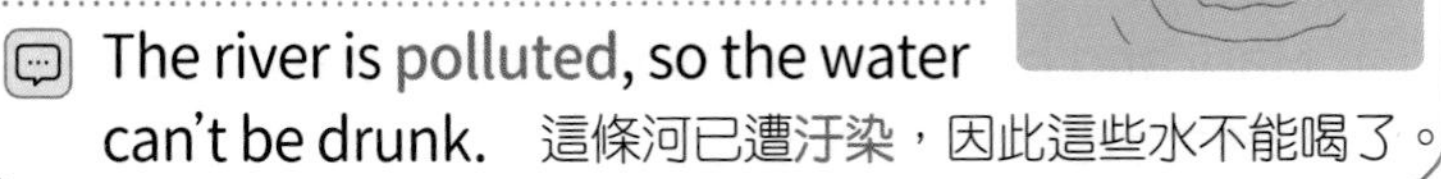

The river is **polluted**, so the water can't be drunk.　這條河已遭汙染，因此這些水不能喝了。

pollution [pə`luʃən]

名 汙染

用法
ⓐ pollution 為不可數。
ⓑ air / noise / water pollution
空氣 / 噪音 / 水汙染

Water pollution is a serious problem in Taiwan. 水汙染在臺灣是個嚴重的問題。

pond [pɑnd]

名 池塘

用法
ⓐ by the pond 在池塘邊
ⓑ in the pond 在池塘裡

It's dangerous to play by the pond.
在池塘邊玩耍很危險。

pool [pul]

名 游泳池；戲水池

用法
「游泳池」的正式說法為 swimming pool [`swɪmɪŋ ˌpul]，但一般均簡稱為 pool。

Mary and her dog are swimming in the pool.
瑪麗和她的狗狗正在水池裡游泳。

poor [pʊr]

形 窮的；可憐的；差勁的

用法 be poor / bad at... 對……不擅長
Eddy is poor at spelling.
（艾迪不擅長拼字。）

Mr. Wei is **poor**, but he is happy.
魏先生很窮，但卻很快樂。

popcorn [ˋpɑpˏkɔrn]

名 爆米花

用法
ⓐ popcorn 為不可數。
ⓑ a bag of popcorn 一袋爆米花
two bags of popcorn 兩袋爆米花

Donald likes to watch a movie and eat **popcorn** at the same time. 唐納德喜歡邊看電影邊吃爆米花。

pop music

[ˏpɑp ˋmjuzɪk]

名 流行樂（不可數）

用法 pop [pɑp] 形 流行的

Does Rose like **pop music**?
蘿絲喜歡流行音樂嗎？

popular [ˋpɑpjələ˞]

形 受歡迎的；流行的

用法 be popular with...　受……的歡迎
John is nice, so he is popular with us.
（約翰人很好，因此他很受我們歡迎。）

Baseball is **popular** in Taiwan.
棒球在臺灣很盛行。

population

名 人口　[ˏpɑpjəˋleʃən]

用法 have a population of + 數字
擁有……人口

The city **has a population of** over 4 million.　該市的人口有四百多萬。

pork [pɔrk]

名 豬肉

用法 pork 為不可數。

Daphne doesn’t eat **pork**. She eats fish.　達芙妮不吃豬肉。她吃魚。

position [pəˋzɪʃən]

名 位置；職位，職缺

用法 Can you find our position on the map?
（你可以在地圖上找到我們的位置嗎？）

Sorry, the position is already filled.
對不起，這個職缺已經補上了。

positive [ˋpɑzətɪv]

形 肯定的；積極的

用法 ⓐ negative [ˋnɛgətɪv] 形 否定的；消極的
ⓑ Vince doesn't give me a positive answer.
（文斯沒有給我一個肯定的答案。）

Polly thinks positive action is necessary. 波莉認為積極的行動是有必要的。

possible [ˋpɑsəbl̩]

形 可能的

用法 It is possible that... 可能……

Is it possible that John will come?
約翰可能會來嗎？

post office [`post ˏɔfɪs]

名 郵局

用法 post 原指「郵政」，這個字也可作動詞用，表示「郵寄」之意。

Danny went to the **post office** to mail a letter. 丹尼到郵局寄了封信。

postcard [`post ˏkɑrd]

名 明信片

用法 send a postcard to + sb
寄一張明信片給某人

Do they sell **postcards** at the post office? 郵局有賣明信片嗎？

pot [pɑt]

名 鍋

用法 pot 指用來煮飯或燉肉的深鍋。
pan [pæn] 指煎蛋用的平底鍋中
炒菜鍋則稱作 wok [wɑk]。

We can cook rice in the **pot**.
我們可以用鍋子煮飯。

potato [pə`teto]

名 馬鈴薯

用法 ⓐ 複數則為 potatoes。
ⓑ a couch potato
成天坐在沙發上看電視的人

Would you like some more potato chips? 你還要些馬鈴薯片嗎？

pound [paʊnd]

名 磅（重量單位）；英鎊（貨幣單位）

用法 pound 也可作動詞，表示「猛敲」。
Somebody is pounding the door.
（有人在猛力敲門。）

The meat costs two dollars a pound. 這些肉一磅要賣兩塊錢。

powder [`paʊdɚ]

名 粉末

用法 cocoa powder 可可粉

Milk is sold in both liquid and powder forms.
牛奶以液體和粉末兩種型態出售。

P p

power [ˋpaʊɚ]

名 權力；電力

用法 power failure　停電
（failure [ˋfeljɚ] 名 故障；失敗）

Dad has a lot of **power** in his office.
爸爸在他辦公室裡很有權力。

practice [ˋpræktɪs]

名 動 練習

用法 practice to sing / to dance (×)
→ practice singing / dancing (○)
練習唱歌 / 跳舞

P

Willy **practices** speaking English every day.　威利每天練習說英語。

praise [prez]

動 稱讚　名 讚美（不可數）

用法 be praised for...　因……受到讚美
Jack was praised for his courage.
（傑克因為他的勇氣而受到讚美。）

Peggy should give her children more **praise**.
佩姬應該給她的孩子多一點讚美。

pray [pre]

動 祈禱

用法 pray for + sb　為某人祈禱

Mary prays before she goes to bed every night.　瑪麗每晚睡前都會禱告。

prepare [prɪˋpɛr]

動 準備；料理（食物）

用法
- ⓐ prepare for a test　準備考試
- ⓑ prepare breakfast / lunch / dinner 準備早 / 午 / 晚餐

Mom is preparing dinner now.
媽媽現在正在準備晚餐。

precious [ˋprɛʃəs]

形 珍貴的

用法
a precious gift　珍貴的禮物
a precious memory　珍貴的回憶

We are wasting our precious time waiting here.　我們在這裡等待是在浪費寶貴時間。

present [ˋprɛznt]

名 禮物　形 到場的，出席的

用法
ⓐ buy + sb + a present　買份禮物給某人
ⓑ Wesley was present at the meeting.
（衛斯理出席了這次的會議。）

Dad bought me a present for my birthday.　爸爸買了一份生日禮物給我。

president [ˋprɛzədənt]

名 總統；大學校長；董事長

用法 preside [prɪˋsaɪd] 動 主持（會議）

The US President is visiting Japan this Friday.　本週五美國總統將訪問日本。

pressure [ˋprɛʃɚ]

名 壓力

用法
put pressure on sb
對某人施加壓力

I didn't put any pressure on Vic.
我並沒有對維克施加任何壓力。

pretty [ˋprɪtɪ]

形 漂亮的（= beautiful） 副 挺，滿

用法 pretty 表示「挺、滿」，程度比 very（很）稍低。
It's very hot today. （今天天氣很熱。）
It's pretty hot today. （今天天氣滿熱的。）

Your sister is pretty.
你妹妹很漂亮。

price [praɪs]

名 價格

用法 price 也有「代價」的意思。
pay a price for... 付出……的代價

The price is too high. Do you have anything cheaper? 這個價錢太貴了。你有沒有便宜一點的？

priest [prist]

名（天主教）神父；（基督教）牧師

用法 minister [ˋmɪnəstɚ] 名 牧師
pastor [ˋpæstɚ] 名 牧師

Wayne made up his mind to be a priest.
韋恩決心要當牧師。

primary [ˋpraɪˏmɛrɪ]

形 主要的；基本的

用法 primary school　小學
= elementary school

My daughter will go to **primary school** next year.　我女兒明年就要上小學了。

prince [prɪns]

名 王子

用法 Prince Charming　白馬王子
Who's your Prince Charming?
（誰是妳心中的白馬王子呀？）

The **prince** and Cinderella finally got married.　王子跟灰姑娘終於結婚了。

princess [ˋprɪnsɛs]

名 公主

用法 童話故事中最有名的公主當屬白雪公主。
「白雪公主」在英文中稱作 Snow White。

The **princess** is really pretty.
這位公主真美。

principal [ˋprɪnsəpḷ]

名 中、小學校長

用法 表示「大學校長」則使用 president 一字。

Mr. Hill is the principal of the school.
希爾先生是該校校長。

principle [ˋprɪnsəpḷ]

名 原則

用法 in principle　原則上

I agree with Peggy in principle.
我原則上同意佩姬的看法。

print [prɪnt]

動 出版；印　名 出版

用法 out of print　絕版
The book is out of print now.
（這本書已絕版了。）

Would you print it out for me?
你可以幫我把它列印出來嗎？

printer [ˋprɪntɚ]

名 印表機

用法 Would you please add paper to the printer?
（可以麻煩你幫印表機加紙嗎？）

The printer is out of order again.
印表機又故障了。

private [ˋpraɪvɪt]

形 私下的；私立的　名 私下

用法 in private　私下
The boss talked to Jack in private.
（老闆私下和傑克談話。）

Penny teaches in a private school.
佩妮在某私立學校教書。

prize [praɪz]

名 獎賞，獎品

用法 win a prize　得獎
win first / second prize
得首獎 / 貳獎

Peter was happy because he won a big prize.　彼得中了大獎，所以他很高興。

probably [ˋprɑbəblɪ]

副 可能

用法 probable [ˋprɑbəbl̩] 形 很可能的
probability [ˌprɑbəˋbɪlətɪ] 名 可能性

Probably it will rain tomorrow.
明天**可能**會下雨。

produce

[prəˋdjus] 動 生產，製造　[ˋprodjus] 名 農產品

用法 ⓐ produce 當名詞時為不可數。
ⓑ producer [prəˋd(j)usɚ] 名 生產者

We **produce** a lot of garbage every day.　我們每天**製造**大量的垃圾。

production

名 生產　[prəˋdʌkʃən]

用法 speed up production　加速生產

We need to increase our **production**.　我們必須增加**生產**。

Pp

professor [prəˋfɛsɚ]

名 （大學）教授

用法 an associate professor
（大學）副教授

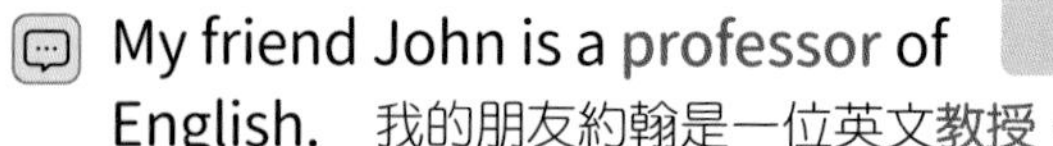

My friend John is a professor of English. 我的朋友約翰是一位英文教授。

problem [ˋprɑbləm]

名 問題

用法 work out a problem 解決問題
= solve a problem
（solve [sɑlv] 動 解決）

Did you finally work out that problem?
你終於解決了那個問題嗎？

program [ˋprogræm]

名 節目；（電腦）程式

用法 watch a program 看節目

There is a good program on TV now. 電視上現在正在播出一個好節目。

P

progress

名 進步（不可數）[ˋprɑgrɛs]

用法
ⓐ make progress　有進步
ⓑ progress 也可當動詞，此時重音在第二音節 [prəˋgrɛs]。

Sally has **made** a lot of **progress** in her English.　莎莉的英語大有進步。

project

[ˋprɑdʒɛkt] 名 計畫　[prəˋdʒɛkt] 動 投射

用法
The first part of the project is completed.
（這個計畫的第一部份已經完成。）

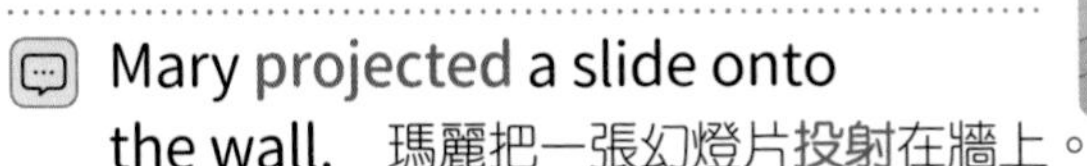
Mary **projected** a slide onto the wall.　瑪麗把一張幻燈片投射在牆上。

promise [ˋprɑmɪs]

名 承諾，諾言　動 承諾，答應

用法
make a promise　作承諾
keep / break one's promise　堅守 / 違背承諾
promise (sb) to + V　承諾（某人）要……

Wesley **promised** me **to** give me a hand.
衛斯理答應會幫我。

Pp

pronounce [prəˋnaʊns]

動 發音

用法 pronunciation [prəˏnʌsɪˋeʃən]
名 發音

How do you pronounce your name?
你的名字怎麼唸？

protect [prəˋtɛkt]

動 保護

用法 protect + sb + from...
保護某人免於……

Parents should protect their children from getting hurt. 父母應該保護孩子不要受傷。

P

proud [praʊd]

形 驕傲的

用法 be proud of...
為……感到驕傲

Edward is very proud of his son.
愛德華很以他兒子為榮。

provide [prə`vaɪd]

動 提供

用法 provide + sb + with + sth
提供某人某物

Phoebe's parents will provide her with everything she needs. 菲比的父母會提供她所需要的每一樣東西。

public [`pʌblɪk]

形 公眾的；公開的 名 公眾；公開

用法
ⓐ the public 公眾，大眾
ⓑ in public 公開地

Do not smoke in public places.
不要在公共場所抽菸。

pull [pʊl]

動 拉；扯

用法
pull the door open 把門拉開
pull one's hair 扯某人頭髮

Don't pull my hair, Johnny.
強尼，別扯我的頭髮。

pump [pʌmp]

名 幫浦　動 抽取；灌注

用法 pump... up / pump up...　將……充氣
First of all, we need to pump up the balloons. （首先，我們必須將汽球充氣。）

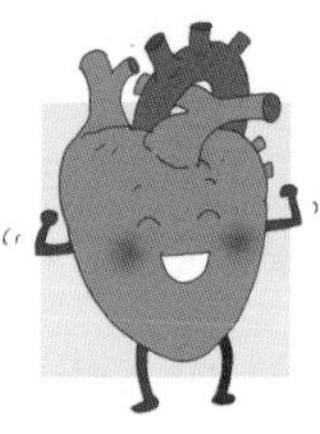

The human heart works like a **pump**.
人類的心臟就像幫浦一樣的運作。

pumpkin [ˋpʌmpkɪn]

名 南瓜

用法 由於南瓜大多是空心的，因此形容某人是笨蛋時會說：He is a pumpkin head.（他是南瓜頭 / 他是笨蛋。）

Mom grows some **pumpkins** in the garden.　媽媽在菜園裡種了一些南瓜。

punish [ˋpʌnɪʃ]

動 處罰

用法 punish sb for + N/V-ing
因……處罰某人

Tim **was punished for** cheating on the exam.　提姆因考試作弊而被處罰。

puppy [ˋpʌpɪ]

名 小狗，哈巴狗

用法 大狗稱作 dog，小型狗或小狗則稱作 puppy。

My pet is a cute **puppy**.
我的寵物是一隻可愛的小狗。

purple [ˋpɝpḷ]

名 紫色　形 紫色的

用法 paint the door purple
把門漆成紫色

Jane looks beautiful in that **purple** dress.　珍穿了那件紫色洋裝真好看。

purpose [ˋpɝpəs]

名 目的，意圖

用法 on purpose　故意
for the purpose of...
為了……的目的

Olivia took a trip to Paris **for the purpose of** learning French.　奧莉薇雅到巴黎去目的是學法文。

purse [pɝs]

名 女用小錢包

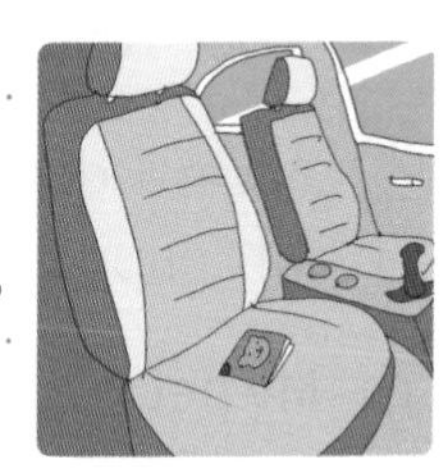

用法 在英式英語中，purse 指女用小錢包，類似男用的皮夾（wallet）。
在美式英語中，purse 就是女用手提包。

Pamela left her purse in the taxi.
潘蜜拉把小錢包掉在計程車上了。

push [pʊʃ]

動 推

用法 push the door open　把門推開

Don't push me!
別推我！

put [pʊt]

動 放

用法
ⓐ 三態同形
ⓐ put down...　把……放下；寫下……

Put the book back on the desk.
把書放回桌上。

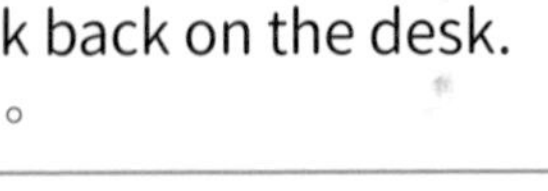

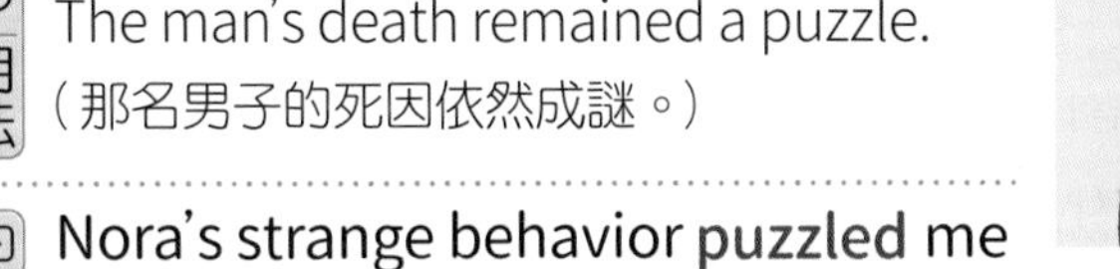

puzzle [ˋpʌzḷ]

動 困惑　名 謎

用法 The man's death remained a puzzle.
（那名男子的死因依然成謎。）

Nora's strange behavior puzzled me for a while. 諾拉的怪異行為讓我困惑了一段時間。

Notes

A B C D E F G H I J K L M N O P Q R S T U V W X Y Z

quarter [ˋkwɔrtɚ]

名 四分之一；十五分鐘；（美金硬幣）二十五分錢

用法
ⓐ cent [sɛnt] 名 一分（美金）
dime [daɪm] 名 十分（美金）
ⓑ It's a quarter past ten.（現在是十點十五分。）

John needs a **quarter** to make a phone call. 約翰需要一枚**二十五分美金**的硬幣打電話。

queen [kwin]

名 皇后；女王

用法
國王則稱作 king [kɪŋ]。

All the people love the **queen**.
所有的百姓都喜歡**皇后**。

question [ˋkwɛstʃən]

名 問題

用法
ⓐ ask + sb + a question　問某人問題
ⓑ answer a question　回答問題

May I **ask** you **a question**?
我可以**問**你**一個問題**嗎？

Q q

quick [kwɪk]

形 動作快的

用法 quick 及 fast 均可表示「快的」，但 quick 指動作或反應方面的「快」，而 fast 則指速度方面的「快」。

You should be **quick**, or you'll be late. 你動作要**快**，否則就會遲到了。

quiet [ˋkwaɪət]

形 安靜的

用法 quiet 也可作動詞，與 down 並用。Quiet down!（安靜下來！）

Be **quiet**. Dad is sleeping. **安靜**。爸爸正在睡覺。

quit [kwɪt]

動 停止；辭去（工作）

用法
ⓐ quit 三態同形。
ⓑ quit smoking 戒菸

Sam **quit** his job and moved to the US last year. 山姆去年**辭職**後搬到美國去了。

A B C D E F G H I J K L M N O P Q R S T U V W X Y Z

quite [kwaɪt]

副 十分，很，相當

用法 quite 接近 very，均表示「很」的意思。
David is quite nice.
（大衛為人相當好。）

It's **quite** cold today.
今天**相當**冷。

quiz [kwɪz]

名 小考

用法 pop quiz　抽考
The teacher gave us a pop quiz yesterday. （昨天老師給我們抽考。）

The teacher gave us a **quiz** this morning.　今天早上老師給我們**小考**。

Notes

rabbit [ˋræbɪt]

名 兔子

用法 bunny [ˋbʌnɪ] 名 小兔子

Rabbits like to eat carrots.
兔子喜歡吃紅蘿蔔。

race [res]

名 賽跑；種族　動 與……賽跑；快速移動

用法
run a race　參加賽跑
win a race　贏了賽跑
rece against time　跟時間賽跑

Daniel runs fast, so I believe he can win the **race**.　丹尼爾跑得很快，因此我相信這次**比賽**他會贏。

radio [ˋredɪˏo]

名 收音機

用法
turn on the radio　打開收音機
turn off the radio　關掉收音機
listen to the radio　聽收音機

Turn on the radio. I want to listen to the news.　**把收音機打開**。我要聽新聞。

A B C D E F G H I J K L M N O P Q R S T U V W X Y Z

railroad [ˋrel͵rod]

名 鐵路

用法 railroad 是美式用法，
railway 為英式用法。

Look around when you cross the railroad tracks. 你穿越鐵路的時候，要看一看四周。

railway [ˋrel͵we]

名 鐵路

用法 the railway station 火車站 [英]
= the train station 火車站 [美]

Do you know where the railway station is? 你知道火車站在哪裡嗎？

rain [ren]

名 雨 動 下雨

用法 ⓐ It looks like rain. （看起來要下雨的樣子。）
ⓑ It's raining cats and dogs.
（正在下大雨。）

It's raining hard now.
現在正在下大雨。

rainbow [ˋren,bo]

名 彩虹

用法 a rainbow above the hill
小山丘頂上的一道彩虹

Cheryl sees a rainbow above the hill. 雪瑞兒看到**山頂上方有一道彩虹**。

raincoat [ˋren,kot]

名 雨衣

用法 rain boots　雨靴 / 鞋
（因為通常是一雙，故常用複數。）

It's raining outside. Don't forget to wear a raincoat.　外面在下雨。別忘了要穿**雨衣**。

rainy [ˋrenɪ]

形 下雨的，雨天的

用法 ⓐ rainy 表示「下雨的」，raining 表示「正在下雨」。
ⓑ a rainy day　雨天（非 a raining day）

Dennis hates rainy days.
丹尼斯討厭**雨天**。

raise [rez]

動 舉起；募集（錢）；撫養；養殖

用法
ⓐ 舉起：raise your hand　舉手
ⓑ 撫養：raise a big family　撫養一個大家庭
ⓒ 養殖：raise pigs　養豬

Dana is **raising money** for poor people.　黛娜正在為清寒人士**募款**。

rare [rɛr]

形 稀少的；煮得嫩的

用法
I'd like my steak rare / medium / well-done.
（我希望我的牛排三分熟 / 五分熟 / 全熟。）

It's **rare** for Doug to be on time.
道格**極少**準時。

rat [ræt]

名 田鼠

用法
rat 指野外的「田鼠」，體型較大，而 mouse [maʊs] 則指「家鼠」，體型較小。

A **rat** is larger than a mouse.
田鼠比家鼠大。

rather [ˋræðɚ]

副 相當地；寧願（與 would 並用）

用法 would rather + V + than + V　寧願……也不願……
Amy would rather stay at home than go out.
（艾咪寧願待在家裡也不要出去。）

It's **rather** hot today.
今天**相當**熱。

reach [ritʃ]

動 到達；伸手去摸

用法 Linda can reach the bank in ten minutes.
= Linda can get to the bank in ten minutes.
（琳達可以在十分鐘後抵達銀行。）

Tommy is too short to **reach** the doorbell.　湯米太矮，按不**到**門鈴。

read [rid]

動 閱讀；唸

用法 ⓐ 三態：read [rid]、read [rɛd]、read [rɛd]
ⓑ read a book　看一本書
read a story to + sb　唸故事給某人聽

Johnny loves to **read storybooks.**
強尼喜歡**看故事書**。

ready [ˋrɛdɪ]

形 **準備好的**

用法 Are you ready to take the test?
= Are you ready for the test?
（你考試準備好了嗎？）

Are you ready to go now?
你現在**準備好**要走了嗎？

real [ˋrɪəl]

形 **真的**

用法 real 及 true 均表示「真的」，real 多指「真的東西」，而 true 則多指「真實的故事」。

Don't touch it. It's a **real** snake.
別碰牠。牠是**真的**蛇。

realize [ˋrɪəˏlaɪz]

動 **了解；實現**

用法 realize one's dream
實現某人的夢想

Finally, Dan **realized** that he was wrong.
丹終於**了解**到他錯了。

really [ˋrɪəlɪ]

副 真正地

用法 really 也可用在問句中，表示「真的嗎？」。
A: I passed the test.（A：我考及格了。）
B: Really?（B：真的嗎？）

Paul is **really** a nice guy.
保羅**實在**是個好人。

reason [ˋrizn̩]

名 理由　動 理論

用法 reason with + sb　與某人講理
It's hard to reason with such a stubborn man.（跟這麼固執的人講理很難。）

Do you know the **reason** why Chelsea quit her job?　你知道雀兒喜辭職的**原因**嗎？

receive [rɪˋsiv]

動 收到；接待

用法 Luke received his guests as they arrived at the dinner party.
（客人來到晚宴時，路克去迎接他們。）

Have you **received** Eddy's letter?
你**收到**艾迪的信了嗎？

record

[rɪˋkɔrd] 動 記錄；錄音　[ˋrɛkɚd] 名 紀錄；唱片

用法
make a record　創紀錄
keep the record　保持紀錄
break the record　破紀錄

Jenny recorded every dollar she spent. 珍妮把她花掉的每塊錢全都**記錄**下來。

recorder [rɪˋkɔrdɚ]

名 錄音機

用法
錄音機的正式說法為 tape recorder。
Put the tape into the recorder.
（把錄音帶放到錄音機內。）

My uncle bought me a tape recorder.
我叔叔買了一臺**錄音機**給我。

recover [rɪˋkʌvɚ]

動 恢復

用法
recover from...　從……中復元

Dave is recovering from the flu.
戴夫的流行性感冒快要**痊癒**了。

rectangle [ˋrɛktæŋgl̩]

名 長方形

用法 square [skwɛr] 名 正方形
circle [ˋsɝkl̩] 名 圓
triangle [ˋtraɪˏæŋgl̩] 名 三角形

The table is a rectangle in shape.
這個餐桌是**長方形**的。

recycle [ˏriˋsaɪkl̩]

動 回收，再利用

用法 Waste paper can be recycled into toilet tissue.
（廢紙可以回收製成衛生紙。）

Old newspapers can be recycled.
舊報紙可以**回收再利用**。

red [rɛd]

名 紅色　形 紅色的

用法 run the red light（開車）闖紅燈
Don't run the red light when you drive.
（你開車時不要闖紅燈。）

That red car is expensive.
那輛**紅色的**車很貴。

refrigerator

[rɪˋfrɪdʒəˌretɚ]

名 電冰箱

用法 也可用 fridge [frɪdʒ] 取代。

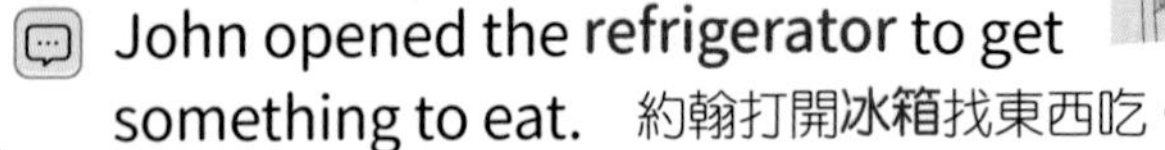

John opened the **refrigerator** to get something to eat. 約翰打開**冰箱**找東西吃。

refuse [rɪˋfjuz]

動 拒絕

用法 refuse to V 拒絕做……

Christina **refused to** do the work.
克莉絲汀娜**拒絕做**這工作。

regret [rɪˋgrɛt]

名 動 後悔；遺憾

用法
ⓐ 三態：regret、regretted [rɪˋgrɛtɪd]、regretted
ⓑ regret + V-ing 後悔曾……
regret to + V 遺憾要……，抱歉要……

I **regret to** tell you that you are fired.
我很**抱歉要**通知你，你被開除了。

Rr

regular [ˋrɛgjələ˞]

形 規律的

用法
on a regular basis　定期
a regular customer　常客

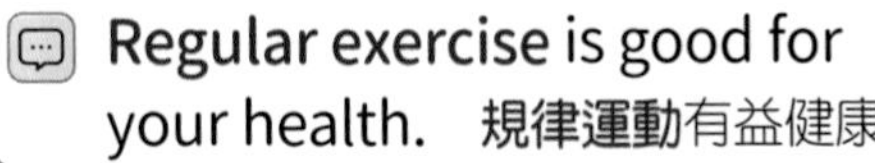

Regular exercise is good for your health.　規律運動有益健康。

reject [rɪˋdʒɛkt]

動 拒絕

用法
rejection [rɪˋdʒɛkʃən]
名 拒絕；排斥

Do you think the boss will **reject** my suggestion?　你認為老闆會**拒絕**我的建議嗎？

relative [ˋrɛlətɪv]

名 親戚

用法
relative 當形容詞用時為「相對的」意思。
be relative to...
與……相應的；與……有關聯

John isn't my **relative**. He is just a friend of mine.　約翰不是我的**親戚**。他只是我的一位朋友。

A B C D E F G H I J K L M N O P Q **R** S T U V W X Y Z

remember

動 記得 [rɪˋmɛmbɚ]

用法 Remember me to your parents.
（代我向你爸媽問好。）

The old man can't **remember** his own name. 這位老伯伯**記**不**得**自己的名字了。

remind [rɪˋmaɪnd]

動 使想起；提醒

用法 remind + sb + of... 使某人想起……
remind + sb + to + V 提醒某人……

This old house **reminds** me **of** my childhood. 這間老房子讓我**想起**我的童年。

rent [rɛnt]

名 租金 動 出租

用法 for rent 出租
This house is not for rent.
（這棟房子不出租。）

What's the **rent** for this house?
這棟房子的**租金**多少？

repair [rɪ`pɛr]

名 動 修理

用法 get sth repaired　將某物送修
Bruce has to get his computer repaired.（布魯斯必須將電腦送修。）

The car is in need of **repair**.
那輛車需要**修理**了。

repeat [rɪ`pit]

動 重複

用法 Repeat after me.
（跟著我唸。）

"**Repeat after me**," the teacher said.
老師說：「**跟著我唸**。」

report [rɪ`pɔrt]

名 報告　動 報告，敘述

用法 report to sb　向某人報告
If you see anything unusual, report it to me.
（你若看到任何不尋常的事就向我報告。）

Our teacher asked us to write a **report** on animals.　我們的老師要我們寫一篇關於動物的**報告**。

reporter [rɪˋpɔrtɚ]

名 記者

用法 reporter 源自 report [rɪˋpɔrt]（報導）一字。
report news　報導新聞

The TV reporter is reporting news.
這位電視**記者**正在報導新聞。

respect [rɪˋspɛkt]

名 動 尊敬

用法 show respect for...　向……表示敬意
Students should show respect for their teachers.（學生應該尊敬老師。）

Bonnie respects Peter as a hero.
邦妮把彼得**尊**為英雄。

responsible

形 負責任的　[rɪˋspɑnsəbḷ]

用法 be responsible for...　為……負責

Chuck has to be responsible for what he did.　查克應**為**他的所作所為**負責**。

rest [rɛst]

名 休息；其餘部分　動 休息

用法
ⓐ take a rest　休息
ⓑ the rest　剩餘部分

Evan is tired. He needs to take a rest.　伊凡累了，需要**休息**一下。

restaurant [ˋrɛstrɑnt]

名 餐廳

用法
Let's eat out tonight.
（咱們今晚到外頭餐廳用餐吧。）
沒有 restaurant，卻有表示「去餐廳用餐之意。」

Let's go to that **restaurant** for dinner.　咱們到那家**餐廳**吃晚飯吧。

restroom [ˋrɛstˏrum]

名 洗手間，廁所

用法
restroom 指公共場所的廁所；家中則稱作 bathroom [ˋbæθˏrum]。均可用 toilet [ˋtɔɪlɪt] 代替（toilet 原指「馬桶」）。

Excuse me. Where is the **restroom**?
不好意思，**廁所**在哪裡？

A B C D E F G H I J K L M N O P Q R S T U V W X Y Z

result [rɪˋzʌlt]

名 結果，後果

用法 as a result of... = because of...　由於……
Millions of people died as a result of the pandemic.（數百萬人因該大流行病而死亡。）

Can you tell me the final **result**?
你可以告訴我最後的**結果**嗎？

return [rɪˋtɝn]

動 返回；歸還　名 回報

用法
ⓐ in return for...　回報……
ⓑ return home　返家

Do not forget to **return** the books by five.　不要忘記在五點以前**歸還**那些書。

review [rɪˋvju]

名 動 複習；評論

用法 review for a test / an exam　為考試來複習
Nina has to review for the math exam.
（妮娜必須複習數學考試。）

Don't forget to **review** the lessons.
不要忘記**複習**功課。

revise [rɪˋvaɪz]

動 修正；校訂

用法 correct [kəˋrɛkt] 動 改正

The book has been **revised** five times. 這本書已經**修正**五次了。

rice [raɪs]

名 米；米飯（不可數）

用法 a bowl of rice　一碗飯
（bowl [bol] 名 碗）

John doesn't like to eat **rice**.
約翰不喜歡吃**米飯**。

rich [rɪtʃ]

形 富有的；豐富的

用法 be rich in...　含有豐富的……
This fruit is rich in vitamin C.
（這個水果含有豐富的維他命 C。）

The **rich man** has five cars.
這個**有錢人**有五輛車。

ride [raɪd]

名 動 騎；乘

用法
- ⓐ 三態：ride、rode [rod]、ridden [ˋrɪdn̩]
- ⓑ ride a horse / bicycle　騎馬 / 騎自行車
- ⓒ give sb a ride　搭便車

Can Elmer **ride a horse**?
艾爾瑪會**騎馬**嗎？

right [raɪt]

形 對的　名 權利；右邊　副 向右

用法
- ⓐ 權利：You have no right to do it.
（你沒有權利做這件事。）
- ⓑ 向右：Turn right.（向右轉。）

The answer is not **right**. Try again.
這個答案不**對**，再試一下。

ring [rɪŋ]

名 鈴聲；戒指　動（鈴聲）響起

用法
- ⓐ 三態：ring、rang [ræŋ]、rung
- ⓑ Thank you for giving me this ring.
（謝謝你送我這枚戒指。）

The telephone is **ringing**.
Go answer it.　電話鈴在**響**。去接一下。

rise [raɪz]

名 動 升起；增加；起來

用法 ⓐ 三態：rise、rose [roz]、risen [ˋrɪzn̩]
ⓑ 起床：I rise at seven every morning.
（我每天早上七點起床。）

Look! The sun is rising.
瞧！太陽正在**升起**。

river [ˋrɪvɚ]

名 河流

用法 riverside [ˋrɪvɚˏsaɪd] 名 河邊
river bank [ˋrɪvɚ ˏbæŋk] 名 河岸

Elaine sees some fish in the river.
伊蓮看到**河裡**有幾條魚。

road [rod]

名 路

用法 ⓐ The road leads to... 這條路通往……
ⓑ on the road 在路上

The **road** leads to our school.
這條**路**通往我們學校。

rob [rɑb]

動 搶劫

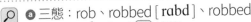

用法
- ⓐ 三態：rob、robbed [rɑbd]、robbed
- ⓑ robber [ˋrɑbɚ] 名 搶匪
- ⓒ rob + sb + of + sth　搶了某人某物

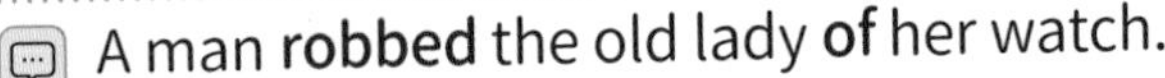

A man **robbed** the old lady **of** her watch.
一名男子**搶走**了老太太的手錶。

robot [ˋrobɑt]

名 機器人

用法 robot 也可指「像機器一樣呆板的人」。

Some **robots** can talk and walk.
有些**機器人**會講話，也會走路。

R.O.C.

名 中華民國

用法 republic [rɪˋpʌblɪk] 名 共和國

R.O.C. stands for the Republic of China.　**R.O.C.** 代表「中華民國」。

rock [rɑk]

名 岩石；搖滾樂　動 搖晃

用法 某個計畫進行很順利，而小明卻愛干預搗蛋，這時我們就可說：Don't rock the boat!（不要搖晃小船——喻「勿興風作浪」。）

Watch out! There is a big **rock** on the road.　小心！路上有一顆大**石頭**。

role [rol]

名 角色

用法 play an important role in...
在……方面扮演重要的角色

Parents **play an important role in** their children's education.　父母親**在**孩子的教育**方面扮演重要的角色**。

roll [rol]

動 滾動　名 一卷；名冊

用法
ⓐ roll up / down the window
把（車）窗搖起來 / 下來
ⓑ call / take the roll　點名

The ball **rolled down** into the pond.
球**向下滾**，滾到池塘裡。

roller skate

[ˋrolɚ ˏsket]

名 四輪溜冰鞋　動 溜冰

用法 roller blades　直排溜冰鞋

My father bought me a pair of roller skates.　我爸爸買了一雙溜冰鞋給我。

roof [ruf]

名 屋頂

用法 under one's roof　住在某人的家裡
When you're under my roof, you follow my rules.（你住我家時，就要遵守我的規定。）

The roof is leaking again.
屋頂又漏水了。

room [rum]

名 房間

用法 我的房間很亂時，爸爸就會說：
Keep your room in order.
（把你的房間弄整齊。）

Someone is crying in the room.
房間裡有人在哭泣。

root [rut]

名 根；根源

用法 by the roots　連根；從根本
The big tree was pulled up by the roots.（那棵大樹被連根拔起。）

The tree has deep roots.
這棵樹的根很深。

rope [rop]

名 繩子

用法 jump rope　跳繩
（非 jump the rope）

Let's jump rope after class.
我們下課後來跳繩吧。

rose [roz]

名 玫瑰花

用法 a rose　一朵玫瑰花
a bunch of roses　一束玫瑰花
（bunch [bʌntʃ] 名 束）

Mary loves red roses.
瑪麗喜歡紅玫瑰。

round [raʊnd]

形 圓的

用法
a round table　圓桌
a square table　方桌

Jane has a **round** face.
珍有一張**圓圓的**臉。

row [ro]

名 一排　動 划（船）

用法
ⓐ sit in a row　坐成一排
ⓑ row a boat　划船

The three little boys are **sitting in a row.**　這三個小男孩正**並排坐著**。

rub [rʌb]

動 擦掉　名 摩擦

用法
ⓐ 三態：rub、rubbed [rʌbd]、rubbed
ⓑ rub salt into the wound
在傷口上灑鹽，雪上加霜

Chris **rubbed** the dust off his shoes.
克里斯把鞋子上的灰塵**擦掉**。

rubber [ˋrʌbɚ]

名 橡膠

用法 a rubber band　橡皮筋

The shoes are made of **rubber**.
這雙鞋是**橡膠**做的。

rude [rud]

形 粗魯的，不禮貌的

用法 rude manners　無禮

It's **rude** to keep people waiting.
讓人家久候是**不禮貌的**。

ruin [ˋruɪn]

動 破壞，毀壞

用法 ruin 當名詞用時有「廢墟、毀壞」的意思。
be / lie in ruins　淪為廢墟

Calvin is **ruining** everybody's fun.
卡文**破壞**了大家的興致。

rule [rul]

名 規則，規定　動 統治

用法
ⓐ follow the rules　遵守規定
ⓑ rule the country　統治國家

Everyone should follow the **rules**.
每個人都應**遵守規定**。

ruler [ˋrulɚ]

名 尺；統治者

用法
draw a line with a ruler
用一把尺畫線

The boy used a **ruler** to draw a straight line.
這個男孩用一把尺畫了一條直線。

run [rʌn]

動 跑；經營

用法
ⓐ 三態：run、ran [ræn]、run
ⓑ run away　逃跑
ⓒ run a restaurant　經營餐廳

John **runs** faster than I.
約翰**跑**得比我快。

rush [rʌʃ]

名 動 匆忙，趕時間

用法 be in a rush 匆忙

There's no need to rush.
不需要這麼匆忙。

Notes

sad [sæd]

形 傷心的，難過的

用法 It is sad to know... 知道……令人難過
It is sad to know that Ted didn't pass the test.（知道泰德考不及格令人難過。）

Linda **feels sad** every time she hears the song. 琳達每次聽到這首歌都會**感到難過**。

safe [sef]

形 安全的

用法 It is safe to... （從事）……很安全
It isn't safe to swim in the river.
（在河裡游泳不安全。）

Don't worry. You are **safe** now.
別擔心。你現在很**安全**。

safety [ˋseftɪ]

名 安全

用法
ⓐ safty 為不可數。
ⓑ for safety's sake 為了安全起見

For your own safety, do not smoke in here. **為了您自身的安全**，請不要在這裡抽菸。

sail [sel]

名（船的）帆　動 航行

用法
ⓐ sail across the ocean
乘船橫渡海洋
ⓑ sail for + 地方　航往某地

The boat will sail for Kaohsiung tomorrow.　這艘船明天會**開往**高雄。

sailor [ˋselɚ]

名 水手

用法
a good / bad sailor
不會暈船 / 會暈船的人

The life of a sailor must be very interesting.　**水手**的生活想必很有趣。

salad [ˋsæləd]

名 沙拉，生菜

用法
have salad for breakfast / lunch / dinner　早餐 / 中餐 / 晚餐吃沙拉
（此處的 for 表示「當作」。）

My sister always has salad for lunch.　我姊姊**中餐**一向都**吃生菜沙拉**。

sale [sel]

名 販售；拍賣

用法
ⓐ for sale 出售
ⓑ have a sale 舉行大拍賣 / 促銷

There is a big sale at that department store. 那家百貨公司正在舉行大拍賣。

salesman [ˋselzmən]

名 男推銷員

用法
ⓐ saleswoman 名 女推銷員
ⓑ salesperson 名 推銷員（男或女）

The salesman sells toy cars.
這位推銷員是賣玩具車的。

salt [sɔlt]

名 鹽

用法
salty [ˋsɔltɪ] 形 鹹的

Pass me the salt, please.
請把鹽罐遞給我。

same [sem]

形 相同的

用法 the same... as...　和……相同的……
I have the same toy as yours.
（我有一個跟你的一樣玩具。）

The two runners arrived at the same time.　這兩名跑者同時到達。

sample [ˋsæmpl̩]

名 樣品

用法 The supermarket gives customers samples of food every day.
（此超市每天都給客人提供試吃。）

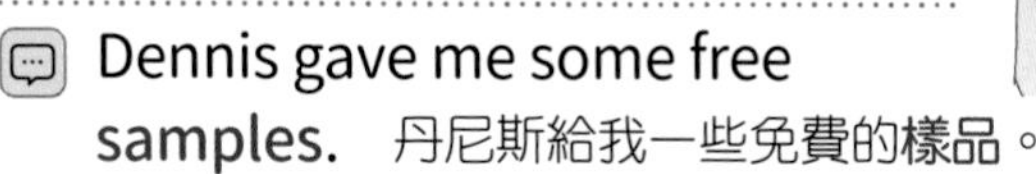

Dennis gave me some free samples.　丹尼斯給我一些免費的樣品。

sand [sænd]

名 沙

用法 a grain of sand　一粒沙
bury / have one's head in the sand　持鴕鳥心態

Many children are playing in the sand.　許多孩子在玩沙。

sandwich [ˋsæn(d)wɪtʃ]

名 三明治

用法
a ham sandwich　火腿三明治
a club sandwich　總匯三明治
a tuna sandwich　鮪魚三明治

Mom is making **sandwiches** for us.
媽媽正在為我們做**三明治**。

satisfy [ˋsætɪsfaɪ]

動 使滿意

用法
ⓐ 三態：satisfy、satisfied [ˋsætɪsfaɪd]、satisfied
ⓑ be satisfied with...　對……很滿意

Eddy is **not satisfied with** my answer.　艾迪不**滿意**我的答案。

Saturday [ˋsætɚde]

名 星期六

用法
on Saturday　星期六那一天
last / next Saturday　上 / 下星期六
every Saturday　每個星期六

Every Saturday Nina goes hiking with her parents.　妮娜**每個星期六**都會跟爸媽去健行。

saucer [ˋsɔsɚ]

名 小碟

用法 a flying saucer　飛碟

Put your teacup on the **saucer**.
把你的茶杯放在**碟子**上。

save [sev]

動 拯救；節省

用法
ⓐ save time　省時
save money　存錢
ⓑ save a life　救一條命

Vic wants to **save money** to buy a computer.　維克要**存錢**買一部電腦。

say [se]

動 說

用法
ⓐ 三態：say、said [sɛd]、said
ⓑ says 要唸成 [sɛz]，不要唸成 [sez]。

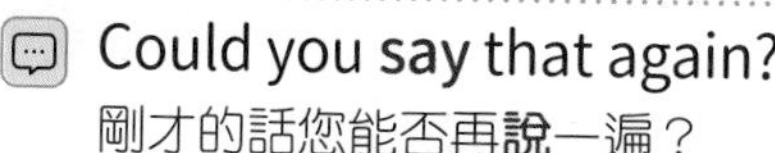

Could you **say** that again?
剛才的話您能否再**說**一遍？

scared [skɛrd]

形 感到害怕的

用法 be scared of... 害怕……
= be afraid of...

The strong boy is scared of nothing.
這個強壯的小子什麼都不怕。

scarf [skɑrf]

名 圍巾

用法 複數形為 scarves [skɑrvz]
或 scarfs [skɑrfs]。

The girl is wearing a scarf around her neck. 這女孩圍了一條圍巾在脖子上。

scene [sin]

名 景觀，景色；(事件的) 現場

用法 at / on the scene (of sth)
在 (某事件的) 現場

We have a lot of beautiful scenes in Taiwan. 臺灣有許多美麗的風景。

scenery [ˋsinərɪ]

名 風景

用法
- ⓐ scenery 為集合名詞不可數。
- ⓑ a lot of scenery　許多風景

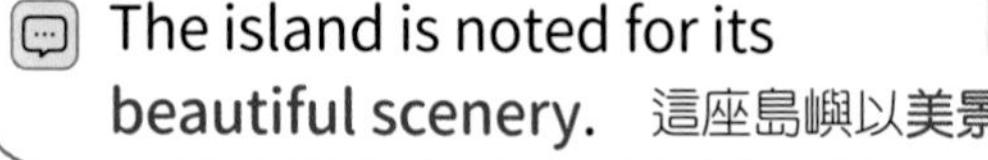

The island is noted for its beautiful scenery.　這座島嶼以美景聞名。

school [skul]

名 學校；魚群

用法
- ⓐ go to school　上學
- ⓑ a school of fish　一群魚

Simon goes to school every day.
賽門每天都會去上學。

scientist [ˋsaɪəntɪst]

名 科學家

用法
scientific [ˌsaɪənˋtɪfɪk]
形 科學的；合乎科學的

My son's dream is to become a famous scientist.　我兒子的夢想是成為知名的科學家。

science [ˋsaɪəns]

名 科學

用法 我們常說的「科技」源自英文的 science and technology。
（technology [tɛkˋnɑlədʒɪ] 名 技術）

Emily is not interested in **science**.
艾蜜莉對**科學**不感興趣。

scooter [ˋskutɚ]

名 輕型機車

用法
ⓐ 輪子較大的重型機車則稱作 motorcycle 或 motorbike。
ⓑ ride a scooter / motorcycle　騎機車

There are many **scooters** in the city.　城市裡有許多**輕型機車**。

score [skɔr]

名 得分；比數　動 得分；進球

用法 The final score was 4-3.
（最後的比數是四比三。）

No one **scored** in the first half.
上半場沒有人**進球**。

screen [skrin]

名 （電影）銀幕；（電視）螢光幕

用法 on the screen　在銀幕 / 螢光幕上

The movie star **on the screen** looks beautiful.　**銀幕上**的那位電影明星模樣真美。

sea [si]

名 海

用法 in the sea　在海裡

There are different fish **in the sea**.
海裡有各種魚類。

seafood [ˋsi͵fud]

名 海鮮

用法 seafood 為不可數。

Eating too much **seafood** makes Chloe feel sick.　吃太多**海鮮**讓克洛伊噁心。

Ss

search [sɝtʃ]

名 動 **搜尋，尋找**

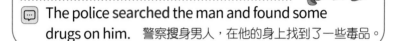

用法 be in search of...　尋找……
= be searching for...

The police searched the man and found some drugs on him.　警察搜身男人，在他的身上找到了一些毒品。

season [ˋsizn̩]

名 **季節**

用法 be in season　（水果）正值盛產季的
Apples are in season now.
（蘋果正值盛產季。）

Spring is Mary's favorite season.
春天是瑪麗最愛的季節。

S

seat [sit]

名 **座位**

用法 客人來訪時，我們可以禮貌地說：
Take a seat, please.
= Have a seat, please.　（請坐。）

Excuse me. Is this seat taken?
不好意思。這個座位有人坐嗎？

second [ˋsɛkənd]

名 第二；秒　形 第二的

用法
ⓐ come in first / second / third...
得第一名 / 第二名 / 第三名……
ⓑ in a second / minute / moment　稍後

John came in second in the race.
約翰這次賽跑得了第二名。

secondary [ˋsɛkən͵dɛrɪ]

形 中等的（學校）；次要的

用法
be secondary to...　與……相比是次要的
All things are secondary to my studies.
（跟課業相比，其它都是次要的。）

Darren teaches Chinese at a secondary school.　達倫在某中學教中文。

secret [ˋsikrɪt]

形 祕密的　名 祕密；祕訣

用法
keep... secret　將……守密
Keep this plan secret.
（這個計畫要守密。）

The place is like a secret garden.　這個地方像是個祕密花園。

Ss

secretary [ˋsɛkrə͵tɛrɪ]

名 祕書

用法 work as a secretary　擔任祕書

My sister is a secretary.
我姊姊是**祕書**。

section [ˋsɛkʃən]

名 部門；（報紙的）版面

用法 Who takes charge of this section?
（誰主管這個部門？）

When Harry gets the newspaper, he reads the sports section first.　哈利拿到報紙時，會先看**體育版**。

S

see [si]

動 看

用法
ⓐ 三態：see、saw [sɔ]、seen [sin]
ⓑ see：無意間看見　watch：注意看
look at：盯著看

I saw John five minutes ago.
五分鐘前我**見**到了約翰。

seed [sid]

名 種子

用法 plant seeds　播種

The farmers are planting seeds.
這些農夫正在**播種**。

seek [sik]

動 尋找

用法 三態：seek、sought [sɔt]、sought

Herman has been seeking a job for three months.　赫曼**找工作**已經找了三個月了。

seem [sim]

動 似乎是；看起來

用法 seem (to be) + Adj　似乎是……
Dora seems very happy with her new boss.（朵拉似乎很滿意她的新老闆。）

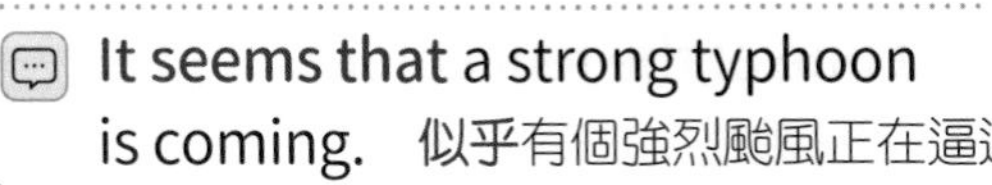

It seems that a strong typhoon is coming.　似乎有個強烈颱風正在逼近。

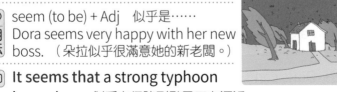

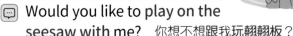

Ss

seesaw [ˋsi͵sɔ]

名 **翹翹板**

用法 play on the seesaw with + sb
與某人玩翹翹板

Would you like to play on the seesaw with me? 你想不想跟我玩翹翹板？

seldom [ˋsɛldəm]

副 **很少，不常**

用法 seldom 是 often [ˋɔfən]（經常）的反義詞。

I seldom call my grandfather, but he often calls me. 我很少打電話給我爺爺，不過他卻常打給我。

S

select [səˋlɛkt]

動 **挑選**

用法 select A for B　挑選 A 給 B，為 B 挑選 A
Parents should select safe toys for their children.（家長應該為小孩挑選安全的玩具。）

Doris can select one of the four colors.
朵瑞絲可以挑選這四種顏色中的其中一種。

selfish [ˋsɛlfɪʃ]

形 自私的

用法 a selfish guy　自私的人

Mr. Johnson is a selfish old man.
強森先生是個自私的老頭子。

sell [sɛl]

動 賣

用法
ⓐ 三態：sell、sold [sold]、sold
ⓑ sell out of...　賣光……

This store sells different kinds of things.　這家店各種東西都有賣。

semester [səˋmɛstɚ]

名 學期

用法 the spring / fall semester
春 / 秋季班

Jason will try to study harder next semester.　傑森下學期會設法更加用功。

send [sɛnd]

動 寄；送

用法 ⓐ 三態：send、sent [sɛnt]、sent
ⓑ send + sb + sth　寄東西給某人
= send + sth + to + sb

My aunt **sent** me a box of toys.
我阿姨**寄**了一盒玩具給我。

senior high school

[ˌsiniɚ ˋhaɪ ˌskul]

名 高中

用法 go to senior high school　念高中

Tom will **go to senior high school** pretty soon.　湯姆很快就要**念高中**了。

sense [sɛns]

名 感覺；意義　動 感覺到，意識到

用法
a sense of humor　幽默感
a sense of duty　責任感
make sense　有意義

Eve **sensed** that she had made a big mistake.　伊芙**察覺到**她犯了一個大錯。

sentence [ˋsɛntəns]

名 句子

用法 make a sentence　造句
write a sentence　寫句子

There is a mistake in this sentence.
這個**句子**有個錯誤。

September [sɛpˋtɛmbɚ]

名 九月

用法 in September　在九月（月分用 in）
on September first　在九月一號
（日期用 on）

We took a trip to America in **September.**　我們**在九月**時到美國走了一趟。

serious [ˋsɪrɪəs]

形 **嚴重的；嚴肅的，認真的**

用法 ⓐ a serious problem　嚴重的問題
ⓑ I'm serious!
（我是認真的 / 我不是開玩笑的！）

Mr. Wilson is a **serious** person. He seldom talks.　威爾遜先生是個**嚴肅的**人。他很少說話。

servant [ˈsɚvənt]

名 僕人

用法 a civil servant　公務員

The rich man has many servants but no friends.　那位有錢人有很多僕人，卻沒有朋友。

serve [sɝv]

動 為……服務 / 效勞；供應（食物）

用法 Leo is busy serving the customers right now.
（李歐現在正忙著服務客人。）

They serve good Italian food at that restaurant.　那家餐廳提供義大利美食。

service [ˈsɝvɪs]

名 服務；幫忙

用法 be at one's service　為某人效勞

I'll be at your service forever, honey.
親愛的，我會一輩子為妳做牛做馬。

set [sɛt]

動 安置；設定　名 一套，一組

用法
❶ 三態同形
❷ set the table　擺餐具（準備吃飯）
❸ set the alarm clock　設鬧鐘

Help me set the table, son.
兒子，幫我擺餐具。

seven [ˋsɛvən]

名 七　形 七個的

用法
seven 作形容詞時，之後名詞用複數。
seven days　七天
seven books　七本書

There are seven days in a week.
一個星期有七天。

seventeen [ˌsɛvənˋtin]

名 十七　形 十七個的

用法
turn seventeen　滿十七歲

My brother just turned seventeen early this year.　我哥哥今年年初剛滿十七歲。

A B C D E F G H I J K L M N O P Q R S T U V W X Y Z

seventy [ˋsɛvəntɪ]

名 七十　形 七十個的

用法 seventy-one　七十一
seventy-two　七十二

Tom's grandfather is seventy years old.　湯姆的爺爺七十歲了。

several [ˋsɛv(ə)rəl]

形 幾個的

用法 a few 及 several 均表示「幾個的」。但 several 相當於「好幾個的」，要比 a few 多一些。

I haven't seen Peter for several years.　我有好幾年沒見到彼得了。

shake [ʃek]

動 搖動；握手　名 搖動

用法
ⓐ 三態：shake、shook [ʃʊk]、shaken [ˋʃekən]
ⓑ shake hands with + sb　與某人握手

The angry girl didn't want to shake hands with the boy.　這個生氣的女孩不願與這男孩握手。

Ss

shall [ʃæl]

助 將要

用法 shall 多與 I 及 we 並用；you、he、she、they 等則與 will 並用。

Shall we leave now?
我們現在**要**離開了嗎？

shape [ʃep]

名 形狀；（身體）狀況

用法 be in good / bad shape
健康很好 / 健康不佳

Paul exercises a lot, so he is in good shape. 保羅常運動，因此他的**身體很好**。

share [ʃɛr]

動 分享

用法 share + sth + with + sb
與某人分享東西

Can I share this cake with you?
我可以**跟**你**分享**這塊蛋糕嗎？

A B C D E F G H I J K L M N O P Q R S T U V W X Y Z

shark [ʃark]

名 鯊魚

用法 shark 也可指專門騙錢的人。
Be careful. That guy is a shark.
（小心。那個人是個騙人錢財的傢伙。）

Sharks have sharp teeth.
鯊魚的牙齒很銳利。

sharp [ʃarp]

形 鋒利的

用法 sharp 亦可表示幾點「整」。
It's ten o'clock sharp.
（現在是十點整。）

This knife is sharp.
這把刀很鋒利。

she [ʃi]

代 她

用法 she 及 her 指女性的「她」，he 及 him 則指男性的「他」。

I like Mary because she is cute.
我喜歡瑪麗，因為她很可愛。

sheep [ʃip]

名 綿羊

用法 sheep 的單複數同形。
one sheep　一隻綿羊
two sheep　兩隻綿羊

There are a few **sheep** on the farm.
農場上有幾隻綿羊。

sheet [ʃit]

名 床單；張，片

用法 a sheet of paper　一張紙
Give me some sheets of paper.
（給我幾張紙。）

My mom changes the **sheets** every week.　我媽媽每個星期換床單。

shelf [ʃɛlf]

名 架子（書架、貨物架）

用法 複數形則為 shelves [ʃɛlvz]。

Could you put the book back on the **shelf**, please?　麻煩您把這本書放回架上好嗎？

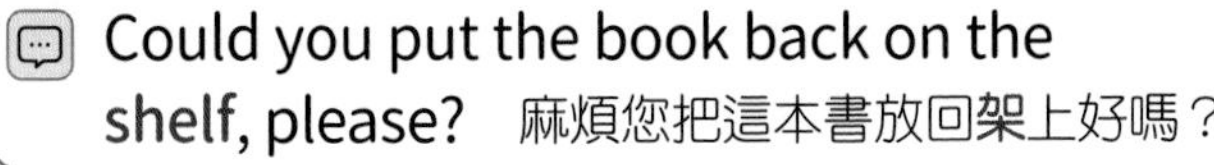

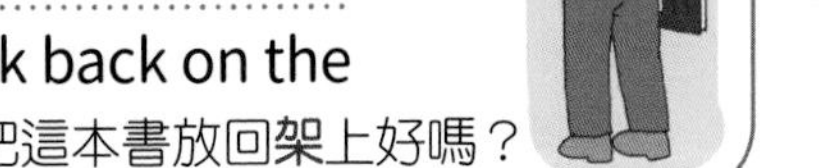

Ss

shine [ʃaɪn]

動 發亮，照耀；擦亮

用法 ⓐ 當「照耀」時三態為：shine、shone [ʃon]、shone。
ⓑ 當「擦亮」時三態為：shine、shined [ʃaɪnd]、shined。

Peter **shines** his own shoes.
彼得**擦**他自己的鞋子。

ship [ʃɪp]

名 船

用法 by ship　搭船
David went to Hong Kong by ship.
（大衛搭船到香港。）

Gary saw a **ship** on the sea.
蓋瑞看到海面上有一艘**船**。

S

shirt [ʃɝt]

名 襯衫

用法 try on a shirt　試穿襯衫
put on the shirt　穿上襯衫
take off the shirt　脫下襯衫

Can I try on this **shirt**?
這件**襯衫**我可以試穿嗎？

shoe [ʃu]

名 鞋子

用法 a pair of shoes　一雙鞋

Amy likes Diana's red shoes.
艾咪喜歡黛安娜的紅**鞋**。

shoot [ʃut]

動 射擊　名（竹的）嫩芽

用法
ⓐ 三態：shoot、shot [ʃat]、shot
ⓑ shoot at...　對……射擊

Flora enjoys eating bamboo shoots.
芙蘿拉喜歡吃**竹筍**。

shop [ʃap]

名 商店　動 購物

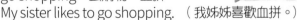

用法
ⓐ 三態：shop、shopped [ʃapt]、shopped
ⓑ go shopping　去購物，血拼
My sister likes to go shopping.（我姊姊喜歡血拼。）

What does that shop sell?
那家**商店**賣的是什麼東西？

shopkeeper

[ˋʃɑpˏkipɚ]

名 店主，店老闆

用法 shopkeeper 也可說 storekeeper。

The shopkeeper is a kind old man.
店主是個和藹的老伯伯。

shore [ʃɔr]

名 海岸；岸邊

用法
on shore　在岸上
off shore　在（海 / 湖等）岸外

A sailor was swimming to the shore.　一名水手正游向海岸。

short [ʃɔrt]

形 短的；矮的

用法
be short of...　短缺……
Fred is a little short of money now.
（弗瑞德現在有點缺錢。）

Henry is short, but his brother is tall.
亨利是矮個子，不過他哥哥卻是高個子。

shorts [ʃɔrts]

名 短褲

用法 如同 pants（長褲）一樣，shorts 有兩條短褲管，所以要用複數。
a pair of shorts　一條短褲（非 a short）

My dad wears shorts when he is at home.　我爸爸在家時都是穿短褲。

should [ʃʊd]

助 應該

用法 should 與 not 並用時，常縮寫成 shouldn't（不應）。
You shouldn't do it.
= You should not do it.（你不應做這件事。）

You should be nice to people.
你對人要和善。

shoulder [ˋʃoldɚ]

名 肩膀

用法 shoulder to shoulder　並肩

Hank's left shoulder hurts.
漢克的左肩很痛。

shout [ʃaʊt]

動 大叫，大吼

用法 shout at + sb　對某人大吼

Don't **shout at** me.
不要**對**我**大吼**。

show [ʃo]

動 顯示　名 節目

用法
ⓐ There is a good show on TV now.
（現在電視正在播放一個好節目。）
ⓑ show off　炫耀

Show me how to do the work.
教我怎麼做這工作。

shower [ˋʃaʊɚ]

名 淋浴；陣雨

用法
take a shower　淋浴
take a bath　盆浴

Take an umbrella with you in case of a **shower**.　帶把傘在身上以防**陣雨**。

shrimp [ʃrɪmp]

名 蝦子

用法 複數形用 shrimp 或 shrimps 皆可。

Jim went down to the creek to catch **shrimps**. 吉姆順溪而下去抓**蝦子**。

shut [ʃʌt]

動 關閉（三態同形）

用法 shut down 關機
John shut down the computer.
（約翰把電腦關機。）

Would you **shut the door** for me, please? 請你幫我**把門關上**，好嗎？

shy [ʃaɪ]

形 害羞的

用法 be shy with + sb 跟某人在一起就會害羞
Peter is shy with girls.
（彼得跟女孩子在一起就會害羞。）

Mary is **shy** in front of strangers.
瑪麗在陌生人面前會**害羞**。

sick [sɪk]

形 生病的

用法 sick 也可表示「厭惡的」，要與 of 並用。
be sick of... 對……厭惡 / 厭煩

Tony is sick, so he can't go to school today. 湯尼生病了，因此今天不能去上學。

side [saɪd]

名 邊，面

用法
on the left-hand side 在左邊
on the right-hand side 在右邊
by my / your side 在我的 / 你的旁邊

Come and sit by my side.
過來坐在我身邊。

sidewalk [ˋsaɪd͵wɔk]

名 人行道

用法
take the sidewalk 走人行道
take the overpass 走天橋
take the underpass 走地下道

We should not play on the sidewalk. 我們不應在人行道上玩耍。

sight [saɪt]

名 視力（不可數）；景象

用法
have good sight　視力很好
have poor sight　視力很差

Though Mr. Li is pretty old, he has good sight.　雖然李先生年紀很大了，他的視力卻很好。

sign [saɪn]

名 標示　動 簽名

用法
Sign your name here, please.
（請在此處簽下大名。）

The sign says, “No Smoking.”
這個標示寫著：「禁止吸菸」。

silence [ˋsaɪləns]

名 沉默；寂靜

用法
in silence　沉默地
Justin and Greta looked at each other in silence.（賈斯汀和葛瑞塔沉默地看著對方。）

The silence was broken by Ken’s coughs.
肯的咳嗽聲打破了寂靜。

A B C D E F G H I J K L M N O P Q R S T U V W X Y Z

silent [ˋsaɪlənt]

形 沉默的；寂靜無聲的

用法 keep silent　保持安靜

It is a silent night with stars shining.　這是個繁星閃耀的**寂靜**夜晚。

silly [ˋsɪlɪ]

形 愚笨的

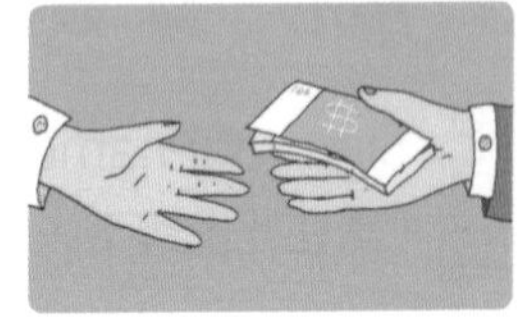

用法 相似字：foolish [ˋfulɪʃ]
形 愚蠢的

It's silly of me to lend Joseph the money.　我真笨，居然借錢給約瑟夫。

silver [ˋsɪlvɚ]

名 銀　形 銀色的；銀製的

用法 a silver coin　銀幣

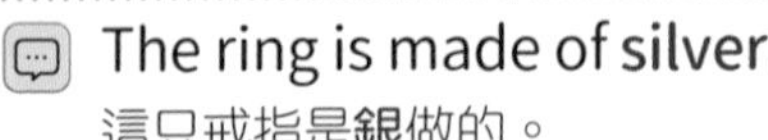

The ring is made of silver.
這只戒指是**銀**做的。

similar [ˋsɪmələ˞]

形 相似的

用法 be similar to... 與……相似

Gina's bike **is similar to** mine.
吉娜的腳踏車**和**我的很**相似**。

simple [ˋsɪmpl̩]

形 簡單的；樸素的

用法 lead a simple life 過著樸素的生活

Even a little child can answer this **simple** question. 甚至小孩子也能回答這個**簡單的**問題。

since [sɪns]

連 自從；因為

用法 自從（要與 have「已經」並用）：
I have lived here since I was born.
（我自出生起就已經住在這裡了。）

I haven't seen Peter **since** last week.
自上星期起我就沒見到彼得了。

sincere [sɪnˋsɪr]

形 真誠的

用法 express one's sincere thanks / apologies to sb
向某人表達誠摯的謝意 / 歉意

Gloria would like to express her sincere thanks to you. 葛蘿莉亞想要向你表達她**真誠的**謝意。

sing [sɪŋ]

動 唱；唱歌

用法 ⓐ 三態：sing、sang [sæŋ]、sung [sʌŋ]
ⓑ sing a song 唱一首歌

The little girl is only three, but she can sing many songs. 這個小女孩才三歲，卻會**唱**許多首歌。

singer [ˋsɪŋɚ]

名 歌手

用法 a pop singer 流行歌手
a rock singer 搖滾歌手
a rap singer 饒舌歌手

George is a famous singer.
喬治是個知名的**歌手**。

single [ˋsɪŋgḷ]

形 單一的；單身的　名 單人房

用法 Is Jane married or still single?
（珍結婚了嗎？還是仍是單身？）

We'll need a single room and a double room for the night.　我們今晚需要一間單人房和一間雙人房。

sink [sɪŋk]

動 下沉　名 水槽

用法 三態：sink、sank [sæŋk]、sunk [sʌŋk]

Look! The boat is sinking.
看啊！這艘船正往下沈。

sir [sɝ]

名 先生

用法 sir 是對男性的尊稱，可譯成「先生」、「長官」。ma' am [mæm] 則是對女性的尊稱，可譯成「女士」、「夫人」。

Thank you, sir.
謝謝您，先生。

sister [ˋsɪstɚ]

名 姊姊；妹妹

用法
an older / elder sister　姊姊
a younger sister　妹妹

Toby has one **older sister** and two **younger sisters.**　托比有一個**姊姊**、兩個**妹妹**。

sit [sɪt]

動 坐

用法
ⓐ 三態：sit、sat [sæt]、sat
ⓑ Sit down!　坐下！

Can I **sit** beside you?
我可以**坐**在妳身旁嗎？

six [sɪks]

名 六　形 六個的

用法
six years　六年
six books　六本書
six o'clock　六點鐘

It's **six o'clock** now.
現在是**六點**。

sixteen [ˌsɪksˋtin]

名 十六 形 十六個的

用法
sixteen books 十六本書
sixteen children 十六名孩子

This book has **sixteen** lessons.
本書有**十六**課。

sixty [ˋsɪkstɪ]

名 六十 形 六十的

用法
sixty boys 六十個男孩
sixty-one books 六十一本書

There are **sixty** parks in this big city.
這座大城市有**六十**座公園。

size [saɪz]

名 尺寸，大小

用法
large-sized [ˋlɑrdʒˌsaɪzd] 形 大號的
medium-sized [ˋmidɪəmˌsaɪzd] 形 中號的
small-sized [ˋsmɔlˌsaɪzd] 形 小號的

My father wears **large-sized** shirts.
我爸爸穿**大號的**襯衫。

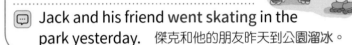

Ss

skate [sket]

名 溜冰鞋　動 溜冰

🔍用法
a pair of skates　一雙溜冰鞋
go skating　去溜冰

💬 **Jack and his friend went skating in the park yesterday.**　傑克和他的朋友昨天到公園溜冰。

ski [ski]

動 滑雪

🔍用法
ⓐ 三態：ski、skied [**skid**]、skied
ⓑ go skiing　去滑雪
ⓒ ski 當名詞為「滑雪板」的意思。

💬 **Skiing is a very exciting sport.**
滑雪是很刺激的運動。

S

skill [skɪl]

名 技巧，技能

🔍用法
skill at / in + N/V-ing　……的技能
I envy Cindy's skill in painting!
（我好羨慕辛蒂的畫功！）

💬 **Craig took that class to learn computer skills.**　克雷格上那門課是為了要學電腦技能。

skillful [ˋskɪlfəl]

形 有技巧的

用法 be skillful at...　擅於……
= be good at...

John is skillful at painting.
約翰對繪畫很在行。

skin [skɪn]

名 皮膚

用法 have (a) thin / thick skin
臉皮很薄 / 厚

Earl likes girls who have light skin.
厄爾喜歡皮膚白皙的女生。

skinny [ˋskɪnɪ]

形 瘦成皮包骨的

用法 skinny 也有「緊身的」意思。
skinny jeans　緊身牛仔褲

John was really skinny when he was young.　約翰年輕的時候真的是瘦到皮包骨。

Ss

skirt [skɜt]

名 裙子

用法 wear a skirt　穿裙子

Cindy looks beautiful when she **wears a skirt.**　辛蒂**穿裙子**時看起來很美。

sky [skaɪ]

名 天空

用法 in the sky　在天空
There is an airplane in the sky.
（天空有一架飛機。）

The **sky** is blue today.
今天的**天空**很藍。

S

sleep [slip]

動 睡覺

用法
ⓐ 三態：sleep、slept [slɛpt]、slept
ⓑ sleep well　睡得很好
ⓒ go to sleep　上床睡覺

When does Jim usually **go to sleep**?
吉姆通常都什麼時候**就寢**？

sleepy [ˋslipɪ]

形 想睡的

用法 be / feel sleepy　覺得很睏，想睡覺

Cassie **felt sleepy** after doing all the work.　凱西把所有的工作做完後**覺得很睏**。

slender [ˋslɛndɚ]

形 苗條的

用法 a slender figure　身材苗條

Susan has a **slender figure**.
蘇珊的**身材**很**苗條**。

slice [slaɪs]

名 片，切片

用法 a slice of bread　一片麵包
= a piece of bread

I'm hungry. Can I have **a slice of bread**?
我餓了，可以吃**一片麵包**嗎？

Ss

slide [slaɪd]

動 滑動，滑行　名 滑梯

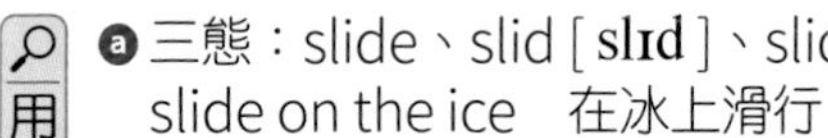

用法 ⓐ 三態：slide、slid [slɪd]、slid
slide on the ice　在冰上滑行
ⓑ slide down the slide　溜滑梯

Watch out! A big rock is sliding down the hill.　小心！一顆大石頭正從山上滾下來。

slim [slɪm]

形 苗條的

用法 stay slim　保持苗條

Jane exercises to stay slim.
珍運動以保持苗條。

S

slipper [ˋslɪpɚ]

名 拖鞋

用法 a pair of slippers　一雙拖鞋

Connie usually wears a pair of slippers indoors.　康妮在室內通常穿拖鞋。

slow [slo]

形 慢的

用法 slow down　速度放慢
You're driving too fast. You should slow down. （你車開得太快了，應該慢下來。）

You are too **slow**. Can you drive a little faster?　你太慢了，可以開快一點嗎？

small [smɔl]

形 （個子、體積）小的

用法 small 是 large（大的）的反義詞。
a small child　一個小孩子
a small tree　一棵小樹

This shirt is too **small**. I need a large one.　這件襯衫太小了，我需要大一點的。

smart [smɑrt]

形 聰明的

用法 small 與 clever [ˋklɛvɚ] 意思相同，均表示「聰明的」。
a smart / clever boy　聰明的男孩

Peter is a **smart** boy.
彼得是個聰明的孩子。

smell [smɛl]

動 聞起來；聞一聞

用法 ⓐ 聞起來（之後接形容詞）：
smell good / bad　聞起來很香 / 很臭
ⓑ 聞一聞：smell the flower　聞一聞這朵花

These flowers **smell good.**
這些花**聞起來很香**。

smile [smaɪl]

名 動 微笑

用法 smile at + sb　對某人微笑

Look! That girl is **smiling at** you.
瞧！那個女孩子正**對**著你**微笑**。

smoke [smok]

名 菸　動 抽菸

用法 give up smoking　戒菸
You should give up smoking, Dad.
（爸，您應該戒菸了。）

You shouldn't **smoke** in the room.
你不應在房間裡**吸菸**。

snack [snæk]

名 點心，零食

用法 表示「正餐」或「一餐」應使用 meal [mil]，正餐以外的食物則稱作 snack。

You'll get fat if you eat **snacks.**
你若吃**零嘴**會發胖的。

snail [snel]

名 蝸牛

用法 at a snail's pace　非常緩慢地

Snails move very slowly.
蝸牛走得很慢。

snake [snek]

名 蛇

用法 Is this snake poisonous?
（這條蛇有毒嗎？）
（poisonous [ˋpɔɪzn̩əs] 形 有毒的）

Is Dennis afraid of **snakes?**
丹尼斯怕**蛇**嗎？

sneaker [ˋsnikɚ]

名 運動鞋

用法 a pair of sneakers　一雙運動鞋

Sneakers are usually used for playing sports.
運動鞋通常是運動時穿的。

sneaky [ˋsnikɪ]

形 鬼鬼祟祟的

用法 a sneaky plan　偷偷摸摸的計畫

Why are you so sneaky? What's going on?　你為什麼那麼鬼鬼祟祟？發生什麼事了？

snow [sno]

名 雪　動 下雪

用法 In our place, it snows in winter.
（在我們這個地方，冬天會下雪。）

Does it snow in your country?
你國家那裡會下雪嗎？

snowman [ˋsno͵mæn]

名 雪人

用法 make a snowman 堆雪人

Several children are making a snowman in the park. 公園裡有幾個小朋友在**堆雪人**。

snowy [ˋsnoɪ]

形 下雪的

用法 描述天氣的形容詞多半用 -y 結尾，類似的有：rainy（下雨的）、foggy（起霧的）、sunny（陽光普照的）。

It's snowy today.
今天下雪。

so [so]

連 因此 副 如此地

用法 so... that... 如此……所以……
Vic is so nice that I like him.
（維克人很好，所以我喜歡他。）

John is tired, so he must go to bed early. 約翰很累，**因此**必須早點入睡。

Ss

soap [sop]

名 肥皂（不可數）

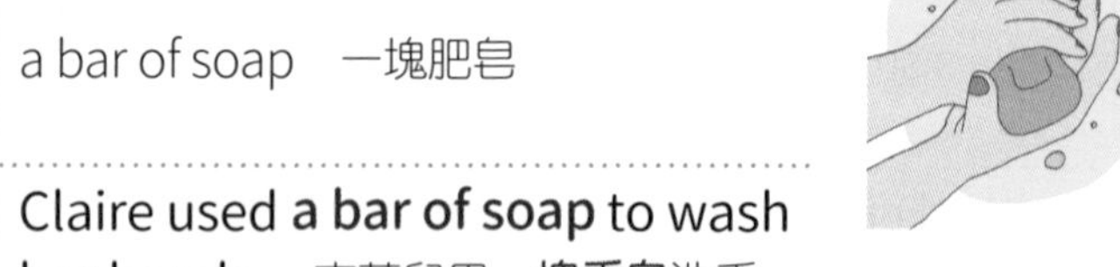

用法 a bar of soap　一塊肥皂

Claire used **a bar of soap** to wash her hands.　克萊兒用**一塊香皂**洗手。

soccer [ˋsakɚ]

名 足球

用法 play soccer　踢足球

Can you **play soccer**?
你會**踢足球**嗎？

S

social [ˋsoʃəl]

形 社會的；社交的

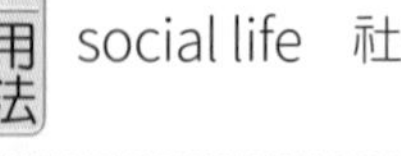

用法 social life　社交生活

Peter has no friends, and he doesn't have any **social life** at all.　彼得沒有朋友，根本沒有**社交生活**。

society [səˋsaɪətɪ]

名 社會

用法 複數為 societies [səˋsaɪətɪz]。

Modern **society** has a lot of problems. 現代**社會**有很多的問題。

sock [sɑk]

名 短襪

用法
a pair of socks　一雙短襪
a pair of stockings　一雙女用長筒襪

Where are my **socks**, Mom?
媽，我的**短襪**在哪裡？

soda [ˋsodə]

名 汽水；蘇打水

用法 an orange soda　柳橙汽水

Harry wants a can of **orange soda**.
哈利想要一罐**柳橙汽水**。

sofa [ˋsofə]

名 沙發

用法 couch 及 sofa 是同義字，指供兩三人坐的長沙發，而 armchair [ˋɑrm͵tʃɛr] 則指單人座的沙發。

Doug likes to sit on the sofa watching TV.
道格喜歡坐在**沙發**上看電視。

soft drink [͵sɔft ˋdrɪŋk]

名 不含酒精的飲料

用法 soft [sɔft] 形 軟的；不含酒精的

Just give me any soft drink.
隨便給我一些**不含酒精的飲料**就好了。

softball [ˋsɔft͵bɔl]

名 壘球

用法 hardball 則為「棒球」。

Debbie played softball when she was young.　黛比年輕的時候打過**壘球**。

soldier [ˋsoldʒɚ]

名 軍人，士兵

用法 soldier 多指「士兵」，軍官則使用 officer 一字。

John's brother is a soldier.
約翰的哥哥是軍人。

solve [sɑlv]

動 解決

用法 solve a problem　解決問題

The problem is really hard to solve.
這個問題真的很難解決。

some [sʌm]

形 代 一些

用法
some money　一些錢
some friends　一些朋友
some of my friends　我的一些朋友

Ivan has some work to do this afternoon.　今天下午艾凡有些工作要做。

someone [ˋsʌm͵wʌn]

代 某人

用法
someone = somebody
anyone（任何人）= anybody
no one（沒有人）= nobody

Helen, come here. **Someone** wants to see you. 海倫，到這兒來。**有人**要見妳。

something [ˋsʌmθɪŋ]

代 某事；某個東西

用法
have something to do　有事要做
have something to say　有話要說
have something to write　有東西要寫

I have **something important** to tell you, Tom. 湯姆，我有**重要的事**要跟你說。

sometimes [ˋsʌm͵taɪmz]

副 有時候

用法
Sometimes we go to the movies.
= We go to the movies sometimes.
（我們有時候會去看電影。）

Sometimes I go shopping with my mom. **有時候**我會跟我媽媽去買東西。

somewhere

[ˋsʌm͵(h)wɛr]

副 某處，某地

用法 go somewhere 到某處

We should hide the candy **somewhere** so that Johnny can't find it. 我們應該把糖果藏在**某處**，這樣強尼就找不到了。

son [sʌn]

名 兒子

用法 daughter 則為「女兒」。

Mr. Johnson has two **sons**.
強森先生有兩個**兒子**。

song [sɔŋ]

名 歌曲

用法 sing a song 唱一首歌

How many **songs** can you sing?
你會唱幾首歌？

soon [sun]

副 不久，很快

用法 as soon as...　一……就……
I will call my mom as soon as I get back.（我一回來就會打電話給我媽媽。）

The train will arrive soon.
火車很快就會到站了。

sore [sɔr]

形（因肌肉拉傷而）痠痛的

用法
have a sore throat　喉嚨痛
have a sore arm　手臂痛

Brenda can't talk much. She has a sore throat today.　布蘭達不能講太多話。她今天喉嚨痛。

sorry [ˋsɔrɪ]

形 抱歉的，遺憾的

用法
I'm sorry that...　我很抱歉……
I'm sorry for...　我對……感到抱歉

I'm sorry that I'm late.
很抱歉，我遲到了。

soul [sol]

名 靈魂；人

用法
ⓐ soul 表示「人」的時候等於 person。
ⓑ a soul mate　心靈伴侶

Erin and her husband are soul mates for each other.　愛倫和她的丈夫是彼此的**心靈伴侶**。

sound [saʊnd]

名 聲音　動 聽起來

用法
ⓐ 聲音：a strange sound　奇怪的聲音
ⓑ 聽起來：sound good　聽起來很棒

Henry's idea sounds good.
亨利的點子**聽起來**挺不錯的。

soup [sup]

名 湯

用法
ⓐ a bowl of soup　一碗湯
ⓑ eat the soup　喝湯

Eat the soup before it gets cold.
趁著湯涼以前喝掉吧。

sour [saʊr]

形 （味道）酸的

用法 turn / go sour 變酸
This milk has turned sour.
（牛奶變酸了。）

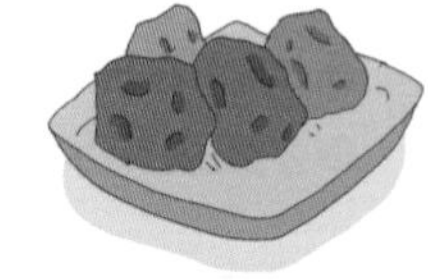

These plums taste **sour.**
這些梅子味道**酸酸的**。

south [saʊθ]

名 南方 副 向南 形 南方的

用法 ⓐ in the south 在南部 / 在南方
I live in the south. （我住在南部。）
ⓑ fly south 向南飛

Birds **fly south** before winter comes.
冬天來臨前，鳥兒都會**往南飛**。

soy sauce [ˋsɔɪ ˏsɔs]

名 醬油（不可數）

用法 soy [sɔɪ] 名 黃豆
（= soybean [ˋsɔɪˏbin]）

You can add some **soy sauce** to the soup. 你可以在湯裡加一點**醬油**。

space [spes]

名 空間；太空

用法 ⓐ 空間：We need space for these books.
（我們需要空間容納這些書。）
ⓑ 太空：in space　在太空

Is there life **in space**?
太空有生物嗎？

spaghetti [spəˋgɛtɪ]

名 義大利麵

用法 spaghetti 為不可數名詞。

Howard doesn't like **spaghetti**. He likes beef noodles.　霍華不喜歡**義大利麵**。他喜歡牛肉麵。

speak [spik]

動 說；演講

用法 三態：speak、spoke [spok]、spoken [ˋspokən]

Excuse me. Do you **speak English**?
不好意思，你會**說英語**嗎？

speaker [ˋspikɚ]

名 演說者；說話者

用法 The speaker seemed a little too nervous.
（主講人看起來似乎有點緊張。）

Is Dale a native speaker of English?
戴爾的**母語是英語**嗎？

special [ˋspɛʃəl]

形 特殊的，特別的

用法 見到一個喜歡的人想要送他 / 她東西時，可說：I have something special for you.
（我有一樣特別的東西要送給你 / 妳。）

What's so special about this toy?
這個玩具有什麼**特別**之處？

speech [spitʃ]

名 演講

用法 make / give / deliver a speech on...
就……發表演講

I feel honored to make a speech to you. 我很榮幸能對諸位**發表演講**。

speed [spid]

名 速度　動 迅速前進

用法
ⓐ 三態：speed、sped [spɛd]、sped
ⓑ at a speed of...　以……的速度

The police car **sped** to the scene of the accident.　警車迅速前往意外發生地點。

spell [spɛl]

動 拼（字）

用法
spell 當名詞為「咒語」的意思。
cast / put a spell (on sb)
對（某人）施魔咒

Can you **spell** your name?
你會拼你的名字嗎？

spend [spɛnd]

動 花費

用法
ⓐ 三態：spend、spent [spɛnt]、spent
ⓑ spend + 時間 + V-ing　花時間從事……

Do not **spend** too much time playing computer games.　不要花太多的時間打電腦遊戲。

spider [ˋspaɪdɚ]

名 蜘蛛

用法 spider's web　蜘蛛網

There is a **spider** on the wall.
牆上有一隻**蜘蛛**。

spirit [ˋspɪrɪt]

名 精神（不可數）；心情（恆用複數）

用法 be in high spirits　心情很好
= be in a good mood

My aunt still feels young in **spirit** at the age of 65.　我的阿姨六十五歲了，但是**內心**卻還很年輕。

spoon [spun]

名 湯匙

用法 eat soup with a spoon　用湯匙喝湯

We **eat soup with a spoon.**
我們**用湯匙喝湯**。

sport [spɔrt]

名 運動

用法 exercise 指個人體能的健身運動，如 跑步、爬山等。有比賽性質的運動，如 賽跑、網球、籃球等則稱作 sport。

What **sports** does Joe like?
喬喜歡什麼**運動**？

spot [spɑt]

名 斑點；地點　動 發現

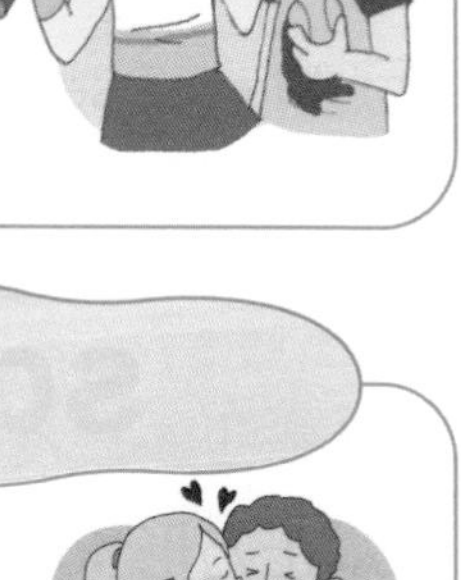

用法
ⓐ 三態：spot、spotted [ˋspɑtɪd]、spotted
ⓑ on the spot　當場，立刻

Christina **spotted** Mary kissing Peter when she opened the door.　克莉絲汀娜開門時，**發現**瑪麗在吻彼得。

spread [sprɛd]

名 動 擴展；蔓延

用法 spread 作動詞時，三態同形。

The **spread** of the disease frightened everyone.　疾病的**擴散**把每個人都嚇壞了。

spring [sprɪŋ]

名 春天；泉，湧泉

用法 a hot spring　溫泉

We can see many beautiful flowers in spring.　春天時我們可以看到許多美麗的花朵。

square [skwɛr]

名 正方形；廣場　形 正方形的

用法
ⓐ square 除表示「正方形」外，也可指市府前或公共大樓前的廣場。
ⓑ draw a square　畫一個正方形

See you in the square at two p.m.
下午兩點在廣場跟你會面。

stair [stɛr]

名 樓梯階

用法 一層樓梯通常有好多階梯，故常用複數 stairs。
walk up / down the stairs　走上 / 下樓梯

These stairs lead to the hilltop.
這些階梯通往山頂。

stamp [stæmp]

名 郵票

用法 stick a stamp onto the envelope
把郵票貼在信封上
（stick [stɪk] 動 黏，貼）

Where can I buy **stamps**?
我在哪裡可以買到**郵票**？

stand [stænd]

動 站；容忍

用法 ⓐ 三態：stand、stood [stʊd]、stood
ⓑ 容忍：I can't stand the hot weather.
（天氣熱得讓我受不了。）

Why are you **standing** over there?
你為什麼**站**在那裡？

star [stɑr]

名 星星

用法 star 也可表示「明星」。
My sister is a movie star.
（我姊姊是電影明星。）

There are many **stars** in the sky.
天上有許多**星星**。

start [start]

名 動 開始

用法 start 與 begin 意思相同。
The meeting will start in five minutes. （會議五分鐘後開始。）

When will the meeting **start**?
會議什麼時候**開始**？

state [stet]

名 狀況；地位；州　動 說明

用法 ⓐ in a state of good health　健康狀況良好
ⓑ There are fifty states in the United States. （美國有五十州。）

Duncan **stated** that he had never seen Mr. Jones before.　鄧肯**聲明**他以前從未見過瓊斯先生。

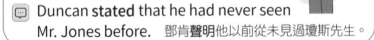

station [ˋsteʃən]

名 車站

用法 train station　火車站
bus station　公車總站

Gail lives very close to the **train station**.　蓋兒住的地方離**火車站**很近。

stationery [ˋsteʃən͵ɛrɪ]

名 文具

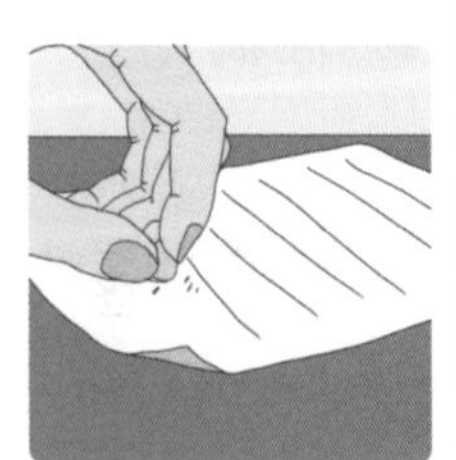

用法 stationery 為集合名詞，不可數，包括紙、筆等。

Daisy is out of stationery.
黛西用完**文具**了。

stay [ste]

動 待在；保持

用法
ⓐ 待在：stay in Taipei　待在臺北
ⓑ 保持：stay healthy　保持健康
ⓒ stay 當名詞為「停留」的意思。

How long will you stay here?
你在這裡會**待**多久？

steak [stek]

名 牛排

用法 牛排幾分熟：Well done.（全熟。）
Medium [ˋmidɪəm].（五分熟。）
Rare [rɛr].（三分熟。）

How would you like your steak?
你的**牛排**要幾分熟？

steal [stil]

動 偷竊

用法 三態：steal、stole [stol]、stolen [ˋstolən]

Somebody has stolen Ella's bicycle.
有人偷了艾拉的腳踏車。

steam [stim]

名 水蒸氣（不可數） 動 蒸

用法 There is a lot of steam on the window glass.
（窗戶玻璃上有好多水蒸氣。）

Mom is steaming fish in the kitchen.
媽媽正在廚房蒸魚。

step [stɛp]

名 腳步；步驟 動 踩（與 on 並用）

用法
ⓐ 三態：step、stepped [stɛpt]、stepped
ⓑ step by step　一步一步地，按部就班
step on...　踩到……

Dora is too tired to take another step.　朵拉累到一步都走不動。

still [stɪl]

副 仍然

用法 still 也可表示「靜止的」。
Keep still. I'm drawing a picture of you.
（別動。我正在畫一張你的畫。）

Kirk still doesn't know the answer to this question. 柯克仍然不知道這個問題的答案。

stingy [ˋstɪndʒɪ]

形 吝嗇的

用法 miserly [ˋmaɪzəlɪ] 形 吝嗇的
cheap [tʃip] 形 小氣的

Jamie doesn't like to spend money. He is stingy. 傑米不喜歡花錢。他很小器。

stomach [ˋstʌmək]

名 胃

用法 have a big stomach
很會吃，食量大

Tom's father has a big stomach.
湯姆的父親食量很大。

stomachache

[ˋstʌmək͵ek]

名 胃痛

用法 等於 stomach ache。

Because Josh ate too much, he had **a stomachache.** 喬許吃太飽了，所以**胃痛**。

stone [ston]

名 石頭

用法 be a stone's throw from + 地方
在某地方附近

Hannah's school is **a stone's throw from** here. 漢娜的學校離這兒**只有幾步遠而已**。

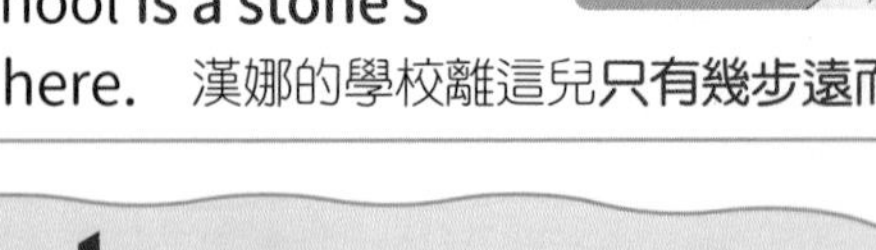

stop [stap]

動 停止　名 停止；(公車) 站牌

用法
ⓐ 三態：stop、stopped [stapt]、stopped
ⓑ stop + V-ing　停止做……
ⓒ The bus came to a stop.（公車停了下來。）

We **stopped** talking when we saw our teacher.
我們看到我們老師時就**停止**說話了。

store [stɔr]

名 商店　動 儲存（食物）

用法 store food　儲存食物

Nick will buy some cold drinks in that store.　尼克要在那家**商店**買些冷飲。

storm [stɔrm]

名 暴風雨

用法 the calm before the storm
暴風雨前的寧靜

The meeting was canceled because of the storm.　因為**暴風雨**的關係，所以會議取消了。

stormy [ˋstɔrmɪ]

形 暴風雨的

用法 stormy 也可表示「激烈的；爭吵的」。
a stormy argument
激烈的爭論

We had a blackout during the stormy night.　**暴風雨**夜晚我們停電了。

story [ˋstɔrɪ]

名 故事

用法 tell a story　講故事
be good at telling stories
很會講故事

My cousin Peter is good at telling stories.　我表哥彼得很會說故事。

stove [stov]

名 爐子

用法 a gas stove　瓦斯爐

Be careful when you use a gas stove.　你使用瓦斯爐時要小心。

straight [stret]

形 直的　副 直直地

用法 go straight ahead　一直往前走
stand straight　直立，站直

The poor old woman cannot stand straight.　這位可憐的老太太無法站直。

strange [strendʒ]

形 奇怪的

用法 Strange to say, ... 說來真怪，……
Strange to say, the dog can sing.
（說來真怪，這隻狗會唱歌。）

That's really a **strange** idea.
那真是個怪點子。

stranger [ˋstrendʒɚ]

名 陌生人

用法 有人向我們問路時，我們也不熟，可說：
Sorry, I'm a stranger here myself.
（抱歉，我自己也不是本地人。）

Do not talk to **strangers**, Johnny.
強尼，別跟**陌生人**說話。

straw [strɔ]

名 稻草；吸管

用法
ⓐ a straw hat 草帽
ⓑ drink juice with a straw
用吸管喝果汁

The two-year-old boy can use a **straw** to drink water. 這個兩歲的小男孩會用**吸管**喝水。

strawberry [ˋstrɔˏbɛrɪ]

名 草莓

用法 複數為 strawberries [ˋstrɔˏbɛrɪz]

💬 **Mr. Wang grows some strawberries in the garden.** 王先生在園子裡種了一些**草莓**。

stream [strim]

名 溪流；流量

用法 The news reported an endless stream of traffic on the highway.（新聞報導高速公路車量川流不息。）

💬 **There is a stream near Ida's house.** 艾達家附近有條**小溪**。

S

street [strit]

名 街，街道

用法

on the street	在街道旁
in the street	在街道中間
live on that street	住在那條街

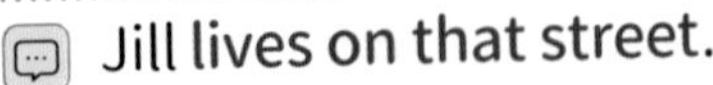

💬 **Jill lives on that street.**
吉兒**住在那條街**。

strike [straɪk]

動 打擊　名 罷工

用法
ⓐ 三態：strike、struck [strʌk]、struck
ⓑ go on strike　罷工

Larry's house was struck by lightning yesterday.　賴瑞的房子昨天被雷擊中。

string [strɪŋ]

名 線，繩子；一串

用法
a piece of string　一條繩子
a string of pearls / beads
一串珍珠 / 珠子

Michael needs a piece of string to tie this box.　麥可需要一條繩子來綁這個箱子。

strong [strɔŋ]

形 強壯的

用法
strong 的反義詞是 weak [wik]（虛弱的）。

The boy is healthy and strong.
那個男孩很健壯。

student [ˋst(j)udənt]

名 學生

用法 a graduate student　研究生
a law / medical student
法律 / 醫學系學生

David is a good student.
大衛是個好學生。

study [ˋstʌdɪ]

動 學習；研究　名 書房

用法 ⓐ 三態：study、studied [ˋstʌdɪd]、studied
ⓑ in the study　在書房

It's time to study now.
現在該是讀書的時候了。

stupid [ˋstjupɪd]

形 愚蠢的

用法 a stupid man　笨蛋
a stupid question　蠢問題

Pigs are not stupid. They are clever.　豬不笨，牠們很聰明。

Ss

style [staɪl]

名 風格；款式

用法 Do you like Karen's singing style?
（你喜歡凱倫的唱歌風格嗎？）

Lena sells different styles of dresses. 莉娜賣各種不同款式的洋裝。

subject [ˋsʌbdʒɪkt]

名 主題；（學校）科目

用法 I don't want to talk about it. Let's change the subject.
（我不想談這件事。咱們換個主題吧。）

What subject is Owen most interested in? 歐文對哪一科最有興趣？

subway [ˋsʌbˏwe]

名 地鐵

用法 take the subway 搭地鐵

Why don't we take the subway? It's faster. 我們為什麼不搭地鐵呢？它比較快。

S s

succeed [sək`sid]

動 成功

用法 succeed in... 在……方面獲得成功

You should work hard if you want to succeed in business. 你經商想**成功**的話，就要努力。

success [sək`sɛs]

名 成功（不可數）；成功的人或事（可數）

用法 Failure is the mother of success.
（失敗為成功之母。—— 諺語）

The party last night was a great success. 昨晚的派對很**成功**。

successful [sək`sɛsfəl]

形 成功的

用法 a successful man 成功的人
a successful plan 成功的計畫

You will not be **successful** if you don't work hard. 你若不努力就不會**成功**。

such [sʌtʃ]

形 如此的，這樣的

用法
ⓐ such + N + that...
如此的……以致於……
ⓑ such as...　例如……

It was such an excellent performance.　這真是場**如此**精彩的表演。

sudden [ˋsʌdn̩]

形 突然的

用法
suddenly [ˋsʌdn̩lɪ] 副 突然地

There was a sudden change in the weather.　天氣**突然**出現了變化。

sugar [ˋʃʊgɚ]

名 糖

用法
drink coffee with sugar　喝咖啡加糖
drink coffee without sugar
喝咖啡不加糖

Dad likes to **drink coffee without sugar**.　爸爸喜歡**喝不加糖的咖啡**。

suggest [sə(g)ˋdʒɛst]

動 建議

用法 suggest 之後接 that 子句時，
該子句恆用助動詞 should，
而 should 往往予以省略。

Lauren suggests that Rick should do it again. 蘿倫建議這件事瑞克重做一遍。

suit [sut]

名 一套西裝 動 適合

用法 Rex is wearing a black suit.
（雷克斯穿著一套黑色的西服。）

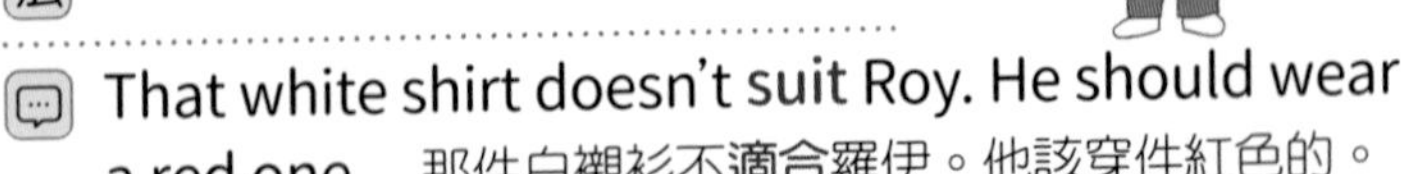

That white shirt doesn't suit Roy. He should wear a red one. 那件白襯衫不適合羅伊。他該穿件紅色的。

summer [ˋsʌmɚ]

名 夏天

用法 Summer is coming. （夏天就要到了。）
It's summer now. （現在是夏天了。）
Summer is over. （夏天過了。）

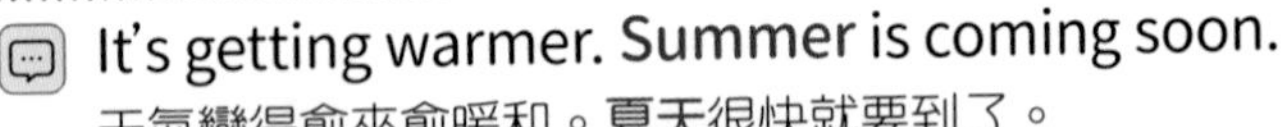

It's getting warmer. Summer is coming soon.
天氣變得愈來愈暖和。夏天很快就要到了。

sun [sʌn]

名 太陽

用法 ⓐ The sun is rising. （太陽正在升起。）
The sun is setting. （太陽正在下沉。）
ⓑ stay in the sun 待在陽光下

Most girls don't like to stay in the sun. 大多數女孩子不喜歡待在陽光下。

Sunday [ˋsʌnde]

名 星期天

用法
on Sunday 在星期天
next Sunday 下個星期天（之前不加 on）
last Sunday 上個星期天（之前不加 on）

Let's go to the movies on Sunday.
星期天咱們看電影去吧。

sunny [ˋsʌnɪ]

形 晴朗的

用法
a sunny day 晴天
a rainy day 雨天

It's sunny today.
今天出太陽。

super [ˋsupɚ]

形 極佳的

用法 superb [sʊˋpɝb] 形 極好的

Mark is a super salesman in the company. 馬克是公司頂尖的銷售人員。

supermarket

[ˋsupɚˏmɑrkɪt]

名 超級市場

用法 現在流行的「大賣場」則稱作 mall [mɔl]。

Mom buys food at that supermarket.
媽媽都在那家超市買東西。

supper [ˋsʌpɚ]

名（家中吃的輕便）晚餐

用法 dinner [ˋdɪnɚ]
名（餐館或家中吃的正式）晚餐

What would you like to eat for supper? 你晚餐想吃什麼？

support [sə`pɔrt]

動 名 支持

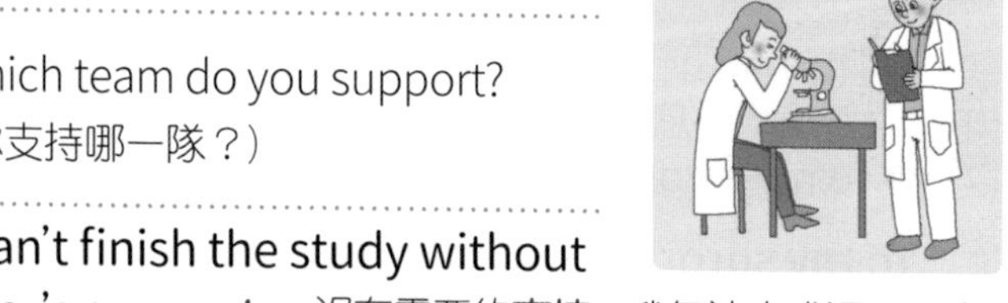

用法 Which team do you support?
（你支持哪一隊？）

I can't finish the study without Lucy's **support**. 沒有露西的**支持**，我無法完成這項研究。

sure [ʃʊr]

形 確定的；確信的

用法 I'm sure that... 我確信……
I'm sure that I'm right.
（我確信我是對的。）

Are you **sure** that John is coming today? 你**確定**約翰今天會來嗎？

surf [sɝf]

動 衝浪；瀏覽（網頁）

用法
ⓐ go surfing 去衝浪
ⓑ surf the internet 上網

My brother will **go surfing** with his friends this weekend. 這個週末我哥哥會跟他朋友**去衝浪**。

Ss

surprise [sɚˋpraɪz]

動 使驚訝　名 驚訝

用法
ⓐ The bad news surprised me.
（這個壞消息令我吃驚。）
ⓑ To my surprise, ...　令我驚訝的是，……

To my surprise, John didn't pass that test.　令我驚訝的是，那次考試約翰沒考及格。

surprised [sɚˋpraɪzd]

形 感到吃驚的

用法
ⓐ be surprised at / by...
對……感到吃驚
ⓑ be surprised to...　很驚訝會……

Lulu was surprised to see Rudy here.　露露很驚訝在這裡見到魯迪。

S

survive [sɚˋvaɪv]

動 存活

用法
survivor [sɚˋvaɪvɚ]
名 生還者，獲救者

The little girl survived the car accident.　那個女孩從車禍中存活下來。

swallow [ˋswɑlo]

名 燕子　動 吞嚥

用法 You can't see any swallows in winter.
（在冬天看不到燕子。）

Roger quickly swallowed the rest of his coffee.　羅傑快速地把剩下的咖啡喝完。

swan [swɑn]

名 天鵝

用法 swan dive　向前跳水

Swans are large white birds with long necks.　天鵝是白色長頸的大型鳥類。

sweater [ˋswɛtɚ]

名 毛衣

用法
wear a sweater　穿毛衣
put on a sweater　穿上毛衣
take off a sweater　脫下毛衣

Ron wears a sweater only when it is cold.　只有在天冷時榮恩才穿毛衣。

sweep [swip]

動 打掃

用法 三態：sweep、swept [swɛpt]、swept

Mom asked me to sweep the floor. 媽媽要我掃地。

sweet [swit]

形 甜的；甜美的

用法 ⓐ 甜的：The coffee is too sweet.（這咖啡太甜了。）
ⓑ 甜美的：a sweet dream 甜美的夢

Mary is a sweet girl.
瑪麗是個甜美的女孩子。

swim [swɪm]

動 名 游泳

用法 ⓐ 三態：swim、swam [swæm]、swum [swʌm]
ⓑ go for a swim 去游泳

Let's go swimming tomorrow.
咱們明天去游泳吧。

swimsuit [ˋswɪm͵sut]

名 泳裝

用法 也可說 swimming suit。

How do I look in this swimsuit?
我穿這件泳衣樣子好看嗎？

swing [swɪŋ]

動 擺動　名 鞦韆

用法
ⓐ 三態：swing、swung [swʌŋ]、swung
ⓑ play on the swing　盪鞦韆

Push me after I sit on the swing.
我坐在鞦韆後請推我一下。

symbol [ˋsɪmbḷ]

名 象徵

用法 as a symbol of...
做為……的象徵

Ron gave Linda a ring as a symbol of his love.　榮恩給琳達一枚戒指以示他對她的愛。

system [ˋsɪstəm]

名 系統；制度

用法 a computer system 電腦系統
an educational / education system 教育制度

The company needs a new system. 這家公司需要新的制度。

Notes

Tt

table [ˋtebḷ]

名 餐桌

用法
set the table　把碗筷擺在桌上（準備吃飯）
clear the table　收拾餐桌
clean up the table　把桌子清潔乾淨

Clean up the table after you finish eating.
你吃完東西後**把桌子清乾淨**。

table tennis

[ˋtebḷ ˏtɛnɪs]

名 桌球

用法 tennis [ˋtɛnɪs] 名 網球

Eric likes to play table tennis on weekends.　艾瑞克喜歡在週末**打桌球**。

tail [tel]

名 尾巴

用法
看到狗狗在搖尾巴時，我們就可說：
The dog is wagging its tail.
（這隻狗正在搖尾巴。）

That dog has a short tail.
那隻狗的**尾巴**很短。

Tt

Taiwan [ˋtaɪˋwɑn]

名 臺灣

用法
ⓐ in Taiwan　在臺灣
ⓑ Taiwanese [ˏtaɪwəˋniz]
名 臺灣人　形 臺灣的；臺灣人的

I live **in Taiwan**. What about you?
我住**在臺灣**，你住在哪裡？

take [tek]

動 帶走；服用（藥物）

用法
ⓐ 三態：take、took [tʊk]、taken [ˋtekən]
ⓑ take medicine　服藥，吃藥

Take this book **to** John. He needs it.
把這本書**帶給**約翰，他需要它。

T

talent [ˋtælənt]

名 才能，天賦

用法
have a talent for...　有⋯⋯的天賦

My younger brother **has a talent for** music.　我弟弟很**有**音樂**天賦**。

Tt

talk [tɔk]

名 動 說話，談話

🔍用法
ⓐ talk about... 談論……
talk about music 談論音樂
ⓑ have a talk 談一談

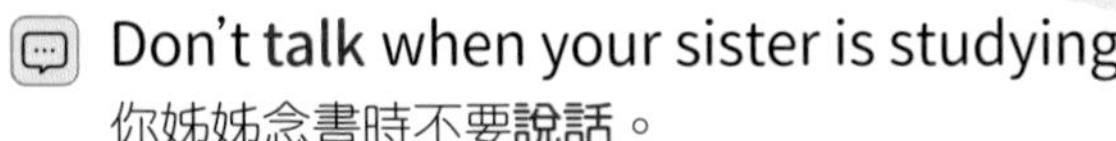

💬 Don't **talk** when your sister is studying.
你姊姊念書時不要**說話**。

talkative [ˈtɔkətɪv]

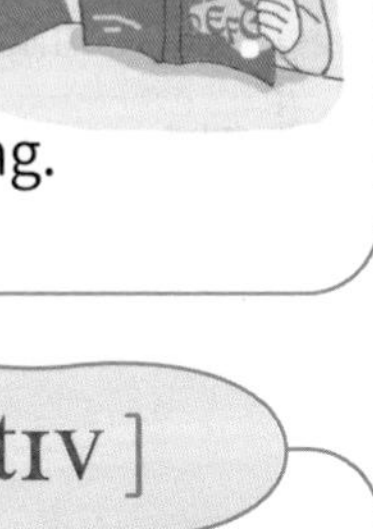

形 愛說話的，聒噪的

🔍用法
a talkative person 聒噪的人

💬 Some people become **talkative** when they get drunk. 有些人喝醉時就會變得很**愛說話**。

tall [tɔl]

形 高的

🔍用法
tall 也有「身高為……」的意思。
Tom is 1.7 meters tall.
（湯姆身高為 1.7 公尺。）

💬 My brother is **tall** and handsome.
我哥哥又**高**又帥。

A B C D E F G H I J K L M N O P Q R S T U V W X Y Z

tangerine

[ˌtændʒəˋrin]

名 橘子

用法 orange [ˋɔrəndʒ] 名 柳橙，柳丁

This tangerine tastes sweet.
這個**橘子**味道很甜。

tank [tæŋk]

名 坦克車

用法 tank 另外也有「槽；油箱」的意思。
a water tank　水箱
a gas tank　油箱

In the past, tanks played an important role in war.
過去，**坦克車**在戰爭中扮演很重要的角色。

tape [tep]

名 膠帶

用法 a roll of tape　一卷膠帶

Mother bought a roll of tape in the store.　媽媽在店裡買了**一卷膠帶**。

taste [test]

動 嚐；嚐起來　名 味道

用法
ⓐ 嚐：Taste the food.（嚐嚐這道食物。）
ⓑ 味道：The taste is good / bad.
（這個味道很好 / 很差。）

The food tastes delicious.
這道食物嚐起來很好吃。

taxi [ˋtæksɪ]

名 計程車

用法
ⓐ 複數為 taxis。
ⓑ take a taxi　搭計程車
hail a taxi　攔計程車

Dad seldom takes a taxi to work.
爸爸很少搭計程車上班。

tea [ti]

名 茶

用法
make tea / coffee　泡茶 / 泡咖啡
green tea　綠茶
black tea　紅茶（非 red tea）

Most Chinese drink tea.
大部分的中國人都喝茶。

teach [titʃ]

動 教，教導

用法
ⓐ 三態：teach、taught [tɔt]、taught
ⓑ Bill teaches us English.
（比爾教我們英文。）

Mr. Wilson **teaches** English very well.
威爾森老師英文**教**得很好。

teacher [ˋtitʃɚ]

名 老師

用法
「王老師」在英文中，男生稱 Mr. Wang；未婚女性則稱 Miss Wang；若是已婚女性則稱 Mrs. Wang。

We all like our **teacher**.
我們大家都喜歡我們的**老師**。

T

team [tim]

名 隊；球隊　動 團結合作

用法
ⓐ There are ten players on the baseball team.（這支棒球隊有十個球員。）
ⓑ team up　團結合作

Let's **team up** and finish the work.
咱們**團結合作**把工作做完吧。

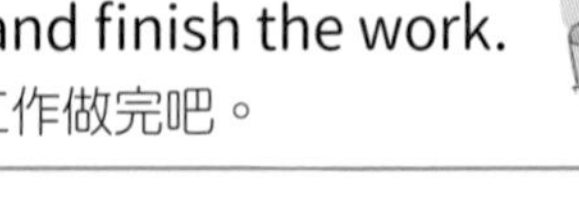

teapot [ˋti͵pɑt]

名 茶壺

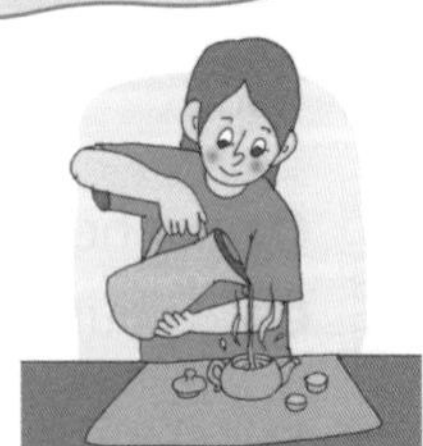

用法 a tempest in a teapot　小題大作
tempest [ˋtɛmpɪst] 名 暴風雨

She poured some hot water into the teapot.　她把一些熱水倒入**茶壺**中。

tear

名 [tɪr] 淚水　動 [tɛr] 撕裂

用法
ⓐ 三態：tear、tore [tɔr]、torn [tɔrn]
ⓑ Amy tore the letter up after reading it.
（艾咪看完信之後就把它撕掉了。）

Tears are falling down her cheeks.
眼淚從她的雙頰滑落。

teenager [ˋtin͵edʒɚ]

名 青少年

用法 teenager 指十三至十九歲的少年。

Pretty soon Tim will be a teenager.
很快提姆就會變成**青少年**了。

telephone [ˋtɛlə͵fon]

名 電話

用法
ⓐ telephone 常簡稱為 phone [fon]。
ⓑ It's your phone call. （這是你的電話。）

May I have your telephone number?
你的電話號碼可以給我嗎？

television [ˋtɛlə͵vɪʒən]

名 電視

用法
ⓐ television 常縮寫成 TV。
ⓑ watch TV　看電視

Don't spend too much time watching television.　別花太多的時間看電視。

tell [tɛl]

動 告訴；說（故事、謊言）

用法
ⓐ 三態：tell、told [told]、told
ⓑ tell a story　說故事
ⓒ tell a lie　說謊

Tell me what to do.
告訴我要做什麼。

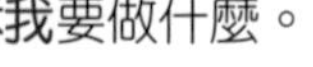

temperature

[ˋtɛmp(ə)rətʃɚ]

名 溫度；體溫

用法 take one's temperature　量某人的體溫

What's the temperature now?
現在溫度幾度？

temple [ˋtɛmpḷ]

名 寺廟

用法 佛教或道教的信徒去的地方叫做 temple；基督教或天主教信徒去的地方叫做 church [tʃɝtʃ]（教會；教堂）。

There are many temples in Taiwan.
臺灣有許多寺廟。

ten [tɛn]

名 十　形 十個的

用法 ⓐ ten 之後的名詞用複數。
ten dollars　十元
ⓑ count from one to ten　從一數到十

My little sister can count from one to ten.　我小妹能從一數到十。

tennis [ˋtɛnɪs]

名 網球（不可數）

用法
play tennis　打網球
tennis shoes　網球鞋

Can you teach me how to play tennis?　你能否教我怎麼**打網球**？

tent [tɛnt]

名 帳篷

用法
pitch a tent　搭帳篷

Our team pitched a tent by the lake.　我們隊在湖邊**紮營**。

term [tɝm]

名 術語

用法
a technical term　專業術語

Avoid using those technical terms.　避免使用那些**專業術語**。

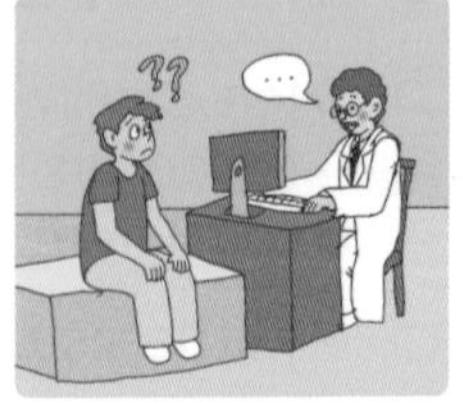

terrible [ˋtɛrəbḷ]

形 可怕的；差勁的，糟糕的

用法
- ⓐ 可怕的：a terrible noise　可怕的聲音
- ⓑ 差勁的：a terrible idea　很爛的想法

My writing is **terrible**. How can I make it better?　我的寫作很**糟**，我要如何改善？

terrific [təˋrɪfɪk]

形 極好的

用法
等於 very good。

Linda feels **terrific** today.
琳達今天**好極了**。

test [tɛst]

名 測驗，考試

用法
- ⓐ take a test　參加測驗
- ⓑ do well on the test　考試考得很好

My brother is going to take a **test** today.　我弟弟今天要**考試**。

textbook [ˋtɛkst͵bʊk]

名 教科書，課本

用法 a reference book　參考 / 工具書

Larry is not interested in these textbooks.　賴瑞對這些教科書沒有興趣。

than [ðæn]

連 介 比

用法 more... than...　比……更……
Amy is more beautiful than Mary.
（艾咪比瑪麗更美。）

John studies harder than Peter.
約翰比彼得用功。

thank [θæŋk]

名 動 謝謝

用法
ⓐ thank 作名詞時，恆用複數。
ⓑ Thank you for...　因……而謝謝你。
= Thanks for...

Thank you for your help.
謝謝你的幫助。

that [ðæt]

形 那個的　代 那個

用法 that（那個）指距離較遠的東西；this（這個）指距離較近的東西。

Mike likes that car.
麥可喜歡那輛車。

the [ðə]

冠 這個；這些；那個；那些

用法 the 在以 a、e、i、o、u 等母音發音起首的字之前唸成 [ði]，在其餘字母起首的字之前唸成 [ðə]。

Finish the work by five o'clock.
五點以前要把這件工作做完。

theater [ˋθɪətɚ]

名 戲院

用法 theater 指有話劇、舞臺劇演出的劇院，但也可指放電影的電影院，等於 movie theater。

There are only five people in the theater.　戲院裡只有五個人。

then [ðen]

副 然後；那時

用法 since then 從那時起
now and then = sometimes 有時，偶爾

Tony was very busy **then.**
湯尼**當時**很忙。

there [ðɛr]

副 那裡

用法 there is / there are 可表示「有」。

There are five people in my family.
我家裡**有**五個人。

therefore [ˈðɛrˌfɔr]

副 因此

用法 therefore 為副詞，故要連接前後兩句可用分號作為連接詞的功能。

Tim is nice; **therefore,** I like him.
提姆很好，**所以**我喜歡他。

these [ðiz]

形 這些的　代 這些東西

用法 these 之後要接複數的名詞。
these books　這些書

Put **these** toys away.
把**這些**玩具收好。

they [ðe]

代 他們；牠們；它們

用法 they 可指人、動物或無生物（如 書、機器等）。
I like these books. They are very good.
（我喜歡這些書。它們是好書。）

I like Tom and Peter. **They** are my classmates.　我喜歡湯姆和彼得。**他們**是我同班同學。

thick [θɪk]

形 厚的

用法 thick 也可指「濃密的」。
Your hair is thick.
（你的頭髮很濃密。）

A good dictionary is usually **thick**.
好字典通常都很**厚**。

thief [θif]

名 小偷

用法 複數為 thieves [θivz]

The thief was caught at last.
小偷最後被抓到了。

thin [θɪn]

形 瘦的；細的；稀疏的

用法 ⓐ 細的：a thin rope　細繩子
ⓑ 稀疏的：His hair is thin.
（他的頭髮很稀疏。）

The poor boy is very thin.
這個可憐的男孩好瘦喲。

thing [θɪŋ]

名 東西；事情

用法 I have many things to do.
（我有很多事情要做。）

John knows many things.
約翰懂很多事情。

think [θɪŋk]

動 想

用法
ⓐ 三態：think、thought [θɔt]、thought
ⓑ I think (that)... 我想 / 認為……
ⓒ think about / of... 想到……

I think we should leave now.
我想我們現在該離開了。

third [θɝd]

名 第三 形 第三的

用法
on July third 七月三日那一天
= on the third of July

Marvin doesn't understand the third question. 馬文不懂第三個問題。

thirsty [ˋθɝstɪ]

形 口渴的

用法
thirsty 除表示「口渴的」以外，也表示「渴望的」：Jane is thirsty for knowledge.（珍渴望知識 / 珍有求知欲。）

I'm thirsty. Can I have something to drink? 我口渴，可不可以喝點東西？

thirteen [ˌθɝˋtin]

名 十三　形 十三個的

用法 thirteen 之後接複數的名詞。
thirteen children　十三個孩子
thirteen days　十三天

Nina will be **thirteen** years old tomorrow.　明天妮娜就十三歲了。

thirty [ˋθɝtɪ]

名 三十　形 三十個的

用法 thirty 之後接複數的名詞。
thirty books　三十本書
thirty boys　三十個男孩子

My aunt is **thirty** years old.
我阿姨三十歲。

this [ðɪs]

形 這個的　代 這個

用法 this and that　各種各樣的事情

This is a very good dictionary.
這是一本相當好的字典。

those [ðoz]

形 那些的　代 那些

用法 如同 these 一樣，those 之後接複數的名詞。
those students　那些學生
those girls　那些女孩子

Those boys are my friends.
那些男孩是我的朋友。

though [ðo]

連 雖然

用法 though 等於 although [ɔlˋðo]，均表示「雖然」，不可與 but 並用，因為英文兩句中只能使用一個連接詞。

Though you are busy, you still have to do it.　**雖然**你很忙，但你仍得做這件事。

thought [θɔt]

名 想法

用法 on second thought
再三考慮後，轉念一想

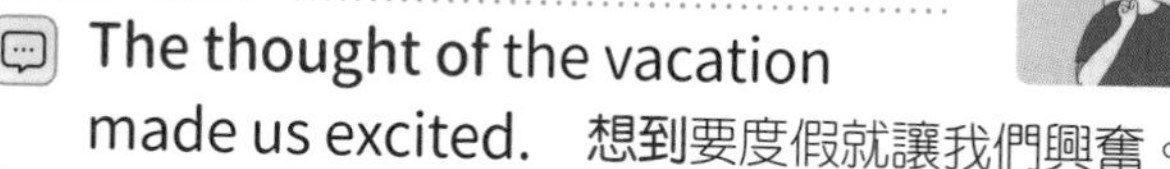

The thought of the vacation made us excited.　**想到**要度假就讓我們興奮。

thousand [ˋθaʊzṇd]

名 千　形 千個的

用法
one thousand students　一千名學生
two thousand books　兩千本書

That bicycle cost Dad two thousand NT dollars. 那輛腳踏車花了爸爸新臺幣兩千元。

three [θri]

名 三　形 三個的

用法
three 之後要接複數的名詞。
three days　三天
three glasses　三個玻璃杯

There are three apples on the table. 桌上有三顆蘋果。

throat [θrot]

名 **喉嚨**

用法
I have a frog in my throat.
（我喉嚨裡有隻青蛙 —— 我喉嚨啞了。）

My brother's throat hurts.
我哥哥的**喉嚨**痛。

throw [θro]

動 丟

用法 ⓐ 三態：throw、threw [θru]、thrown [θron]
ⓑ throw up　嘔吐

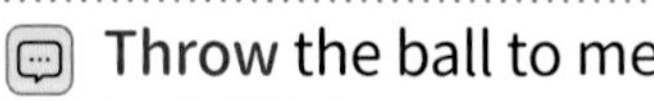

Throw the ball to me.
把球丟給我

through [θru]

介 副 穿過；經由

用法 Many people keep in touch through the internet.
（許多人用網際網路保持聯繫。）

The train was running through a tunnel.　火車正穿越隧道。

thumb [θʌm]

名 姆指

用法 ⓐ thumbs up　贊成
ⓑ all thumbs　笨手笨腳

Bell's thumb hurts.
貝爾大姆指很痛。

thunder [ˋθʌndɚ]

名 雷　動 打雷

用法 It started to pour after it thundered several times.
（打了幾聲雷後就下起了傾盆大雨。）

The thunder scared the baby.
雷聲嚇壞了小寶寶。

Thursday [ˋθɝzde]

名 星期四

用法
on Thursday　在星期四那一天
last Thursday　上星期四
next Thursday　下星期四

Today is **Thursday**.
今天是**星期四**。

ticket [ˋtɪkɪt]

名 票；入場券

用法
train ticket　火車票
movie ticket　電影票

Give me three **tickets**, please.
請給我三張**票**。

Tt

tidy [ˋtaɪdɪ]

形 整潔的

用法 keep... clean and tidy
將……保持整潔

Keep the room **clean and tidy.**
把房間**保持整潔**。

tie [taɪ]

名 領帶

用法 tie 當動詞用時有「綁；繫」的意思：
The little boy can tie his shoelaces.
（這個小男孩會綁鞋帶。）

Dad wears a **tie** to work every day.
爸爸每天都打**領帶**上班。

tiger [ˋtaɪgɚ]

名 老虎

用法 tiger 可指公的或母的老虎，不過 tigress [ˋtaɪgrɪs] 則指母老虎。

Can **tigers** climb trees?
老虎會爬樹嗎？

A B C D E F G H I J K L M N O P Q R S T U V W X Y Z

till [tɪl]

介 連 直到……為止

用法 等於 until [ʌnˋtɪl]。

My father won't be back till ten o'clock. 我爸爸要到十點鐘才會回來。

time [taɪm]

名 時間；次數

用法
once 一次
two times 兩次

What time is it, please?
請問現在幾點了？

tiny [ˋtaɪnɪ]

形 極小的

用法 a tiny flower 極微小的花

It's only a tiny mistake.
這只是個小小的錯誤。

tip [tɪp]

名 小費　動 給小費

用法
ⓐ 三態：tip、tipped [tɪpt]、tipped
ⓑ The man tipped me NT$100 for the service.（那名男子給我新臺幣一百元小費。）

Don't forget to leave a tip before you go. 離開前別忘了留下小費。

tired [taɪrd]

形 **感到累的；厭倦的**

用法
be tired of... 厭倦……
Larry is tired of this job.
（賴瑞厭倦了這份工作。）

Bill was tired after all the work.
比爾做完所有工作後便累了。

title [ˋtaɪtl̩]

名 **標題，名稱；頭銜**

用法
John's new title is general manager.
（約翰的新頭銜是總經理。）

The title of this book is *True Love*.
這本書的書名叫做《真愛》。

to [tu]

介 到；對

用法 To me, this is a good book.
（對我而言，這是本好書。）

Ken went to the beach yesterday.
肯昨天**到**海邊去了。

toast [tost]

名 吐司麵包

用法 表示「一片吐司」，不可說：a toast (×)
而要說：a piece / slice of toast (○)

Can I have one more piece of toast?
我可不可以再來一片**吐司**？

today [tə`de]

名 副 今天

用法 ⓐ today 一字通常置於句尾。
ⓑ a week from today　下禮拜的今天

It's a fine day today.
今天天氣不錯。

toe [to]

名 腳趾

用法 step on someone's toes　踩到某人的腳趾
Be careful. Don't step on my toes.
（小心。別踩到我的腳趾。）

I have ten toes.
我有十個**腳趾頭**。

tofu [ˋtofu]

名 豆腐

用法 tofu 為不可數名詞。

Sally enjoys eating tofu and vegetables.　莎莉喜歡吃**豆腐**和青菜。

together [təˋgɛðɚ]

副 一起

用法
stay together　待在一起
work together　一起工作
get together　聚在一起

Let's sing together.
咱們**一起唱**吧。

toilet [ˋtɔɪlət]

名 洗手間；馬桶

用法 flush the toilet　沖馬桶

Excuse me. I'd like to go to the toilet.　很抱歉，我想要上洗手間。

tomato [təˋmeto]

名 番茄

用法 tomato 的複數是 tomatoes。

Most tomatoes are red.
大部分的番茄都是紅色的。

tomorrow

名 副 明天　[təˋmɔro]

用法 如同 today 一樣，tomorrow 多置於句尾。

See you tomorrow.
明天見。

Tt

tonight [tə`naɪt]

名 副 今晚

用法 tonight 也多置於句尾。
What are you going to do tonight?
（你今晚將要做什麼？）

Kevin will go to bed early tonight.
凱文今晚要早一點睡覺。

tongue [tʌŋ]

名 舌頭；語言

用法 mother tongue　母語
John's mother tongue is French.
（約翰的母語是法文。）

Nancy burned her tongue on the hot coffee.　南西的舌頭被熱咖啡燙到了。

too [tu]

副 太；也

用法 too 表示「也」時要放在句尾，且之前要有逗點。
Dora can sing, and she can dance, too.
（朵拉會唱歌，也會跳舞。）

You are too lazy, Peter.
彼得，你太懶惰了。

tool [tul]

名 工具；器具

用法 do something with a tool
用工具做某件事

The store sells all kinds of **tools.**
那家店販賣各類**工具**。

tooth [tuθ]

名 牙齒

用法 複數為 teeth [tiθ]。

This **tooth** needs to be pulled out.
這顆**牙齒**必須拔掉。

toothache [ˋtuθ͵ek]

名 牙痛

用法 have a toothache　牙痛

Billy had a **toothache** this morning.
比利今早**牙痛**。

toothbrush

名 牙刷　[ˋtuθˏbrʌʃ]

用法 toothpaste [ˋtuθˏpest]
名 牙膏（不可數）

Gary needs to buy a new **toothbrush**.
蓋瑞需要買一支新**牙刷**。

top [tɑp]

名 頂端

用法
ⓐ on top of...　在……的頂端
ⓑ top 也可作形容詞用，表示「最棒的」。
a top student　最優秀的學生

There is a temple **on top of** that hill.
那座山丘**頂上**有一座廟。

topic [ˋtɑpɪk]

名 主題

用法 topical [ˋtɑpɪkəl]
形 熱門話題的；時下關注的

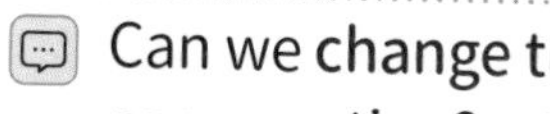

Can we **change** the **topic** of our conversation?　我們可以**轉換**一下談話的**主題**嗎？

A B C D E F G H I J K L M N O P Q R S T U V W X Y Z

total [ˋtotl̩]

名 **總數**

用法 a total of + 數字　總共……
= 數字 + in total

Owen has two hundred dollars in total.　歐文一共有兩百元。

touch [tʌtʃ]

名 動 **接觸**

用法 touch 也可表示「感動」，常用於下列的結構：
be touched by...　被……感動

Don't touch anything here.
這裡的任何東西都不要碰。

toward [tɔrd]

介 **朝向**

用法 等於 towards [tɔrdz]

Mary saw a stranger coming toward her.　瑪麗看見一個陌生人向她走來。

towel [ˋtaʊəl]

名 毛巾

用法 towel 指洗臉的「毛巾」或「浴巾」，bath towel 則專指「浴巾」。（bath [bæθ] 名 盆浴）

John dries his body with a towel.
約翰用毛巾把身體擦乾。

tower [ˋtaʊɚ]

名 塔

用法 the Eiffel tower　艾菲爾鐵塔

The tower has a history of 300 years.　這座塔有三百年的歷史。

town [taʊn]

名 城鎮

用法
in town　在城裡
out of town　出城，不在城裡

Nancy lives in a small town.
南西住在一座小鎮上。

toy [tɔɪ]

名 玩具

用法 play with toys　玩玩具

My little sister is **playing with** her **toys**.　我小妹正在**玩**她的**玩具**。

trace [tres]

動 追蹤；追溯　名 蹤跡

用法 be traced back to + 過去的時間
被追溯到某個過去時間

The team just disappeared without a **trace**.　那支隊伍就這樣不見了，一點**蹤跡**也找不到。

trade [tred]

名 貿易　動 交易

用法 trade A for B　以 A 交換 B
Can I trade my watch for your pen?
（我可以用我的錶來換你的筆嗎？）

Global trade seems to be increasing.　**全球貿易**似乎日益增加。

tradition [trəˋdɪʃən]

名 傳統

用法 by tradition　按傳統

By **tradition**, we eat rice dumplings on the Dragon Boat Festival.　**按傳統**，我們端午節會吃粽子。

traditional [trəˋdɪʃənḷ]

形 傳統的

用法 classic [ˋklæsɪk] 形 傳統的；經典的

Zack prefers the **traditional** music of his homeland to Western music.　查克喜歡家鄉的**傳統音樂**甚於西洋音樂。

traffic [ˋtræfɪk]

名 交通（不可數）

用法 traffic 指「馬路上行進的眾多車輛」。
traffic light　紅綠燈號誌

The **traffic** is heavy at this time.
目前**車流量**很大。

train [tren]

名 火車

用法 take the train　搭火車

David takes the train to school.
大衛坐火車上學。

trap [træp]

名 陷阱　動 困住

用法 三態：trap、trapped [træpt]、trapped

The police set a trap to catch the thief.　警察設了陷阱來追捕那個小偷。

trash [træʃ]

名 垃圾（不可數）

用法 trash 與 garbage 意思相同，均表示無用而要丟掉的「垃圾」。

There is a lot of trash in the park.
公園裡有許多垃圾。

travel [ˋtrævḷ]

名 動 旅行

用法 Nora's dream is to travel (around) the world.
（諾拉的夢想是環遊世界。）

Space travel is possible in the near future.　太空旅行最近將會成真。

treasure [ˋtrɛʒɚ]

動 珍惜　名 寶藏

用法 I treasure your love.
（我很珍惜妳的愛。）

The museum has many art treasures.　這間博物館有許多藝術寶藏。

treat [trit]

動 對待；請客

用法
ⓐ 對待：treat people well　善待人們
ⓑ 請客：treat John to dinner / a movie
請約翰吃晚餐 / 看電影

You should treat people politely.
你應待人有禮貌。

tree [tri]

名 樹

用法
plant a tree　種樹
climb a tree　爬樹

Sophie loves those green **trees.**
蘇菲很喜歡那些綠**樹**。

trick [trɪk]

名 惡作劇；把戲

用法
play tricks on + sb
對某人惡作劇，整某人

Don't **play tricks on** John.
別**整**約翰。

triangle [ˋtraɪˏæŋgl̩]

名 三角形

用法
triangular [traɪˋæŋgjələ]
形 三角形的

The child is learning to draw a **triangle.**　這個小朋友正在學習畫**三角形**。

trip [trɪp]

名 旅行

用法 go on a trip to + 地方　到某地旅行
= take a trip to + 地方

We'll **take a trip to** America next week.
我們下個星期會**到**美國**旅行**。

trouble [ˋtrʌbḷ]

名 麻煩

用法 be in trouble　陷入麻煩，倒楣
have trouble + V-ing　做……有困難

You'll **be in trouble** if you don't listen to me.　你若不聽我的話就會**有麻煩**。

trousers [ˋtraʊzɚz]

名 褲子

用法 trousers 多為英國人使用的字，美國人則多用 pants。因褲管有兩條，故 trousers 或 pants 恆用複數。

Johnson bought **a pair of trousers** today.　強森今天買了**一條褲子**。

truck [trʌk]

名 卡車

用法 drive a truck　開卡車

a truck driver　卡車司機

Paul's father is a truck driver.

保羅的爸爸是卡車司機。

true [tru]

形 真實的；忠實的

用法 ⓐ 真實的：a true story　真實的故事

ⓑ 忠實的：Mr. Wang is true to his wife.

（王先生對他太太很忠實。）

That's a true story.

那是真實的故事。

trumpet [ˋtrʌmpɪt]

名 喇叭

用法 trumpeter [ˋtrʌmpɪtɚ] 名 喇叭手

Kevin is good at playing the trumpet.

凱文擅長吹喇叭。

trust [trʌst]

名 動 信任

用法 Just put your trust in me!
（你只要信任我就好了！）

We have to trust each other.
我們必須信任彼此。

truth [truθ]

名 真相

用法 To tell (you) the truth, ...
老實（跟你）說，……

To tell the truth, I don't trust David. 老實說，我不信任大衛。

tube [t(j)ub]

名 管子；管狀物

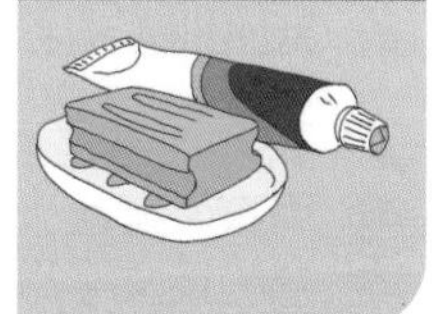

用法 a tube of toothpaste 一條牙膏

My mom bought a tube of toothpaste and a bar of soap at the supermarket. 我媽媽在超市買了一條牙膏及一塊肥皂。

tunnel [ˋtʌnl̩]

名 隧道

用法 an undersea tunnel　海底隧道

Our car stalled as we were driving through the tunnel.　我們開車經過**隧道**時，車子拋錨了。

try [traɪ]

名 動 設法；嘗試

用法
ⓐ 三態：try、tried [traɪd]、tried
ⓑ try to...　設法……
I'll try to call William.（我會設法打電話給威廉。）

Let me try again.
讓我**再試試**看。

T-shirt [ˋti͵ʃɝt]

名 短袖圓領衫

用法 T-shirt 就是無領的短袖運動衫，用衣架撐起來時，形狀就像個大寫的英文字母 T。

This T-shirt looks good on you.
這件 **T 恤**穿在你身上很好看。

tub [tʌb]

名 浴缸

用法 fill the tub with hot water
把浴缸加滿熱水

The tub is full of water.
浴缸裡充滿了水。

Tuesday [ˋtjuzde]

名 星期二

用法 on Tuesday　在星期二那一天
What are you going to do on Tuesday?
（你星期二要做什麼？）

It's Tuesday today.
今天是**星期二**。

turkey [ˋtɝkɪ]

名 火雞

用法 cold turkey　一次就斷然地（放在句尾）
You should give up smoking cold turkey. （你應一次就把菸戒掉。）

Grandmother raises two turkeys.
奶奶養了兩隻**火雞**。

Tt

turn [tɝn]

動 轉動　名 轉動；輪班

用法 ⓐ turn on / off...　打開 / 關掉（電燈、電視、收音機等電器設備）
ⓑ It's your turn.（輪到你了。）

Turn off the light, please.
請熄燈。

turtle [ˋtɝtḷ]

名 烏龜

用法 turtle 多指「海龜」，陸地上的烏龜則稱 tortoise [ˋtɔrtəs]。

David has a pet turtle.
大衛有一隻寵物龜。

twelve [twɛlv]

名 十二　形 十二個的

用法 twelve 之後要放複數的名詞。
twelve days　十二天
twelve boys　十二個男孩

Karen will be twelve years old next year.
明年凱倫就十二歲了。

twenty [ˋtwɛntɪ]

名 二十　形 二十個的

用法 twenty 之後要放複數的名詞。
twenty books　二十本書
twenty students　二十個學生

That store is open twenty-four hours a day. 那家商店全天二十四小時營業。

twice [twaɪs]

副 兩次

用法 once　一次
twice　兩次（= two times）
three times　三次

Lisa visits her grandmother twice a month. 莉莎一個月會去探視她奶奶兩次。

two [tu]

名 二　形 兩個的

用法 two 之後接複數的名詞。
two boys　兩個男孩
two books　兩本書

Mr. Lai has two sons.
賴先生有兩個兒子。

type [taɪp]

動 打字　名 類型

用法
ⓐ 類型：I don't like this type / kind of man.
（我不喜歡這種人。）
ⓑ 打字：type very quickly　打字很快

Can you **type** this document for me?
你能否替我**打字**這份文件？

typhoon [taɪˋfun]

名 颱風

用法
typhoon 這個字還真是從中文「颱風」譯音過來。「豆腐」在英文中稱作 tofu [ˋtofu]，顯然也是從中文譯音過來。

A **typhoon** is coming.
颱風就要來了。

Notes

ugly [ˋʌglɪ]

形 醜的

用法 an ugly duckling　醜小鴨

Tom is **ugly** but kind.
湯姆雖醜，但心地善良。

umbrella [ʌmˋbrɛlə]

名 雨傘

用法 umbrella 一字通稱「雨傘」或「陽傘」。

You'd better carry an **umbrella** with you.　你最好隨身帶把傘。

uncle [ˋʌŋkḷ]

名 叔叔；伯父

用法 uncle 也可指「姑丈」、「姨丈」、「舅舅」。

My **uncle** and aunt live in the country.
我叔叔及嬸嬸住在鄉下。

under [ˋʌndɚ]

介 在……的下面

用法 under 與 below 均指「在……的下面」。under 強調「正下方」；below 則可指「在下方的前一點或邊邊一點」。

There is a cat under the table.
桌子下有一隻貓。

underline [ˏʌndɚˋlaɪn]

動 在……下劃線

用法 underline 當名詞用時，意思為「底線」。

Underline all the words you don't know. 把你不懂的字全都劃底線。

underpass [ˋʌndɚˏpæs]

名 地下道

用法 overpass [ˋovɚˏpæs] 名 天橋，陸橋

Please use the underpass to go across the road. 請利用地下道穿越馬路。

Uu

understand

動 了解 [ˌʌndɚˋstænd]

用法 三態：understand、understood [ˌʌndɚˋstʊd]、understood

Do you **understand** that language?
那種語言你懂嗎？

underwear [ˋʌndɚˌwɛr]

名 內衣

用法 underwear 為集合名詞，不可數。

The man was only wearing his **underwear**. 這個男人只穿著內衣。

unhappy [ʌnˋhæpɪ]

形 不快樂的

用法 be unhappy about... 對……感到不高興
Paula is unhappy about Will's words.
（威爾的話讓寶拉不高興。）

Why is Simon so **unhappy**?
賽門為什麼那麼不快樂？

uniform [ˋjunəˏfɔrm]

名 制服

用法 wear a uniform　穿制服

In our school, everyone **wears a uniform.**　我們學校每個人都**穿制服**。

unique [juˋnik]

形 獨一無二的

用法 be unique to + 地方　為某地方所獨有
Kiwi birds are unique to New Zealand.
（鷸鴕為紐西蘭所獨有。）

Everyone's face is **unique.**
每個人的臉都是**獨一無二的**。

universe [ˋjunəˏvɝs]

名 宇宙

用法 ⓐ 前面加定冠詞 the。
ⓑ in the universe　在宇宙中

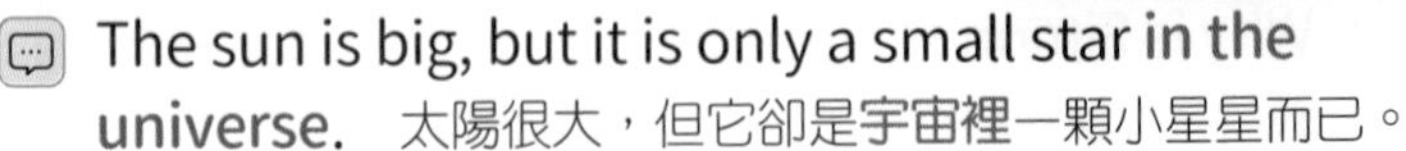

The sun is big, but it is only a small star in the **universe.**　太陽很大，但它卻是**宇宙**裡一顆小星星而已。

university

[ˌjunəˋvɝsətɪ]

名 大學

用法 a university student　大學生

Iris hopes to go to a good **university.**　艾麗絲希望能上一所好大學。

until [ənˋtɪl]

連 介 直到

用法 口語中常用 till [tɪl] 取代 until。
We'll work until / till five p.m.
（我們會工作到下午五點才收工。）

Owen will wait **until** ten o'clock.
歐文會等到十點鐘。

up [ʌp]

副 介 往上

用法 get up　起床
walk up the hill　走上山

Get up, you lazy boy.
起床了，你這懶小子。

Uu

upload [ʌp`lod]

動（電腦）上傳

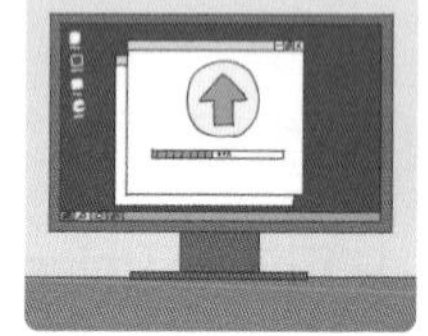

用法 download [`daʊn,lod]
動（電腦）下載

It takes a while to **upload** these images to my blog.
把這些圖片上傳到我的部落格要花一點時間。

upon [ə`pɑn]

介 在……之上

用法 upon 等於 on。

Leo **sat upon the ground**.
李歐坐在地上。

upper [`ʌpɚ]

形 上面的，上部的

用法 lower [`loɚ] 形 下面的，下部的

Randy's **upper** arm hurts badly.
藍迪的上手臂很痛。

upstairs [ˏʌpˋstɛrz]

副 形 在樓上

用法 downstairs [ˏdaʊnˋstɛrz]
副 形 在樓下

Could you **go upstairs** to answer the phone? 你可以上樓去接電話嗎？

USA [ˏjuɛsˋe]

名 美國

用法 USA 是美利堅合眾國的縮寫。
united [juˋnaɪtɪd] 形 聯合的
state [stet] 名 州

USA is short for the United States of America.
USA 是 the United States of America 的縮寫。

use

[juz] 動 使用 [jus] 名 用途；使用

用法 ⓐ 使用：use the phone 使用電話
ⓑ 用途：What's the use of this machine?
（這個機器的用途是什麼？）

May I **use** your telephone?
我可以用你的電話嗎？

useful [ˋjusfəl]

形 有用的

用法
a useful tool　實用的工具
a useful man / woman　有用的人

A knife is a **useful** tool.
刀子是很實用的工具。

usual [ˋjuʒuəl]

形 通常的

用法
as usual　一如往常

As usual, Warren was late again.
一如往常，華倫又遲到了。

usually [ˋjuʒuəlɪ]

副 通常

用法
usually 有時也可用 often 取代，
表示「通常」或「經常」。

Carol **usually** gets up at seven o'clock.　卡蘿通常都在七點起床。

vacation

[veˋkeʃən / vəˋkeʃən]

名 假期

用法 be on vacation　在度假

Mom and Dad **are on vacation** somewhere.　爸媽正在某地度假。

valley [ˋvælɪ]

名 山谷

用法 canyon [ˋkænjən]
名 峽谷

The river flows through the valley.　河流流過山谷。

valuable [ˋvæljuəbl̩]

形 很有價值的，珍貴的

用法 valuable advice　寶貴的建議
I'd like to thank you for your valuable advice.（我很感謝你寶貴的意見。）

Nothing is as **valuable** as our friendship.　我們的友誼比什麼都珍貴。

value [ˋvælju]

名 價值

用法 be of great value
很重要，很有價值

This book is of great value.
這本書很有價值。

vegetable [ˋvɛdʒ(ə)təbl̩]

名 蔬菜

用法 vegetarian [ˏvɛdʒəˋtɛrɪən]
名 素食者

We should eat more vegetables.
我們應多吃蔬菜。

vendor [ˋvɛndɚ]

名 販賣者

用法 peddler [ˋpɛdlɚ] 名 小販

Daisy bought the hat from a street vendor. 黛西跟街頭小販買了這頂帽子。

very [ˋvɛrɪ]

副 很

用法 very 之後一定接 good、bad、nice 等形容詞，也可接 hard（努力地）、slowly（慢慢地）等副詞。

John's English is very good.
約翰的英文很棒。

vest [vɛst]

名 背心

用法 vest 可以指男士的西裝背心。男士的整套西裝稱作 suit [sut]，西裝的上衣稱作 jacket [ˋdʒækɪt]，褲子則稱作 pants [pænts]。

Peter is wearing a vest.
彼得穿了一件背心。

victory [ˋvɪktrɪ / ˋvɪktərɪ]

名 勝利

用法 win a victory　贏得勝利
= score a victory

Our team finally won a victory.
我們的隊伍終於贏得勝利。

video [ˋvɪdɪˏo]

名 錄影（帶） 形 錄影的

用法
a video camera 攝影機
a video game 電動玩具

The two brothers are playing video games in the living room. 這兩兄弟正在客廳打電動玩具。

village [ˋvɪlɪdʒ]

名 村落

用法
villager [ˋvɪlɪdʒɚ] 名 村民

Eddie grew up in a small village in the mountains. 艾迪是在山中的一座小村落裡長大的。

vinegar [ˋvɪnɪgɚ]

V

名 醋（不可數）

用法
sugar [ˋʃugɚ] 名 糖
salt [sɔlt] 名 鹽
MSG 味精

Doris doesn't like vinegar because it tastes sour. 朵瑞絲不喜歡醋，因為它味道很酸。

violin [ˌvaɪəˋlɪn]

名 小提琴

用法 play the violin　拉小提琴

Can you play the violin?
你會拉小提琴嗎？

visit [ˋvɪzɪt]

名 動 拜訪；參觀

用法 I'll visit Tom tomorrow.
= I'll pay Tom a visit tomorrow.
（我明天會去拜訪湯姆。）

Tony visited his grandmother yesterday.　湯尼昨天去探視他奶奶。

visitor [ˋvɪzɪtɚ]

名 訪客

用法 a visitor to + 地方　造訪某地的人

There are many visitors to the museum on Sundays.　每逢週日便有許多遊客去參觀博物館。

vocabulary

[vəˋkæbjə͵lɛrɪ]

名 字彙

用法 have a large vocabulary　懂很多字

Our teacher has a large vocabulary.
我們的老師知道的字彙很多。

voice [vɔɪs]

名 聲音

用法
have a beautiful voice　有甜美的嗓音
have a loud voice　嗓門很大
have a soft voice　有柔和的嗓音

Mary has a beautiful voice.
瑪麗的嗓音很甜美。

volleyball [ˋvɑlɪ͵bɔl]

名 排球

用法 play volleyball　打排球

Would you like to play volleyball with us?　你要跟我們一起打排球嗎？

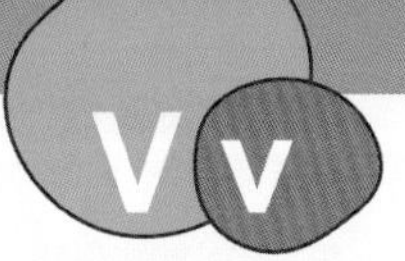

vote [vot]

名 動 投票

用法
vote for... 對……投贊成票
vote against... 對……投反對票

Who will you vote for?
你將投票給誰？

Notes

Ww

waist [west]

名 腰

用法 lap [læp] 名（人坐著時的）大腿部
hip [hɪp] 名 臀部，屁股（常用複數）
ankle [ˋæŋkḷ] 名 腳踝

I forgot to wear a belt around my **waist.**
我忘記在**腰**間繫條皮帶。

wait [wet]

動 等待

用法 wait for + sb　等待某人

Gordon is **waiting for** his girlfriend at the post office.　戈登正在郵局**等待**他女友。

waiter [ˋwetɚ]

名（男）服務生

用法 waiter 指餐廳的男侍。

My brother is a **waiter** at that restaurant.　我哥哥是那家餐廳的**服務生**。

waitress [ˋwetrɪs]

名 （女）服務生

用法 waitress 指餐廳的女侍。

The **waitress** gave us the menu.
這位**女服務生**把菜單拿給我們。

wake [wek]

動 睡醒

用法
ⓐ 三態：wake、woke [wok]、woken [ˋwokən]
ⓑ wake + sb + up　把某人叫醒 / 吵醒

Erin **wakes up** at six thirty every morning.　艾琳每天早上都在六點半**醒來**。

walk [wɔk]

動 走路；陪……走路　名 散步

用法
ⓐ 陪……走路：Let's walk the dog.（咱們遛狗去吧。）
ⓑ 散步：Let's take a walk.（咱們散個步吧。）

Walk faster! You are too slow.
走快一點！你太慢了。

wall [wɔl]

名 牆壁

用法 Walls have ears.
(隔牆有耳。)

There is a picture on the wall.
牆上有一幅畫。

wallet [ˋwalɪt]

名 皮夾

用法 purse [pɝs] 名（女用）錢包

Joe lost his wallet on the bus.
喬把皮夾丟在公車上了。

want [want]

動 想要

用法 want to... 想要……
Matt wants to go to bed.
(麥特想要去睡覺。)

What do you want?
你要什麼？

W

war [wɔr]

名 戰爭

用法 be at war　正在作戰

These two countries are at war now.　這兩個國家正在交戰。

warm [wɔrm]

形 暖和的；溫暖的

用法 warm 也可作動詞。
warm up　暖身

The weather is getting warmer and warmer.　天氣愈來愈暖和了。

wash [waʃ]

動 洗

用法 wash / do the dishes　洗碗盤

Wash your hands before eating.
你洗手後再吃東西。

waste [west]

名 動 浪費

用法 waste one's time + V-ing　浪費時間……
Don't waste your time playing games.
（不要把你的時間浪費在玩遊戲上。）

It was a **waste** of time.
那只是**浪費**時間而已。

watch [watʃ]

名 手錶　動 觀看

用法 watch TV　看電視

Dad bought me a new **watch**.
爸爸買了一只新**手錶**給我。

water [ˈwatɚ]

名 水（不可數）

用法 water 也可作動詞，表示「用水澆」。
Don't forget to water the garden.
（別忘了花園要澆水。）

You should **drink** more **water**.
你應該多**喝水**。

watermelon

[ˋwɑtɚˏmɛlən]

名 西瓜

用法 a piece of watermelon　一片西瓜

Can I have **a piece of watermelon**?
我可不可以吃**一片西瓜**？

wave [wev]

動 揮動　名 波浪

用法
ⓐ wave at + sb　向某人揮手
ⓑ make waves　興風作浪

Peter is **waving at** us.
彼得正**向**我們**揮手**。

way [we]

名 路，方向；方法

用法
ⓐ on the / one's way to + 地方
某人前往某地的途中
ⓑ a way to V　做……的方法

Could you show me the **way** to the train station?　可否請您指引我到火車站的**路**嗎？

we [wi]

代 我們

用法 we 用作動詞的主語，受詞為 us。

We are family.
我們都是一家人。

weak [wik]

形 虛弱的

用法 weak 也可指「不精通的」。
John is weak in / at math.
（約翰數學不在行。）

Luke feels tired and weak.
路克感到又累又虛弱。

wear [wɛr]

動 穿著

用法 三態：wear、wore [wɔr]、
worn [wɔrn]

Mrs. Wilson is wearing a pink dress today. 威爾遜太太今天穿了一件粉紅色的洋裝。

A B C D E F G H I J K L M N O P Q R S T U V W X Y Z

weather [ˋwɛðɚ]

名 天氣

用法 ⓐ weather 為不可數。
ⓑ good / bad weather　好 / 壞天氣

What's the weather like today?
今天天氣怎麼樣？

wedding [ˋwɛdɪŋ]

名 婚禮

用法 a wedding ring　婚戒
a wedding dress　婚紗

Many people were invited to the wedding.　許多人應邀參加婚禮。

Wednesday

名 星期三　[ˋwɛnzde]

用法 on Wednesday　在星期三那一天

Today is Wednesday.
今天是星期三。

week [wik]

名 星期

用法
this week 本星期
last week 上星期

We'll have two tests **this week.**
這個星期我們會有兩次考試。

weekday [ˋwikˏde]

名 平日（指星期一到星期五）

用法
on weekdays 平日

Is Clara busy **on weekdays?**
克萊拉**平日**忙嗎？

weekend [ˋwikˏɛnd]

名 週末

用法
this weekend 本週末
last weekend 上週末
on the weekend 在週末時

What are you going to do **on the weekend?** 這個**週末**你要做什麼？

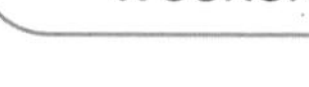

weight [wet]

名 體重

用法 lose weight　瘦下來
gain weight　變胖

Nana tried to **lose weight** by going on a diet.　娜娜設法利用節食來**減肥**。

welcome [ˋwɛlkəm]

動 名 歡迎　形 受歡迎的

用法 對方表示謝謝時，我們可這樣回答：
You're welcome.（別客氣。）

"Thank you very much." "**You are welcome.**"
「非常謝謝您。」「**別客氣。**」

well [wɛl]

形（健康）好的　副 很棒地

用法 You will get well.
（你身體會好起來。）

Peter **speaks** English **very well.**
彼得英語**說得很好**。

A B C D E F G H I J K L M N O P Q R S T U V **W** X Y Z

west [wɛst]

名 西方，西邊　副 在西方，在西邊

用法
ⓐ in the west　在西方，在西邊
ⓑ go west　往西行
ⓒ west 也可當形容詞，為「西方的」。

The sun rises in the east and sets in the west.　太陽從東方升起，西方落下。

wet [wɛt]

形 溼的

用法
get wet　弄溼
Stay inside. Don't get wet.
（待在屋內。別淋溼了。）

Be careful! The floor is wet.
小心！地板是溼的。

whale [(h)wel]

名 鯨魚

用法
go whale watching　去賞鯨

The whale is the biggest animal in the sea.　鯨魚是海洋中最大的動物。

what [(h)wɑt]

代 限 感歎 什麼

用法 What does your boyfriend do?
（妳男友是做哪一行的？）

What is this?
這是**什麼**？

wheel [wil]

名 輪子

用法 汽車的方向盤也叫 wheel。

Dad bought a four-wheel drive jeep last week.
爸爸上星期買了一輛**四輪傳動**的吉普車。

when [(h)wɛn]

連 當　副 代 何時

用法 When will he come?
（他何時會來？）

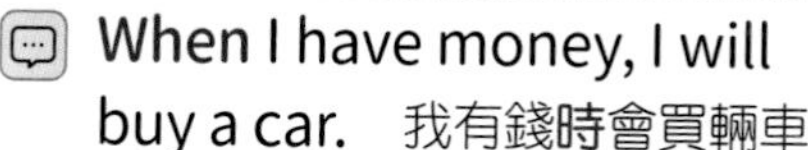

When I have money, I will buy a car.　我有錢**時**會買輛車。

A B C D E F G H I J K L M N O P Q R S T U V W X Y Z

where [(h)wɛr]

副 連 代 何處

用法 Where are you going?（您要去哪裡？）
The train station, please.
（麻煩到火車站。）

Where are you from?
你是哪裡人？

whether [(ˋh)wɛðɚ]

連 是否

用法 whether 與 or not 並用，or not 也可省略。

I don't know **whether** Mary is coming **or not.** 我不知道瑪麗**是否**要來。

which [(h)wɪtʃ]

W

代 哪一個

用法 which 用以指同類東西的「哪一個」。

Which book do you like best?
你最喜歡**哪一**本書？

while [waɪl]

連 當時，在……時　名 一段時間

用法
(for) a while　一會兒
once in a while　偶爾

Please take care of my baby while I'm away.　我外出的時候，請照顧我的小寶寶。

white [(h)waɪt]

名 白色　形 白色的

用法
white 及 black 可分別指「白人」及「黑人」。
John is a white, and Peter is a black.
（約翰是白人，彼得則是黑人。）

My dad wears white shirts only.
我爸爸只穿白襯衫。

who [hu]

代 誰

用法
Who are you?（你是誰？）→不知對方身分
Who is it?（你是誰 / 哪位？）
→沒看到對方（如 打電話或敲門）

Who can answer this question?
誰能回答這個問題？

whole [hol]

形 全部的　名 全部

用法
on the whole　大體上來說
the whole of...　整個……

Tell me the whole story, please.
請告訴我故事的**整個**經過。

whose [huz]

代 誰的

用法
Whose book is this?　（這是誰的書？）
= Whose is this book?　（這本書是誰的？）

Whose book is this?
這是**誰的**書？

why [(h)waɪ]

副 為什麼

用法
老師指定小毛參加英文演講比賽，小毛自覺比不上另一位同學優秀，便反問老師：Why me?（為什麼是我呢？）

Why are you crying, Mary?
瑪麗，妳**為何**在哭？

wide [waɪd]

形 寬的

🔍用法 a wide variety of... 各式各樣的……

The bed is eight feet wide.
這張床寬八英尺。

wife [waɪf]

名 妻子，太太

🔍用法 husband [ˋhʌzbənd]
名 丈夫，先生

Mr. Johnson’s wife is a doctor.
強森先生的太太是位醫生。

wild [waɪld]

形 野生的；野的

用法 go wild 變得放肆，狂野起來

There will be fewer and fewer wild animals on earth. 地球上的野生動物會愈來愈少。

will [wɪl]

助 將，會　名 意願

用法 我們若欲表示「未來」或「以後」要做的動作，就可使用 will。
Will Ben come tomorrow?（班明天會來嗎？）

💬 **Don't worry. I will help you.**
別擔心，我會幫助你。

win [wɪn]

動 贏

用法 三態：win、won [wʌn]、won

💬 **Did you win the race?**
這次賽跑你贏了嗎？

wind [wɪnd]

名 風

用法 a gust of wind　一陣風

💬 **The wind is blowing hard.**
風正猛烈地颳著。

window [ˋwɪndo]

名 窗戶

用法
open the window 打開窗戶
close the window 關閉窗戶

Open the window, please.
請打開窗戶。

windy [ˋwɪndɪ]

形 風大的

用法
cloudy [ˋklaʊdɪ] 形 多雲的
snowy [ˋsnoɪ] 形 下雪的

It's windy today.
今天風很大。

wing [wɪŋ]

名 翅膀

用法
take wing 飛走
The bird took wing before the hunter shot.
（獵人開槍前，那隻鳥早飛走了。）

Most butterflies have beautiful wings.
大部分的蝴蝶都有很漂亮的翅膀。

A B C D E F G H I J K L M N O P Q R S T U V W X Y Z

winner [ˋwɪnɚ]

名 勝者；得獎者

用法 loser [ˋluzɚ] 名 失敗者

Who is the winner of this game?
這場比賽誰是贏家？

winter [ˋwɪntɚ]

名 冬天

用法
Winter is coming. （冬天就要來了。）
Winter is here. （冬天到了。）
Winter is over. （冬天過去了。）

It's cold in winter.
冬天很冷。

wise [waɪz]

形 有智慧的

用法
be wise (of sb) to V （某人）做……很明智
It's wise of you to prepare in advance.
（你提前做好準備真明智。）

Mr. Chang is a wise old man.
張先生是個有智慧的長者。

wish [wɪʃ]

動 希望　名 願望

用法 make a wish　許個願

I wish I could help Max, but I'm too busy.　我真希望能幫助麥克斯，但我太忙了。

with [wɪð]

介 和；有

用法
ⓐ 和：work with sb　和某人共事
ⓑ 有：with one's help　有某人的幫助

Would you like to take a walk with me?　你想不想跟我散個步？

without [wɪð'aʊt]

介 沒有

用法 cannot... without...　若沒有……就無法……
I cannot do it without your help.
（若沒有你的幫助，這件事我就做不了。）

Fish can't live without water.
沒有水，魚就無法存活。

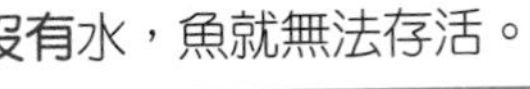

wok [wɑk]

 弧形鐵鍋

ⓐ wok 源自「鍋」或「鑊」的廣東話發音。

ⓑ pan [pæn] 名 西式平底煎鍋

Woks are used in Chinese cooking.
中式的烹飪使用**弧形鐵鍋**。

wolf [wʊlf]

 狼（單數）

複數為 wolves [wʊlvz]。

The man was attacked by a pack of wolves. 那個人被狼群攻擊。

woman [ˋwʊmən]

 女人

複數為 women [ˋwɪmən]。

The woman there is our teacher.
那位女士是我們老師。

women's room

[ˋwɪmənz ˏrum]

名 女洗手間

用法 men's room [ˋmɛnz ˏrum] 名 男洗手間

Can you show me where the women's room is? 你能告訴我女廁在哪裡嗎？

wonderful [ˋwʌndɚfəl]

形 美好的；棒的；奇妙的

用法 Wonderful!（太棒了！）
= Great!
= Cool!

What a wonderful idea!
好棒的點子！

wood [wʊd]

名 木頭（不可數）

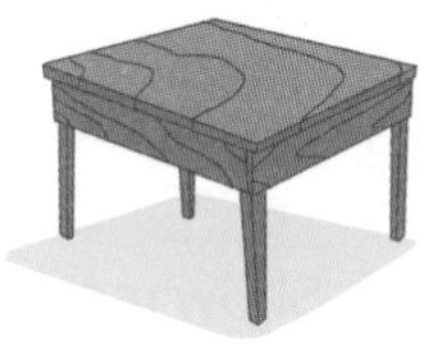

用法 woods 為「森林」，恆用複數。
The hikers were lost in the woods.
（有幾名健行客在森林裡迷路了。）

The desk is made of hard wood.
這張書桌是硬木製的。

word [wɝd]

名 字；話

用法 have a word with + sb　與某人談一談
I would like to have a word with you after school. （放學後，我想跟你談一談。）

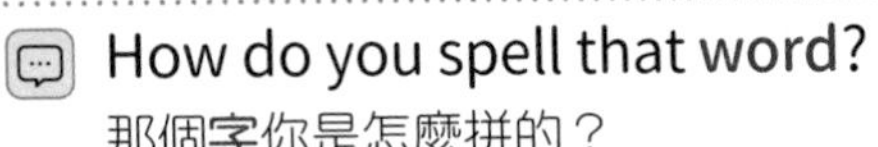

How do you spell that word?
那個字你是怎麼拼的？

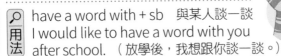

work [wɝk]

名 動 工作

用法 a lot of work　許多工作

Jason has a lot of work to do today.　傑森今天有好多工作要做。

workbook [ˋwɝk,bʊk]

名 作業本

用法 workbook 指的就是有練習題的作業本。

Show me your workbook, Johnny.
強尼，把你的作業本拿給我看。

worker [ˋwɝkɚ]

名 員工；工人

用法 worker 一字可指一般勞動工人，但在公司行號工作的人也稱 worker（員工）。

The workers are building a house.
這些工人正在蓋房子。

world [wɝld]

名 世界

用法 in the world　在世界上
Helen is the most beautiful girl in the world.（海倫是世上最美的女孩子。）

This is a small world.
這世界真小。

worm [wɝm]

名 蟲

用法 worm 也可當動詞，表示「蜷縮著身子走」的意思。

The early bird catches the worm.
早起的鳥兒有蟲吃。—— 諺語

A B C D E F G H I J K L M N O P Q R S T U V W X Y Z

worry [ˈwɜɪ]

動 名 擔心

用法
ⓐ 三態：worry、worried [ˈwɜɪd]、worried
ⓑ worry about... 擔心……

There is nothing to worry about.
沒什麼好擔心的。

wound [wund]

名 傷口 動 使受傷

用法
The soldier was seriously wounded in the battle.（這名士兵在作戰時受到重傷。）

There was a knife wound in my arm.
我的手臂上有一道刀傷。

wrist [rɪst]

名 手腕

用法
a wristband 護腕

The policeman took the thief by the wrist. 那個警察抓住小偷的手腕。

write [raɪt]

動 寫

用法 ⓐ 三態：write、wrote [rot]、written [ˋrɪtn̩]
ⓑ write a book / an e-mail　寫書 / 寫 e-mail

Peter is writing a letter.
彼得正在寫一封信。

writer [ˋraɪtɚ]

名 作家

用法 writer 指以寫作謀生的「作家」。若指某本書的「作者」，則應使用 author [ˋɔθɚ] 一字。

John's father is a famous writer.
約翰的父親是個知名作家。

wrong [rɔŋ]

形 錯誤的　名 錯誤

用法 tell right from wrong　分辨是非
You should learn to tell right from wrong. （你應學習明辨是非。）

Jim's answer is wrong.
吉姆的答案錯了。

X-ray [ˋɛksˏre]

名 X 光

用法 The X-ray shows (that)... X 光片顯示……
The X-ray shows your legs are not broken.
（X 光片顯示你的雙腿沒有骨折。）

That is an X-ray machine.
這是 X 光機。

xylophone [ˋzaɪləˏfon]

名 木琴

用法 play the xylophone 演奏木琴

Can Gina play the xylophone?
吉娜會演奏木琴嗎？

Notes

yard [jɑrd]

名 院子；碼

用法
backyard [ˋbækˌjɑrd] 名 後院
a yard　一碼（= 0.9144 公尺）

We have a small yard behind our house.　我們家後面有個小院子。

year [jɪr]

名 年；歲

用法
Jay is ten years old.
（傑十歲了。）

Gary has lived here for ten years.
蓋瑞在這裡住了十年。

yell [jɛl]

動 大吼，大叫

用法
yell at + sb　對某人大吼，大罵某人

Don’t yell at me. I haven’t done anything wrong.　別對我大吼，我又沒做錯事。

A B C D E F G H I J K L M N O P Q R S T U V W X Y Z

yellow [ˋjɛlo]

名 黃色　形 黃色的

用法 yellow 在俚語中也表示「膽小的」。
Don’t be yellow.
（別膽小嘛。）

All taxis are yellow in this city.
這座城市所有計程車都是黃色的。

yes [jɛs]

副 是的

用法 只要不是 what、when、how、where、why 等起首的問句，均可用 yes 或 no 回答。

Yes, sir. I’ll do it.
是的，長官。我會做這件事的。

yesterday [ˋjɛstɚde]

名 副 昨天

用法 yesterday 與 today 一樣，作副詞時，多置於句尾。

I saw Peter yesterday.
我昨天看到彼得。

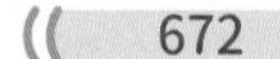

yet [jɛt]

副 還沒　連 但是

a 還沒（與 not 並用）：I haven't done it yet.（我還沒把這件事做完。）

b 但是：等於 but。

John hasn't come yet.
約翰還沒來。

you [ju]

代 你 / 妳；你們 / 妳們

從 you 衍生出 your（你 / 妳的；你們 / 妳們的）及 yours（你 / 妳的東西；你們 / 妳們的東西）。

Can you help me?
你可以幫我忙嗎？

young [jʌŋ]

形 年輕的；幼小的

a young man　年輕人
a young woman　年輕女子
a young child　幼兒

Eric is a young man now.
艾瑞克現在是個青年了。

A B C D E F G H I J K L M N O P Q R S T U V W X Y Z

youth [juθ]

名 青春（不可數）；年輕人（可數）

用法
- ⓐ the youth （統稱）年輕人
- ⓑ in one's youth 某人年輕時

In his youth, Mark was very active. 馬克在年輕時很活躍。

yummy [ˋjʌmɪ]

形 好吃的

用法 yummy 是口語的用法，表示「好吃的」。一般正式的字是 delicious 或 tasty [ˋtestɪ]。

Yummy! This ice cream really tastes good. 好好吃喲！這個冰淇淋味道真棒。

Notes

zebra [ˋzibrə]

名 斑馬

用法 zebra crossing [ˋzibrə ˏkrɑsɪŋ]
名 斑馬線

We can see zebras in the zoo.
我們可以在動物園見到斑馬。

zero [ˋzɪro]

名 零

用法 below zero　零下
It's five degrees below zero.
（現在溫度是零下五度。）

We all know that zero means nothing.
我們都知道零就是表示空無一物。

zoo [zu]

名 動物園

用法 in the zoo　在動物園

Children like to visit the zoo.
小朋友喜歡逛動物園。

索引

B

索引

I

A B C D E F G H I J K L M N O P Q R S T U V W X Y Z 索引

A B C D E F G H I J K L M N O P Q R S T U V W X Y Z 索引

N

索引

Notes

Notes

國家圖書館出版品預行編目（CIP）資料

看圖學英文超好記：國中小實用 2000 單字辭典 /
賴世雄作. -- 初版. -- 臺北市：常春藤有聲出版股份有限公司, 2022.11 面； 公分.
--（常春藤國中小系列；N02）
ISBN 978-626-7225-03-5（精裝）
1. CST：英語教學 2. CST：詞彙 3. CST：中小學教育
523.318 111017545

常春藤國中小系列【N02】

看圖學英文超好記：國中小實用 2000 單字辭典

總編審 賴世雄
終 審 李 端
執行編輯 許嘉華
編輯小組 畢安安
設計組長 王玥琦
封面設計 胡毓芸
排版設計 王玥琦・王穎婕・林桂旭
錄 音 劉書吟・李鳳君・張智傑
播音老師 Stephanie Buckley・Jacob Roth
法律顧問 北辰著作權事務所蕭雄淋律師
出 版 者 常春藤數位出版股份有限公司
地 址 臺北市忠孝西路一段 33 號 5 樓
電 話 (02) 2331-7600
傳 真 (02) 2381-0918
網 址 www.ivy.com.tw
電子信箱 service@ivy.com.tw
郵政劃撥 50463568
戶 名 常春藤數位出版股份有限公司
定 價 620 元

©常春藤數位出版股份有限公司 (2022) All rights reserved. X000012-5947
本書之封面、內文、編排等之著作財產權歸常春藤數位出版股份有限公司所有。未經本公司書面同意，請勿翻印、轉載或為一切著作權法上利用行為，否則依法追究。

如有缺頁、裝訂錯誤或破損，請寄回本公司更換。 【版權所有 翻印必究】

請沿虛線剪下，對折寄回，謝謝！

郵票黏貼處

100009 臺北市忠孝西路一段 33 號 5 樓

常春藤有聲出版股份有限公司　行政組　啟

讀者問卷【N02】

看圖學英文超好記：國中小實用 2000 單字辭典

感謝您購買本書！為使我們對讀者的服務能夠更加完善，請您詳細填寫本問卷各欄後，寄回本公司或傳真至（02）2381-0918，**或掃描 QR Code 填寫線上問卷**，我們將於收到後七個工作天內贈送「常春藤網路書城熊贈點 50 點（一點 = 一元，使用期限 90 天）」給您（每書每人限贈一次），也懇請您繼續支持。若有任何疑問，請儘速與客服人員聯絡，客服電話：（02）2331-7600 分機 11～13，謝謝您！

姓　　名：＿＿＿＿＿＿　**性別**：＿＿＿　**生日**：＿＿年＿＿月＿＿日

聯絡電話：＿＿＿＿＿＿　**E-mail**：＿＿＿＿＿＿

聯絡地址：□□□□□□

教育程度：□國小　□國中　□高中　□大專 / 大學　□研究所含以上

職　　業：1 □學生　2 社會人士：□工　□商　□服務業　□軍警公職　□教職　□其他＿＿＿＿

1 您從何處得知本書：□書店　□常春藤網路書城　□FB / IG / Line@ 社群平臺推薦　□學校購買　□親友推薦　□常春藤雜誌　□其他＿＿＿＿

2 您購得本書的管道：□書店　□常春藤網路書城　□博客來　□其他＿＿＿＿

3 最滿意本書的特點依序是（限定三項）：□字詞解析　□編排方式　□印刷　□音檔朗讀　□封面　□售價　□信任品牌　□其他＿＿＿＿

4 您對本書建議改進的三點依序是：□無（都很滿意）　□字詞解析　□編排方式　□印刷　□音檔朗讀　□封面　□售價　□其他＿＿＿＿

原因：＿＿＿＿

對本書的其他建議：＿＿＿＿

5 希望我們出版哪些主題的書籍：＿＿＿＿

6 若您發現本書誤植的部分，請告知在：書籍第＿＿＿頁，第＿＿＿行

有錯誤的部分是：＿＿＿＿

7 對我們的其他建議：＿＿＿＿

感謝您寶貴的意見，您的支持是我們的動力！　常春藤網路書城 www.ivy.com.tw